Life
in a
Medieval
City

Medieval city gate. Among the finest surviving is that of the Porte
St.-Jean at Provins, one of the four Champagne Fair towns. The two
towers are connected on three levels: under the roadway, above the
entry, and on top of the wall. (French Government Tourist Office)

Life
in a
Medieval
City

Joseph and Frances Gies

■ HarperPerennial
A Division of HarperCollinsPublishers

This book was originally published by Thomas Y. Crowell Company.

First HARPER COLOPHON edition published 1981.

ISBN: 0-06-090880-7

93 94 95   CWI   30 29 28 27 26 25 24 23 22 21

To
Jane Sturman Gies
and
Frances Gibson Carney

Nos ignoremus quid sit matura senectus,
scire aevi meritum, non numerare decet.

Acknowledgments

The authors, who are amateur historians, owe a debt to four professional historians for invaluable criticism and assistance: Dr. Sylvia L. Thrupp, Alice Freeman Palmer professor of history at the University of Michigan; Dr. John F. Benton, professor of history at the California Institute of Technology; Dr. J. Lee Shneidman, assistant professor of history at Adelphi College; and Dr. Peter Riesenberg, professor of history at Washington University, St. Louis. The debt is especially large to John Benton, a leading authority on medieval Champagne, who made many valuable suggestions, supplied otherwise unobtainable reference material, and read the manuscript not once but twice.

Most of the research was done in two great libraries: the Sterling Library of Yale University, and the Newberry Library of Chicago.

Special acknowledgment is due to four people who helped make the construction of a Gothic cathedral come to life: Rowan and Irene Le Compte, stained-glass artists and creators of windows for the Washington Cathedral; and R. T. Feller and John Fanfani, Clerk of the Works and Assistant Clerk of the Works at the Washington Cathedral.

Finally, mention should be made of the numerous French citizens, from archivists to First World War widows in charge of national monuments, who helped us during our research in France.

vii

Contents

Illustrations

Maps

xiii

Prologue

The western European city, with all its implications for the future, was born in the Middle Ages. By 1250 it was alive and flourishing, not only on the ancient Mediterranean coast but in northwest Europe. The narrative that follows is an attempt to depict life at the midpoint of the thirteenth century in one of the newly revived cities: Troyes, capital of the rich county of Champagne, seat of a bishop, and, above all, site of two of the famous Fairs of Champagne.

Back in the days when Julius Caesar camped in Gaul and bivouacked in Britain, there were few places in northwest Europe that could be called cities. Lutetia (Paris) was sufficiently important for Caesar's Commentaries to record its destruction by fire. But in most of the region political organization was too undeveloped, commerce too scanty, and religion too primitive to permit the creation of communities larger than villages. Vast areas remained wilderness.

The Roman legions built roads, provided a market for local farm produce, and offered shelter to traders in their fortified camps. One place they fortified was a hamlet at the confluence of the Seine and an important military road, the Via Agrippa. Marcus Aurelius built a tower there, and later emperors, notably Aurelian, employed it as a base. Along with other camp towns, "Tricasses" took on the appearance

I

of a permanent settlement as garrisoned soldiers married local girls, raised families, and stayed on after their discharges to farm outside the walls or perform craftsmen's jobs inside. Graduating from army base to administrative center, the town acquired masonry walls and attracted new inhabitants: tax collectors, bureaucrats, army purveyors, and skilled and unskilled laborers, including prisoners of war brought back from the wilds of Germany and Friesland. Troyes hardly rivaled the opulent cities of Southern Europe or even Paris, which by the third century boasted three baths, a theater, and a racetrack. Troyes may have had one bath, which would have made it the equal in amenity of most of the other northern towns.

The Christian Church furnished a powerful new impetus to the development of many backwoods towns in the north, although the first apostles were not always appreciated by the pagan civil and religious authorities. At Troyes, as elsewhere, a number of martyrs were created by governors and emperors who held with the faith of their fathers. But once the Church had made a believer out of the Emperor Constantine, it had clear sailing. In the fourth and fifth centuries bishoprics sprang up all over the map. The natural place for a bishop to establish himself was in a Roman administrative center, usually a former legionary camp. The new clerical establishments required the services of a secular population of farmers and craftsmen. A new word described these episcopal towns—cité (city)—a derivation of the Latin civitas that usually took on the meaning of a populated place inside walls.

As the power of the Roman Empire faltered, local Roman officials lost their authority, creating a vacuum that was filled by Christian bishops. By the middle of the fifth century the prestige of the bishop of Troyes was such that when the

Huns appeared in the neighborhood everyone turned to him for protection.

The town had just been sacked once by the Vandals, and Attila's Huns were reputed to be even less amicable. Bishop Lupus first sent a deacon and seven clerks to propitiate the enemy, but an unlucky accident caused the mission to miscarry. The clerics' white vestments made Attila's horse rear. Concluding that his visitors were magicians, the Hun chieftain had them slain on the spot, one young clerk escaping to tell the tale. Attila then went off to fight the Romans, Goths, Burgundians, and Franks, who momentarily stopped fighting among themselves to take him on. Beaten, though not badly, Attila returned eastward, with Troyes directly in his path. It was an ominous moment, and once more everyone turned to Bishop Lupus. This time Lupus negotiated in person, and he scored a surprising success. Attila spared Troyes, and, taking the bishop with him as far as the Rhine, sent him home laden with honors. For this diplomatic feat Lupus was first denounced as a collaborator and exiled, but later, on sober second thought, restored to his see, to be eventually canonized as St.-Loup.

By the end of the fifth century the western half of the Roman Empire had slid into chaos. Nearly all the cities, old and new, large and small, declined catastrophically. People borrowed stones and bricks from public monuments to patch up their houses and strengthen walls against hordes of unwelcome immigrants. Commerce, already slowed down by a long-drawn-out, deeply rooted agricultural crisis, was nearly brought to a halt by the turmoil of the great migrations, or invasions, from the north and east. Towns like Troyes remained stunted, half military, half rural. Apart from crude ecclesiastical buildings—bishop's palace, basilica-cathedral, the abbey and a couple of priories—the walls of

Troyes enclosed only a few score hovels. Most of the town's forty-acre area was given over to vineyards, vegetable gardens, and pasturage.

Yet the marauding barbarians did contribute something to the growth of such settlements. After pillaging a Roman province, they set up a headquarters that generally metamorphosed into a petty capital. Reims, north of Troyes, became the capital of the Franks, and Troyes a Frankish sub-capital of Champagne. The Franks' chief, Clovis, hardly less truculent a fellow than Attila, was more completely vanquished by St.-Rémi, bishop of Reims, than Attila had been by St.-Loup of Troyes. As St.-Rémi eloquently narrated the story of Jesus' martyrdom, Clovis exclaimed, "If only I'd been there at the head of my valiant Franks!" Clovis received baptism, and all his valiant Franks promptly did likewise.

In the sixth and seventh centuries a new ecclesiastical source of cities appeared—the Benedictine monastery. The institution spread rapidly, establishing itself sometimes in towns, sometimes in open country, and immediately attracting craftsmen, farmers, and traders. In the Bavarian forest appeared "Monks' Town"—Munich. In Flanders a Benedictine abbey built at the point where the river Aa becomes navigable formed the nucleus of the future manufacturing city of Saint-Omer.

On the Mediterranean littoral many of the old Roman cities did business in the Dark Ages much as they had done under the Empire. Marseilles, Toulon, Arles, Avignon, and other Provençal ports continued active commerce with the eastern Mediterranean. They imported papyrus and spices, for which the Benedictine monasteries helped provide a market. As a return cargo, the Provençal ships often carried slaves.

This state of affairs came to an end in the seventh century. The electrifying military successes of the followers of Mohammed in the Near East and North Africa were accompanied by a major dislocation of Mediterranean trade. Modern scholars have modified Henri Pirenne's thesis on the causal connection between Mohammed and the Dark Ages, pointing out other influences at work. But it is fact that as Moslem fleets appeared in the western and central Mediterranean, the old Roman-Christian trading cities were thrown on the defensive and were frequently raided and pillaged. Genoa, once a busy port, declined to a fishing village. New cities, flying the banner of the Prophet, blossomed along the shores of North Africa—Cairo, Mahdia, Tunis. Ancient Greek and Roman ports took on new life under the conqueror's administration. In the harbor of Alexandria, guarded by the lighthouse that had been a wonder of the world for a thousand years, new shipyards furnished the vessels for Moslem commerce and piracy, the products of which, in turn, made Alexandria's markets the largest in the Mediterranean. One Christian—if not exactly European—port was even busier: Constantinople, capital of the eastern Roman Empire, strategically seated astride major trade routes from east, west, north and south. But except for Greek Constantinople the Moslem merchants and raiders virtually took over the maritime world. In the eighth century their advance enveloped Spain and the Balearic Islands, and even a piece of Provence, from which foothold they raided all the ancient cities of the Rhône valley. One party roamed far enough north to sack Troyes.

Sacking was something to which citizens of an early medieval city had to be resigned. Not only pagan invaders, but Christian lords, and even bishops, did their share—

Troyes was sacked by the bishop of Auxerre. But the champion raiders, who appeared in the late ninth century, were the Vikings.

By the time they reached Troyes these red-bearded roughnecks from the far north had taken apart nearly every other town on the map—Paris, London, Utrecht, Rouen, Bordeaux, Seville, York, Nottingham, Orléans, Tours, Poitiers; the list is an atlas of ninth-century western Europe. In Champagne the invaders were led by a local freebooter named Hasting, who was noted for his prodigious strength. Reversing the custom by which Vikings sometimes settled in southern Europe, Hasting had traveled to Scandinavia and lived as a Northman, returning to lead his adopted countrymen on devastating forays into Normandy, Picardy, Champagne, and the Loire valley.

Troyes was plundered at least twice, perhaps three times. Here, as elsewhere, repeated aggression bred resistance. Bishop Anségise played the role of King Alfred and Count Odo, rallying the local knights and peasants, joining forces with other nearby bishops and lords, and fighting heroically in the pitched battle in which the Vikings were routed. The renegade Hasting, who had carved out a handsome fief for himself, bought peace by ceding Chartres to one of the coalition of his foes, the count of Vermandois,[1] who thereby acquired the basis of a powerful dynasty.

Paradoxically, the Vikings sometimes contributed to the development of cities. Often their plunder came to more than they could carry home, and they sold the surplus. A town strong enough to resist attack might thereby profit from the misfortune of its less prepared neighbors. The Vikings even founded cities. Where the looting was good, they built base camps to use as depots for trading. One such was Dublin. And they gave a helpful stimulus to York by making it their headquarters, though the original inhabitants may not have appreciated the favor.

This aspect of Viking activity notwithstanding, the ninth century was the nadir of city life. Besides the Vikings, the Moslems were still on the prowl, cleaning out St.-Peter's Church outside Rome in 846. Toward the end of this century of calamity the Hungarians—named for an affinity in appearance and manners with the unforgettable Huns— went on a rampage through Germany, northern Italy, and eastern France.

After vast losses of life and property while makeshift solutions were tried—hiding, bargaining, fighting—Europe hit on the answer to invasion: wall-building. Existing towns built walls and prospered by offering security. The lords of the countryside built walls to strengthen their crude castles, thereby enhancing their own importance. Monasteries built walls. Sometimes walls built to protect castle or monastery had the unexpected effect of attracting coopers, blacksmiths, trappers, and peddlers, and so becoming the nuclei of new towns.

A few places even built their walls before they were attacked. The citizens of Saint-Omer dug a wide, deep moat, filled it with water, and erected a rampart with the excavated material, topping it with pointed stakes. Inside was a second, stronger fortification. The Vikings were repelled in 891 and did not venture a second attack. Invigorated by success, the Saint-Omer burghers turned their monastery-village into a real town, with three principal streets. Much the same thing happened at other towns in this low-lying, vulnerable corner of Europe. Arras, Ghent, Bruges, Lille, Tournai, Courtrai, all began to emerge from obscurity. More was going on than defense against raiders. Some towns, notably Ypres, grew up without benefit of

Town wall. The twelfth-century rampart of Provins is punctuated
by alternating round and square towers, some sixty feet high.
(Touring-Club de France)

any lord, bishop, or fort. They were simply well situated for the manufacture of wool cloth.

The new walls built from scratch in the tenth century were nearly all of the earthwork-palisade variety, like the walls of Saint-Omer. Adequately manned, they sufficed against enemies armed only with the hand-missile weapons of the Vikings. The old Roman cities, like Troyes, had let their masonry ramparts fall into disrepair and so had come to grief in the violent ninth century. By the middle of the tenth, Troyes had repaired its walls, which served the city well, not against the Vikings, but against its former defender, Bishop Anségise himself. Battling his rival, the count of Vermandois, Anségise borrowed a Saxon army from Emperor Otto the Great and besieged Troyes until another doughty prelate, the archbishop of Sens, relieved the city. Otto interceded for Anségise and got him restored to his see, where he lived peacefully until his death ten years later, but never again did a bishop of Troyes try to contest the primacy of the secular counts. Six hundred years after inheriting authority from the Roman governors, the bishops had to take a back seat.

The newly fortified towns were usually called "bourgs" or "burhs" (later, boroughs) in the Germanic dialects that were evolving into new languages. People who dwelt in the bourgs were known as bourgeois, or burghers, or burgesses. By the middle of the tenth century town-fortresses dotted western and northern Europe as far as the newly fortified bishopric of Hamburg, at the mouth of the Elbe, and Danzig, at the mouth of the Vistula. They were not worthy of comparison with the populous and wealthy centers of Islam—Baghdad, Nishapur, Alexandria, Granada, Cordova—where rich merchants patronized poets and architects. The cities of Europe were full of cattle barns and pigsties, with hovels and workshops clustered around church, castle, and bishop's palace. But growth was unmistakable. By the tenth century the crumbling Roman villas outside the walls of Troyes were interspersed with abbeys and houses.

It was certainly a beginning, and in Italy there was a little more than a beginning. Certain towns, nonexistent or insignificant in Roman times, were suddenly emerging. Venice appeared on the mud flats of the Adige at the head of the Adriatic, and Amalfi, south of Naples, thrust up into the space between the Sorrentine cliffs and the sea. The fact that their locations were inhospitable was no coincidence. A set of immigrants called the Lombards, somewhere between the Franks and the Huns in coarseness of manners, had taken over the Italian interior. The Lombards were strictly landlubbers, so the ideal place for a merchant was a sheltered bit of coastline easy to get at from the water, hard to get at from the land. By the late tenth century Venetian and Amalfitan sails were part of the seascape in the Golden Horn of Constantinople. And though it was considered scandalous, not to mention dangerous, to do business directly with the Moslems, a number of Venetian, Amalfitan, and other Italian businessmen found the necessary hardihood.

Over a lengthy interval in the tenth and eleventh centuries two major developments stimulated city growth. One was land clearance, in which the new Cluniac and Cistercian monastic establishments took a leading role. Behind land clearance lay a number of improvements in agricultural technology that taken as a whole amounted to a revolution. The heavy wheeled plow, capable of breaking up the rich, deep north European bottomlands, came into wide use. At first drawn by the slow-gaited ox, the plow was eventually harnessed, with the aid of the new padded but rigid collar, to the swifter horse. This change was in turn related to changes in crops and crop rotation, as oats and legumes were introduced and in many areas the more productive three-field system supplanted the old Roman two-field method.

The new cities played a considerable role in the agricultural revolution. The old manorial workshops tended to be usurped by better, more efficient forges, smithies, mills, and workshops in the towns. The peasants of northwest Europe harvested their crops with iron-bladed sickles and scythes and plowed them with iron plowshares and coulters that would have been the envy of prosperous Roman farmers. The increased food supply was both a cause and an effect of unmistakable population growth.

The second major influence on urban development was the beginning of medieval mining. The Romans and Greeks had dug mines, but the technique had to be reinvented when silver was discovered in the mountains of Saxony. Saxon miners carried their know-how abroad, mining iron in the Carpathians and Balkans, and teaching the men of Cornwall how to mine their native tin. Saxon silver flowed in especial abundance to Milan, which outgrew old walls built by the Emperor Maximilian. Milan boasted a hundred towers in the tenth century. Its prosperity had derived originally from its fertile countryside and the road and river network of which it was the hub. But during the tenth and eleventh centuries it became the chief workshop of Europe. Its smiths and armorers turned out swords, helmets, and chain mail for the knights of Italy, Provence, Germany, and even more distant lands, while its mint struck over twenty thousand silver pennies a year.

Improved agriculture and more money brought a boom

in business outside Italy also. In Flanders, Ghent burst through the ancient walls of the Vieux Bourg, which had enclosed only twenty-five acres. The new merchants' and weavers' quarter, the Portus, more than tripled the town's size.

In many places the growth of towns involved a special symbiosis with the neighboring countryside. In regions that were well suited to a particular form of agriculture, such as wine growing, cities both marketed the local product and procured imports. At the same time twelfth-century towns continued to take over the old manorial functions. In Troyes eleven mills were established between 1157 and 1191. The wheels in city streams began to provide the power not only for milling grain but for oil presses, working hammers and the forges that manufactured iron for farm implements.

Inside city walls there was less room for orchards, vineyards, and gardens. Towns were losing some of their rural look. Wealthy merchants built large houses. Luxury shops, goldsmiths, and silversmiths appeared side by side with the basic crafts. Horse and donkey traffic made the narrow streets as foul as they were congested. The more closely houses and shops were crowded together, the greater the danger of fire. The water supply was limited. In many towns servants and housewives had to stand in line at the wells with their buckets and jars. By the end of the twelfth century urbanization with all its problems had arrived in the cities of Flanders, not to mention Cologne and Hamburg, London and Paris, Provins and Troyes.

The last two were the scene of a significant new development. In Roman times certain dates and seasons had been set aside for markets and fairs. Throughout the following centuries, even when trade had dwindled to a trickle, the idea had stayed alive; in fact, the less buying and selling there was, the more important it became to have fixed times and places for merchants to meet customers.

But merchants also had to meet merchants. This was not an important problem in the Dark Ages, but when the manufacture of woolen cloth in western Europe began to find an outlet in the Mediterranean, via the Italian cities, and when, reciprocally, Mediterranean luxury products began to sell in western Europe, a pressing need arose for a wholesale market. Venetian and Genoese merchants carried spices over the Alps by pack train to trade for Flemish woolen cloth. In the latter half of the eleventh century the Flemings took to meeting them partway. They did not, however, meet them halfway, which would have been in Burgundy. Instead the rendezvous was in Champagne, nearer Flanders than Italy. The reason for this probably lies in the realm of politics.

The adventures of the embattled Bishop Anségise left Troyes in the hands of the counts of Vermandois, who ran out of direct heirs in the eleventh century. A combative cousin named Count Eudes seized Troyes, announced that he was henceforth the count of Champagne, and dared anybody to contradict him. After a turbulent career, Count Eudes died as he had lived, by the sword, or perhaps by the battle ax—his widow had to identify his body by a birthmark. Eudes' two sons divided up his domain and started a war with the king of France, after which one son died and the other, Thibaut the Trickster, duly tricked his nephew out of his share of the inheritance.

Thibaut the Trickster did something else—he gave organization and impetus to the trade fairs that were attracting foreign merchants to Troyes and some of his other towns. His sons, Hugo of Troyes and Etienne, and his grandson, Thibaut II, continued to encourage them. The twelfth century brought boom times, and the Champagne Fairs became the permanent year-round commodity market and money exchange for western Europe. They were so successful that Thibaut II won the sobriquet "Great," along with a reputation for hospitality and charity. An admiring chronicler hailed him as "father of orphans, advocate of widows, eye of the blind, foot of the lame." Approved for his philanthropy, Thibaut the Great was respected even more for his wealth, the source of which was easy to identify. A surviving letter of Thibaut attests the value he attached to the fairs. A rude young baron whose father was a vassal of the king of France waylaid a party of money-changers from Vézelay on their way to Champagne. Thibaut wrote a strong protest to Suger, the minister of Louis VII: "This insult cannot go unpunished, because it tends toward nothing less than the destruction of my fairs."

Eventually, discussion of the problem led to a remarkable treaty by which the kings of France pledged themselves to take under their protection all merchants passing through royal territory on the roads to and from the Champagne Fairs.

Diplomatic relations between count and king were not uniformly cordial. Thibaut the Great had a misunder-standing with Louis VII and a royal army invaded Champagne. The countryside suffered, but Troyes closed the gates of its well-maintained ancient walls and waited till St.-Bernard mediated peace.

Troyes' walls were in good shape, but they were too confining. By the middle of the twelfth century new districts had to be protected. Two large abbeys to the east and south had attracted settlements, but the main thrust of the town's growth was toward the west and southwest, the quarters of St.-Rémi and St.-Jean, two new churches after which the two fairs held in Troyes each year were named. This large district, twice the size of the ancient *cité*, was thinly populated for half the year, but during July and August (the Fair of St.-Jean) and again during November and December (the Fair of St.-Rémi) it was bursting with men, wagons, animals, and merchandise.

Apart from its seasonal fluctuations of population, Troyes in the twelfth century was much like a score of other growing cities of western Europe. All had strong walls. All had abbeys and monasteries, as well as many churches—most of timber, a few of stone with timber roofs. A feature of many cities, including Troyes, was the palace of a secular prince. There were still empty spaces in these municipalities—swampy land along a river, or an unexploited meadow. Most cities ranged in area from a hundred acres to half a square mile, in population from two or three thousand to between ten and twenty thousand. Some, like Troyes, had excavated canals or canalized rivers. Many had built timber bridges on stone piers, and in London a stone-arch bridge had actually been constructed. London Bridge fell short of Roman quality in design and workmanship, but its nineteen arches, mounted on massive piers of varying sizes, and loaded with shops and houses, formed a monument that tourists admired for the next six hundred years. The houses on the roadways of bridges did nothing to improve traffic conditions but they were in great demand because of their unusual access to both water supply and sewage disposal.

But despite their advances the western cities continued to lag behind those of Italy. Twelfth-century Venice, Genoa, Pisa, and the other Italian maritime towns were sending out fleets of oared galleys that hauled the priceless spices of the Indies across the eastern Mediterranean; they were planting

colonies on the shores of the Black Sea, fighting and barter-
ing with the Moslems of Egypt and North Africa, giving
powerful support to the Crusaders and taking valuable
privileges in return, attacking the "Saracens" in their own
backyards, and wresting from them islands and ports.
Plunder helped build many of the truculent towers that
sprouted in the Italian cities, from which wealthy and
quarrelsome burghers defended themselves against their
neighbors. In Pisa plunder contributed to the construction
of a large tower designed to house the bells of a new
cathedral; unfortunately this edifice did not settle properly.
Venice crowned its Basilica of St. Mark with a huge dome,
and built many other churches and public buildings. One
public work of no aesthetic value had enormous practical
significance. The Arsenal of Venice comprised eight acres
of waterfront filled with lumberyards, docks, shipyards,
workshops, and warehouses, where twenty-four war
galleys could be built or repaired at one time.

While Venice wielded a naval power that kings envied,
inland Milan put on a convincing demonstration of a city's
ground-force prowess. At the head of a "Lombard League,"
the Milanese had the effrontery to face up to their lord, the
Holy Roman Emperor Frederick Barbarossa, and to give his
German army a good beating at the Battle of Legnano,
assuring their city's freedom. By that date (1176) Venice,
once a dependency of Greek Constantinople, was as
sovereign as pope or emperor. For all intents and purposes,
so was Genoa, so was Pisa, so were Florence, Piacenza,
Siena, and many other Italian cities. Dominated by wealthy
merchants, and frequently embroiled in civil strife ranging
from family feuding to class warfare, the Italian cities
launched a movement that the cities of the northwest sought
to follow.

The essence of the new movement was the "commune," a sworn association of all the businessmen of a town. In Italy, where the nobility lived in towns, many nobles had gone into business, and some of them helped found communes. But the commune, even in Italy, was a burgher organization; in northwest Europe nobles, along with the clergy, were specifically excluded. Cloth merchants, hay merchants, helmet makers, wine sellers—all the merchants and craftsmen of a town—joined together to defend their rights against their secular and ecclesiastical lords. Enlightened princes like Thibaut the Great and Louis VII favored communes as beneficial to town development and therefore to princely revenues. A tithe from a busy merchant was better than every possession of a starving serf. Nevertheless, the communes came in for considerable disapproval, mostly from clerical critics who saw in them a threat to the social order—which indeed they were. A cardinal[2] accused the communes of abetting heresy, of declaring war on the clergy, and of encouraging skepticism. An abbot[2] wrote bitterly: "Commune! New and detestable name! By it people are freed from all bondage in return for a simple annual tax payment; they are not condemned for infraction of the laws except to a legally determined fine, and they no longer submit to the other charges levied on serfs."

Mere settlement in a town automatically provided escape from such feudal duties as bringing in the lord's harvest, repairing his castle, presenting him with sheep's dung. By the annual tax payment to which the abbot alluded, town people won freedom from a variety of other payments.

Bishops, living cheek-by-jowl with burghers, and seeing these once-servile fellows growing saucy, often had materialistic as well as ideological reasons for disapproving. At Reims the king of France recognized the commune formed by the burghers living inside the old Roman *cité*. Burghers living outside the *cité*, on the bishop's land, also joined. The bishop objected strenuously because he wanted to keep collecting feudal dues. Eventually he had to yield, in return for an annual money payment from his burghers. Bishops and abbots did not scruple any more than secular lords to employ dungeon and rack in their quarrels with their subjects, and they usually could count on the support of the Pope. In strong language Innocent II commanded the king of France to suppress "the guilty association of the people of Reims, which they call a commune." Innocent III excommunicated the burghers of Saint-Omer for their conflict with the local abbey.

In Troyes conflict between burgher and church did not develop, probably because by the twelfth century the counts of Champagne had completely eroded the bishop's authority, as the history of the local coinage attests. In Carolingian times the bishop of Troyes had minted coins. In the early twelfth century the monogram of Count Thibaut— TEBO—appeared on one face of the coins of Troyes, the bishop's inscription in the name of St. Peter (BEATUS PETRUS) on the other. On the coins of the later twelfth century the name of Thibaut's successor, Henry the Generous, appeared alone.

Pope and bishops notwithstanding, the commune swept western Europe. Even villages formed communes, buying their collective freedoms from old feudal charges. Usually the freedoms they received were written down in "charters," which were carefully guarded. Louis VII and other progressive rulers founded "new cities"—with such names as Villeneuve, Villanova, Neustadt—and accorded them charters of freedom to attract settlers. The charter of the town of Lorris, in the Loire Valley, became a model for a hundred other towns of France, while that of Breteuil, in Normandy, became the model for many in England. In Flanders, as early as the eleventh century, towns copied the charter of Saint-Omer. "Charter" joined "commune" as a fighting word to reactionaries.

Interestingly, Troyes and its sister Champagne Fair cities were late in getting charters. This was because of, rather than in spite of, the progressive views of the counts of Champagne. The counts' zeal in protecting and promoting the fairs undercut much of the need for a commune. The businessmen of Troyes enjoyed advantages beyond those that other towns obtained by charter. Nevertheless, in 1230, Troyes received a charter, which was afterward accorded to several other Champagne towns that did not already possess their own.

The sovereign who granted Troyes its charter was Thibaut IV, whose talent as a poet won him the dashing sobriquet of *Thibaut le Chansonnier* ("Songwriter"). Even before he inherited the kingdom of Navarre (after which he signed himself Thibaut, king of Navarre and Champagne), his territories were extensive, though held from seven different lords—the king of France, the emperor of Germany, the archbishops of Sens and Reims, the bishops of Paris and Langres, and the duke of Burgundy. For administrative purposes, the complex territory of Champagne was divided into twenty-seven castellanies, each of which included several barons and a number of knights who owed military service—altogether more than two thousand. (There were also a few hundred knights in Champagne who owed military service to somebody else.)

Throughout the territory Thibaut profited from high justice—the fines and forfeits for major crimes not involving clergy—and a number of imposts, varying from place to

place, such as the monopoly of flour mills and baking ovens
or fees from noble widows seeking permission to remarry.
But far more important were his revenues from the towns,
especially Troyes and Provins. Some years after Thibaut's
death in 1253 a catalogue of the count's properties and
prerogatives was drawn up by committees of citizens
(*prud'hommes*) from the towns: the *Extenta terre comitatus
Campanie et Brie*. A few citations from the section on Troyes
give an illuminating insight into the nature of the count's
revenues:

> The Count has the market of St.-Jean . . . estimated to be worth
> 1,000 pounds (livres), besides the fiefs of the holders of the
> market, worth 13 pounds.
> He also has the markets of St.-Rémi, called the Cold Fair . . .
> estimated to be worth 700 pounds . . .
> The Count also has the house of the German merchants in the
> Rue de Pons . . . worth 400 pounds a year, deducting expenses . . .
> The Count also has the stalls of the butchers in the Rue du
> Temple and the Rue Moyenne . . . paid half on the day of St.-
> Rémi, and half on the day of the Purification of the Blessed
> Virgin. The Count also has jurisdiction in cases arising in regard
> to the stalls of the butchers.
> He also has the hall of the cordwainers . . .
> The Count and Nicolas of Bar-le-Duc have undivided shares
> in a house back of the dwelling of the provost, which contains 18
> rooms, large and small . . . rented for 125 shillings, of which half
> goes to the said Nicolas . . .
> The Count and the said Nicolas have undivided shares in
> seventeen stalls for sale of bread and fish . . . now rented for 18
> pounds and 18 shillings.
> He has the halls of Châlons . . . worth 25 s. in St.-Jean and 25 s.
> in St.-Rémi . . .

The fact that Thibaut the Songwriter was chronically in
debt and at one point even had to mortgage Troyes merely
underlines a truth about princes: the more money they have,

the more they spend. Whatever his foibles, Thibaut carried on his family's tradition of supporting the fairs. During his reign revenues achieved, record heights.

While the Hot Fair (St.-Jean) or the Cold Fair (St.-Rémi) was on, Troyes was one of the biggest and certainly one of the richest cities in Europe. In the off-seasons its population decreased, but remained at a very respectable level. Its permanent population[3] was about ten thousand, a figure exceeded by only a handful of cities in northern Europe: Paris with (about) 50,000; Ghent, 40,000; London, Lille, and Rouen, 25,000. Among many northern European cities of about Troyes' size were Saint-Omer, Strasbourg, Cologne, and York. In populous southern Europe the largest cities were Venice, 100,000; Genoa and Milan, 50,000 to 100,000; Bologna and Palermo, 50,000; Florence, Naples, Marseille, and Toulouse, 25,000. Barcelona, Seville, Montpellier, and many Italian cities were about the size of Troyes.

To pursue demography a little further, it should be noted that the population of western Europe in the mid-thirteenth century was only about sixty million. The pattern of distribution was radically different from that of later times. France, including royal domain and feudal principalities, but excluding eastern areas that became French later on, accounted for more than a third of the total, probably some twenty-two million. Germany, which included much of modern France and Poland, had perhaps twelve million people. Italy had about ten million, Spain and Portugal seven million. The Low Countries supported about four million, as did England and Wales; Ireland had less than a million, Scotland and Switzerland no more than half a million each.

These figures, though far below those produced by the Industrial Revolution, represented an enormous upsurge from Roman and Dark Age times. Practically all the increase was in northwest Europe. There the future lay.

In 1250, when our narrative takes place, Louis IX, St.-Louis, was king of the broad and disparate realm of France. The royal domain, where the king made laws and collected taxes, comprised about a quarter of the whole country; the remainder was parceled out among a score of princes and prelates and hundreds of minor lords and barons, whose relationships with each other were hopelessly intricate. Scientific-minded Frederick II, "the Wonder of the World," was in the last year of his reign as Holy Roman emperor and king of Sicily. Henry III occupied the throne of England, enjoying an uneventful reign, though the loss of the old Plantagenet lands in France had left him less wealthy and powerful than his predecessors. Innocent IV wore the papal tiara in a Rome which had recovered a little of the prestige of its pagan days. In Spain the Moors were hard-pressed by the Christian kingdoms, while on the opposite side of Europe the Mongols, having lately taken over Russia, were raiding Hungary and Bohemia.

For much of Europe 1250 was a relatively peaceful time. As such, it may not have suited the fierce barons of the countryside, but it was congenial to the city burghers whose lives and activities constituted the real history of the period.

I.

Troyes: 1250

A Bar, à Provins, ou à Troies
Ne peut estre, riches ne soies.

[*At Bar, at Provins or at Troyes*
You can't help getting rich.]

—CHRÉTIEN DE TROYES (*Guillaume d'Angleterre*)

In the first week of July, dust clouds rise along the roads that crisscross the broad plain of Champagne. From every direction—Paris and the west, Châlons and the north, Verdun and the northeast, Dijon and the southeast, Auxerre and Sens, and the south—long trains of pack animals plod to their common destination—the Hot Fair of Troyes.

Some have already covered hundreds of miles by the time they reach the borders of Champagne. The cloth caravans from Flanders move south along the old Roman road from Bapaume. Merchants of the German Hanse follow the Seine in their oceangoing boats as far as Rouen, where they transship to shallow-draft vessels or hire animals. Italians sail from Pisa or Genoa to Marseille, or take the "Strada Francesca" from Florence to Milan. If they go by the latter route, they climb the Little St.-Bernard Pass in the Savoy Alps, led along precipices, through drifts, and around crevasses by guides in woolen caps, mittens, and spiked

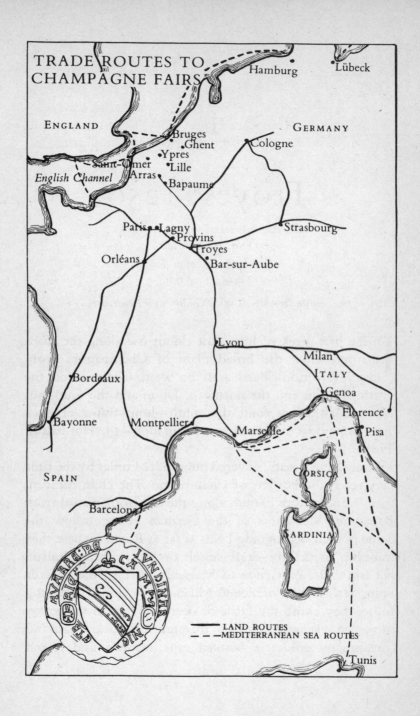

TRADE ROUTES TO CHAMPAGNE FAIRS

Hamburg

Lübeck

ENGLAND

GERMANY

Bruges
Ghent
Ypres
Saint-Omer
Lille
Arras
Bapaume

Cologne

English Channel

Paris Lagny
Provins
Troyes
Bar-sur-Aube

Strasbourg

Orléans

Lyon

Milan

ITALY

Bordeaux

Genoa

Florence

Bayonne
Montpellier
Marseille

Pisa

SPAIN

CORSICA

Barcelona

SARDINIA

———— LAND ROUTES
– – – – MEDITERRANEAN SEA ROUTES

Tunis

boots. Descending the western slopes, they follow the valley of the Isère to Vienne and Lyon. Here they are joined by merchants from Spain and Languedoc for the last leg of their trip, following the Saône valley north, or cutting northwest by way of Autun, or hiring boats and ascending the Saône.

In level country pack animals can make fifteen to twenty-five miles a day, carrying three to four hundred pounds. Couriers travel faster; the Flemish cloth merchants operate a service between the Champagne Fairs and Ghent which covers two hundred miles in four days. But it takes a company of merchants traveling from Florence to Champagne three weeks, even barring accidents. Because carts mire down in rainy weather, pack animals—horses, asses, and mules—make up the merchant trains.

Among the worst nuisances to merchants are the tolls. River crossings that range from the magnificent Pont d'Avignon to bad ferries and worse fords all charge tolls. So do many roads, even though built by the Romans.

Most of the fair traffic journeys in convoy, sometimes preceded by a standard-bearer, and with crossbowmen and pikemen guarding the flanks—a martial display which serves to advertise the value of the goods. Roads are actually safe enough, at least in the daytime. Besides, merchants en route to the fair enjoy extraordinary guarantees as the result of the treaties made by the counts of Champagne with neighboring princes. This very year, 1250, a merchant was robbed of a stock of cloth and squirrel skins while passing through the territory of the duke of Lorraine. Honoring his treaty obligation, the duke indemnified the merchant.

The countryside through which the merchants approach Troyes is heavily wooded, but the past two centuries have witnessed considerable clearing and cultivating. Castles,

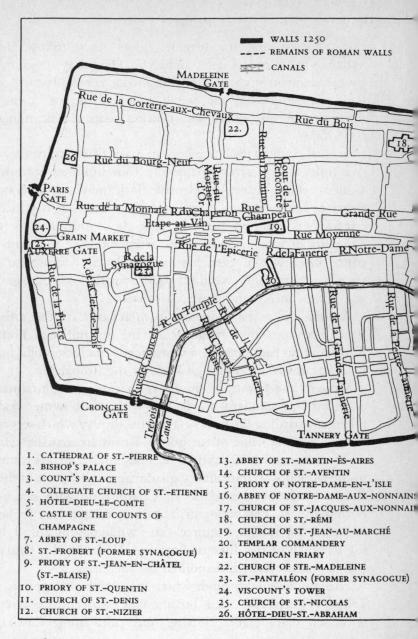

WALLS 1250
REMAINS OF ROMAN WALLS
CANALS

MADELEINE GATE

Rue de la Corterie-aux-Chevaux

Rue du Bois

22.

26

Rue du Bourg-Neuf

Rue du Mortier d'Or

Rue du Domino

Cour de la Rencontre

PARIS GATE

Rue de la Monnaie R. du Chaperon

Rue Champeau

Grande Rue

Etape-au-Vin

19.

Rue Moyenne

24.

GRAIN MARKET

25.

Rue de l'Epicerie

R. de la Fanerie

R. Notre-Dame

AUXERRE GATE

R. de la Synagogue

23.

R. de la Clef-de-Bois

20.

Rue de la Pierre

R. du Temple

R. de la Corderie

Rue de la Grande-Tannerie

Rue de la Petite-Tannerie

R. du Cheval Blanc

R. de Croncels

CRONCELS GATE

Trévois Canal

TANNERY GATE

1. CATHEDRAL OF ST.-PIERRE
2. BISHOP'S PALACE
3. COUNT'S PALACE
4. COLLEGIATE CHURCH OF ST.-ETIENNE
5. HÔTEL-DIEU-LE-COMTE
6. CASTLE OF THE COUNTS OF CHAMPAGNE
7. ABBEY OF ST.-LOUP
8. ST.-FROBERT (FORMER SYNAGOGUE)
9. PRIORY OF ST.-JEAN-EN-CHÂTEL (ST.-BLAISE)
10. PRIORY OF ST.-QUENTIN
11. CHURCH OF ST.-DENIS
12. CHURCH OF ST.-NIZIER

13. ABBEY OF ST.-MARTIN-ÈS-AIRES
14. CHURCH OF ST.-AVENTIN
15. PRIORY OF NOTRE-DAME-EN-L'ISLE
16. ABBEY OF NOTRE-DAME-AUX-NONNAINS
17. CHURCH OF ST.-JACQUES-AUX-NONNAINS
18. CHURCH OF ST.-RÉMI
19. CHURCH OF ST.-JEAN-AU-MARCHÉ
20. TEMPLAR COMMANDERY
21. DOMINICAN FRIARY
22. CHURCH OF STE.-MADELEINE
23. ST.-PANTALÉON (FORMER SYNAGOGUE)
24. VISCOUNT'S TOWER
25. CHURCH OF ST.-NICOLAS
26. HÔTEL-DIEU-ST.-ABRAHAM

26

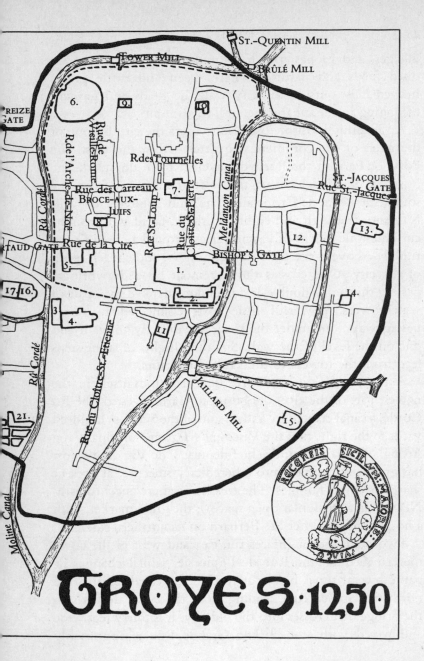

ST.-QUENTIN MILL

TOWER MILL

BRÛLÉ MILL

PREIZE
GATE

6.

9.

10.

Rue de
Vieille-Romme

R de l'Arche-de-Noé

R des Fournelles

R du Corde

Rue des Carreaux
BROCE-AUX-
JUIFS

7.

8.

St.-Pierre

Rue du Cloître St.-Pierre

Meldançon Canal

ST.-JACQUES
GATE
Rue St.-Jacques

13.

12.

TAUD GATE

Rue de la Cité

Rue St.-Loup

BISHOP'S GATE

S.

1.

17. 16.

2.

14.

3.

4.

11.

Rue du Cloître St.-Etienne

JAILLARD MILL

15.

Rᵈ Cordé

21.

Moline Canal

ΤROΥES · 1250

27

villages, and monasteries have multiplied, surrounded by tilled fields and pastures where sheep and cattle graze. Immediately outside the city walls lie fields and gardens belonging to the inhabitants of Troyes itself.

An incoming visitor to the fair enters the city by one of the gates of the commercial quarter—from the west, the Porte de Paris or the Porte d'Auxerre; from the north, the Porte de la Madeleine or the Porte de Preize; from the south, the Porte de Cronciaus. The sand-colored city wall[1] is twenty feet high and eight feet thick, faced with rough-cut limestone blocks of varying sizes, around a core of rock rubble. Above it rise the roofs, chimneys, and church spires of the city. One crosses the dry moat by a drawbridge, passing through a double-leaf iron door flanked by a pair of watchtowers, powerful little forts connected by three passageways, one under the road, one directly above it and one on the level of the wall. Spiraling flights of stone steps lead from the towers to the vaulted interiors.

A party entering the Porte de Paris finds itself in the newest part of the city, the business quarter west of the Rû Cordé, a canal created by a diversion of the Seine. A hundred yards to the right rises the Viscount's Tower,[2] originally the stronghold of the count's chief deputy. The Viscount's post has gradually evolved into a hereditary sinecure, at present shared by three families. The tower is a mere anachronism. Nearby, in a triangular open space, is the grain market, with a hospital named after St.-Bernard on its northern side.

Two main thoroughfares run east and west in the commercial section—the Rue de l'Epicerie, which changes its name several times before it reaches the canal, and to the north the Grande Rue, leading from the Porte de Paris to the bridge that crosses into the old city. It is thirty feet wide and paved with stone.[3] The Grande Rue is appreciably

Cats' Alley (Ruelle des Chats), Troyes' most picturesque street, looks today much as it did in the thirteenth century, barely seven feet wide, with housetops leaning against each other.

broader and straighter than the side streets, where riders and even pedestrians sometimes must squeeze past each other. The Ruelle des Chats—"Cats' Alley"—is seven feet wide. Even on the Grande Rue one has a sense of buildings crowding in, the three- and four-story frame houses and shops shouldering into the street, their corbelled upper stories looming irregularly above. Façades are painted red and blue, or faced with tile, often ornamented with paneling, moldings, and sawtooth. Colorful signboards hang over the doors of taverns, and tradesmen's symbols identify the shops. The shops open to the street, the lowered fronts of their stalls serving as display counters for merchandise—boots, belts, purses, knives, spoons, pots and pans, paternosters (rosaries). Inside, shopkeepers and apprentices are visible at work.

Most traffic is on foot—artisans in bright-colored tunics and hose, housewives in gowns and mantles, their hair covered by white wimples, merchants in fur-trimmed coats, here and there the black or brown habit of a priest or monk. Honking geese flutter from under the hooves of horses. Dogs and cats lurk in the doorways or forage for food with the pigeons.

The streets have been freshly cleaned for the fair, but the smells of the city are still present. Odors of animal dung and garbage mingle with pleasanter aromas from cookshops and houses. The most pungent districts are those of the fish merchants, the linen makers, the butchers and, worst of all, the tanners. In the previous century the expanding business of the tanners and butchers resulted in a typical urban problem. The bed of the Vienne became choked with refuse. Count Henry the Generous had a canal dug from the upper Seine, increasing the flow into the Vienne and flushing out the pollution. But the butchers' and tanners' district remains the most undesirable neighborhood in town. Cities such as Troyes legislate to make householders and shop-keepers clean the streets in front of their houses, and to forbid emptying waste water into the streets. But such ordinances are only half effective. Rain compounds the problem by turning the unpaved streets to mud.

The heart of the fair district surrounds the church of St.-Jean-au-Marché, a warren of little streets where the money-changers have their headquarters, and where the public scales and the guards' quarters are located. This area, half asleep all spring, is now humming. Horses clomp, hammers bang, and bales thud. Commands and curses resound in several languages, as sacks and bales from the ends of the earth are unloaded—savory spices, shimmering silks, pearls from the bottom of the sea, and wagonload after wagon-load of rich wool cloth.

Fair merchants can lodge where they wish, but fellow-countrymen tend to flock together—businessmen from Montpellier on the Rue de Montpellier, near the Porte de Paris; those from Valencia, Barcelona, and Larida in the Rue Clef-du-Bois; Venetians in the Rue du Petit Credo, where the count's provost has his lodge; Lombards in the Rue de la Trinité.

Tents and stalls are used only for the sale of secondary merchandise. The main transactions, in wool, cloth and spices, take place in large permanent halls scattered through-out the fair quarter, whose limits are carefully marked to insure collection of tolls from merchants. Several of the great cloth manufacturing cities have their halls in the Rue de l'Epicerie—Arras, Lucca, Ypres, Douai, Montauban. The hall of Rouen is in the Rue du Chaperon, that of Provins between the Rue de la Tannerie and the Commandery of the Knights Templar.

Near the canal, the Rue de l'Epicerie passes the ancient and powerful convent of Notre-Dame-aux-Nonnains and becomes the Rue Notre-Dame. Here, in stalls maintained by the convent, the Great Fire of 1188 began. To the south is the twenty-year-old Dominican friary (the Franciscans are outside the town, near the Porte de Preize). A little to the north, at the end of the Grand Rue, the Pont des Bains crosses the canal into the ancient Gallo-Roman citadel. On the right bank, above the bridge, are the public baths, where the traveler can scrub off the dust of the roads.

Across the canal lies the old city, still enclosed within its dilapidated Roman walls. Wealthy families live there, along with numerous clergy, officials serving the count, Jews in the old ghetto, some of the working class, and the poor. In the southwest corner of the square enclosure, its back to the canal, stands a large stone building, the count's palace. The great hall rises over an undercroft, with the living quarters in the rear. In front of the palace stands the pillory, a wooden structure resembling a short ladder, which often pinions a petty thief or crooked tradesman. The count's own church of St.-Etienne forms an "L" with the palace, so that he can hear masses from a platform at the end of his hall. Immediately to the north is the hospital founded by Count Henry the Generous, and at the northwest extremity of the old city rises the castle, a grim rectangular tower surrounded by a courtyard with a forbidding wall. The ancient donjon of the counts, the tower is today used as a ceremonial hall for knightings, feasts, and tourneys.

Near the center of the old city is the Augustinian abbey of St.-Loup, named after the bishop who parleyed with Attila. Originally it lay outside the walls, but following the Viking attack in 891, Abbot Adelerin moved the establishment into the city, St.-Loup's remains included. The Rue de la Cité, principal street of the old town, separates the abbey from the cathedral, which is at the southeast corner of the enclosure. Workmen are busy on the scaffolding that sheathes the mass of masonry. A huge crane, standing inside the masonry shell, drops its line over the wall. Masons' lodges and workshops crowd the space between the cathedral and the bishop's palace.

Near the old donjon is the ghetto. Well-to-do Jewish families live in the Rue de Vieille Rome, just south of the castle wall; farther south, others inhabit the Broce-aux-Juifs, an area enclosed by lanes on four sides.

This is Troyes, an old town but a new city, a feudal and ecclesiastical capital, and major center of the Commercial Revolution of the Middle Ages.

2.

A Burgher's Home

*They live very nobly, they wear a king's clothes,
have fine palfreys and horses. When squires go to
the east, the burghers remain in their beds; when the
squires go get themselves massacred, the burghers go
on swimming parties.*

—RENARD LE CONTREFAIT
a fourteenth-century clerk of Troyes

In a thirteenth-century city the houses of rich and poor
look more or less alike from the outside. Except for a
few of stone, they are all tall timber post-and-beam
structures, with a tendency to sag and lean as they get older.
In the poor quarters several families inhabit one house. A
weaver's family may be crowded into a single room, where
they huddle around a fireplace, hardly better off than the
peasants and serfs of the countryside.

A well-to-do burgher family, on the other hand, occupies
all four stories of its house, with business premises on the
ground floor, living quarters on the second and third,
servants' quarters in the attic, stables and storehouses in the
rear. From cellar to attic, the emphasis is on comfort, but it
is thirteenth-century comfort, which leaves something to be
desired even for the master and mistress.

Entering the door of such a house, a visitor finds himself
in an anteroom. One door leads to a workshop or counting

Romanesque house at Cluny. Several twelfth- and thirteenth-century houses survive in France, in Cluny, Provins, Dol-de-Bretagne, Perigueux, Le Puy, and elsewhere. (Touring-Club de France)

Thirteenth-century house. No. 6, Rue d'Avril, Cluny, this was the home of a wealthy moneychanger. The irregular stone courses, Romanesque windows, and steeply pitched roof are characteristic of medieval house construction. The brick wall is a modern addition.

room, a second to a steep flight of stairs. The greater part of
the second floor is occupied by the hall, or solar, which
serves as both living and dining room. A hearth fire blazes
under the hood of a huge chimney. Even in daytime the
fire supplies much of the house's illumination, because the
narrow windows are fitted with oiled parchment.[1] Suspended by a chain from the wall is an oil lamp, usually not
lighted until full darkness. A housewife also economizes on
candles, saving fat for the chandler to convert into a smoky,
pungent but serviceable product. Beeswax candles are
limited to church and ceremonial use.

The large low-ceilinged room is bare and chilly. Walls
are hung with panels of linen cloth, which may be dyed or
decorated with embroidery; the day of tapestry will come
in another fifty years. Carpets are extremely rare in
thirteenth-century Europe; floors are covered with rushes.
Furniture consists of benches, a long trestle table which is
dismantled after meals, a big wooden cupboard displaying
plate and silver, and a low buffet for the pottery and tin-
ware used every day. Cupboards and chests are built on
posts, with planks nailed lengthwise to form the sides. In
spite of iron bindings, and linen and leather glued inside or
out, the planks crack, split and warp. It will be two centuries before someone thinks of joining panels by tongue
and groove, or mortise and tenon, so that the wood can
expand and contract.

If furniture is drab, costume is not. A burgher and his
wife wear linen and wool in bright reds, greens, blues, and
yellows, trimmed and lined with fur. Though their garments are similar, differentiation is taking place. A century
ago both sexes wore long, loose-fitting tunics and robes that
were almost identical. Now men's clothes are shorter and
tighter than women's, and a man wears an invention of the

Middle Ages that has already become a byword for masculinity: trousers, in the form of hose, a tight-fitting combination of breeches and stockings. Over them he wears a long-sleeved tunic, which may be lined with fur, then a sleeveless belted surcoat of fine wool, sometimes with a hood. For outdoors, he wears a mantle fastened at the shoulder with a clasp or chain; although buttons are sometimes used for decoration, the buttonhole has not been invented. (It will be by the end of the century.) His clothes have no pockets, and he must carry money and other belongings in a pouch or purse slung from his belt, or in his sleeves. On his feet are boots with high tops of soft leather.

A woman may wear a tunic with sleeves laced from wrist to elbow, topped by a surcoat caught in at the waist by a belt, with full sleeves that reveal those of the tunic underneath. Her shoes are soft leather, with thin soles. Both sexes wear underclothes—women long linen chemises, men linen undershirts and underdrawers with a cloth belt.

Hair is invariably parted in the middle, a woman's in two long plaits, which she covers with a white linen wimple, a man's worn jaw-long, sometimes with bangs, and often topped with a soft cap. Men's faces are stubbly. Only a rough shave can be achieved with available instruments, and a burgher may visit the barber only once a week.

At mealtime a very broad cloth is laid on the trestle table in the solar. To facilitate service, places are set along one side only. On that side the cloth falls to the floor, doubling as a communal napkin. At a festive dinner it sometimes gets changed between courses. Places are set with knives, spoons, and thick slices of day-old bread, which serve as plates for meat. There are several kinds of knives—for cutting meat, slicing bread, opening oysters and nuts—but no forks.

Wooden casket, thirteenth century. This ironbound box ornamented with enameled medallions may have held a wealthy burgher's valuables. (Metropolitan Museum of Art, Gift of J. Pierpont Morgan, 1917)

Between each two places stands a two-handled bowl, or *écuelle*, which is filled with soup or stew. Two neighbors share the *écuelle*, as well as a winecup and spoon. A large pottery receptacle is used for waste liquids, and a thick chunk of bread with a hole in the middle serves as a salt shaker.

When supper is prepared, a servant blows a horn. Napkins, basins, and pitchers are ready; everyone washes his

A thirteenth-century banquet. The scene is from an illuminated manuscript, "The Tale of Meliacin." A suitor for the hand of the princess displays his gift, a copper figurine that plays a silver trumpet. The guests sit on a bench at a trestle table, each pair sharing a wine cup and an *écuelle* knives and pieces of bread lie on the tablecloth. (Bibliothèque Nationale)

hands without the aid of soap. Courtesy requires sharing a basin with one's neighbor.

If there is no clergyman present, the youngest member of the family says grace. The guests join in the responses and the amen.

Supper may begin with a capon brewet, half soup, half stew, with the meat served in the bottom of the *écuelle*, broth poured over, and spices dusted on top. The second course is perhaps a porray, a soup of leeks, onions, chitterlings, and ham, cooked in milk, with stock and bread crumbs added. A civet of hare may follow—the meat grilled, then cut up and cooked with onions, vinegar, wine, and spices, again thickened with bread crumbs. Each course is washed down with wine from an earthenware jug. At a really elaborate meal roast meats and other stews and fish dishes follow. The meal may conclude with frumenty (a kind of custard), figs and nuts, wafers and spiced wine.

On a fast day a single meal is served after Vespers. Ordinarily it is sparse, no more than bread, water, and vegetables. However, the faithful are not uniformly austere, and in fact the clergy often find loopholes in the law. In the last century St.-Bernard testily described a fast day at a Cluniac monastery:

> Dish after dish is served. It is a fast day for meat, so there are two portions of fish . . . Everything is so artfully contrived that after four or five courses one still has an appetite . . . For (to mention nothing else) who can count in how many ways eggs alone are prepared and dressed, how diligently they are broken, beaten to froth, hard-boiled, minced; they come to the table now fried, now roasted, now mixed with other things, now alone . . . What shall I say of water-drinking, when not even watered wine is admitted? Being monks, we all suffer from poor digestions, and are therefore justified in following the Apostle's counsel [Use a little wine for thy stomach's sake]: only the word "little," which he puts first, we leave out.

Though everything except soup and sauce is finger food, table manners are important.[2] Gentlefolk eat slowly, take small bites, do not talk while eating, do not drink with their mouths full. Knives are never put in the mouth. Soup must be eaten silently, and the spoon not left in the dish. One does not belch, lean on the table, hang over his dish, or pick

his nose, teeth, or nails. Food is not dipped into the salt cellar. Bread is broken, not bitten. Blowing on food to cool it is commonly practiced but frowned upon. Because the wine cup is shared, one must wipe the grease from one's lips before putting them to the cup.

When the family has eaten, servants and apprentices take their turn at the table. They are permitted to eat their fill but not to linger. Then the table is cleared; bowls, knives and spoons washed; and pots and kettles cleaned. One servant takes a pair of buckets and heads for the well down the street. Another collects the leftovers from the meal and takes them to the door, where a pauper or two generally waits; in bad times there will be a crowd. In the last century, beggars were permitted to enter great houses and solicit directly from the table, but now they are restricted to the doorstep.

After the solar, the principal room on the second floor is the large kitchen. Its focus is the fireplace, back to back and sharing the chimney with the main hearth in the solar. Tall enough for a man to walk into, the fireplace burns logs that are three and a half feet long. The fire is rarely allowed to die. If it does, the servants must start it again with a fire-iron, a three-inch piece of metal shaped like a flatiron, which is struck against a piece of flint to produce sparks.

On the hearth, a toothed rack supports an iron kettle where water is kept heating. Other kettles and cauldrons stand on trivets. Skimmers, spoons, shovels and scoops, pokers, pincers, spits and skewers, and a long-handled fork hang in front of the chimney. Nearby is the kitchen garbage pit, emptied periodically, and a vat which holds the water supply. Live fish swim in a leather tank, next to a wooden pickling tub. On a long table against the wall are casseroles of varying sizes. Small utensils are stored on a

Another fine example of a thirteenth-century house. Known as the Hôtel de Vauluisant, it is situated in Provins. (Archives Photographiques, Paris)

shelf above: sieves, colanders, mortars and pestles, graters. Hand towels hang out of the reach of mice.

Next to the table stands a spice cupboard—locked, because some of its contents are fabulously expensive. Saffron, of which a rich man's wife may hoard a minute quantity, is worth a good deal more than its weight in gold. Ginger, nutmeg, cinnamon, and several other seasonings imported from the distant East are nearly as dear. Less prohibitive are clove, cannel, mace, cumin. Pepper is just costly enough to be a rich man's table seasoning, as is mustard. Apart from these condiments, the housewife relies on the herbs from her own garden, which hang drying in bunches from the kitchen beams: basil, sage, savory, marjoram, rosemary, and thyme.

On the floor above the solar and kitchen are the family bedrooms. Master and mistress sleep on a great canopied bed as much as eight feet long and seven feet wide, the straw-filled mattress hung on rope suspenders, and covered with linen sheets, blankets of wool and fur, and feather pillows. Children's beds are smaller, with serge and linsey-woolsey covers. Bedrooms are sparsely furnished—a wash-basin on a stand, a table, a few chairs, a chest. Perhaps once a week a wooden tub for bathing is set up, and servants lug up buckets that have been heated over the kitchen fire. In the interval between baths members of the household may take shampoos.

Along the wall above the head of the bed runs a horizontal pole, or perch, for hanging up clothes at night. Modesty dictates that husband and wife get in bed in their undergarments, removing them after snuffing the candle and tucking them under the pillows. People sleep naked.

The toilet is usually a privy in the stable yard. A few city houses have a "garderobe" off the sleeping room, over a chute to a pit in the cellar that is emptied at intervals. Ideally such a convenience is built out over the water, an arrangement enjoyed by the count's palace on the canal. Next best is a drainpipe to a neighboring ditch or stream.

Ceaseless war is carried on against fleas, bedbugs, and other insects. Strategies vary. One practice is to fold coverlets, furs, and clothes so tightly in a chest that the fleas will suffocate. A housewife may spread birdlime or turpentine on trenchers of bread, with a lighted candle in the middle. More simply, she may cover a straw mattress with a white sheepskin so that the enemy can be seen and crushed. Netting is used in summer against flies and mosquitoes, and insect traps have been devised, of which the simplest is a rag dipped in honey.

Even for a well-to-do city family, making life comfortable is a problem. But arriving at a point where comfort becomes a problem for a fair number of people is a sign of advancing civilization.

3.

A Medieval Housewife

*He is upheld by the hope of his wife's care . . . to
have his shoes removed before a good fire, his feet
washed and to have fresh shoes and stockings, to be
given good food and drink, to be well served and well
looked after, well bedded in white sheets . . . well
covered with good furs, and assuaged with other
joys and amusements . . . concerning which I am
silent; and on the next day fresh shirts and garments.*

—THE GOODMAN OF PARIS

At daybreak cathedral bells sound the first note in a
clangorous dialogue that keeps time all day for the
citizens of Troyes. The cathedral, as the bishop's
church, has the right to speak first—before the count's
chapel or Notre-Dame-aux-Nonnains—a precedence con-
ceded to Bishop Hervée after an acrimonious dispute.
Troyes has so many bells that a verse runs:

> Where are you from? I'm from Troyes.
> What do you do there? We ring.

The bells do not ring the hours, but at three-hour
intervals,[1] marking the offices of the Church. People do not
care exactly what time it is; they want to know how much
daylight is left. The bells are their only timekeepers.
Monasteries, churches, and public buildings may have sun-

46

dials or clepsydras (water clocks). The weight-driven clock has yet to be invented.

The dawn bells—"Prime"—launch the day's activity. The men of the guard go off duty as thieves slink to their cellars and honest men begin work. Blacksmiths and butchers are among the first. Shutters rattle and shops open. Cows, sheep, and pigs, mooing and squealing their way out of stable yards to pastures outside the walls, meet sleepy maidservants going to the wells with buckets and basins.

In the tall houses, people crawl out of bed, grope for their underclothes beneath the pillow and their outer garments on the perch, and splash their faces and hands with cold water. An honest housewife completes her morning grooming by combing and plaiting her hair. She has heard more than one sermon censuring women who indulge in cosmetics. The preachers like to remind their lady parishioners that wigs are made of the hair of persons who are now likely to be found in hell or purgatory, and that "Jesus Christ and his blessed mother, of royal blood though they were, never thought of wearing" the belts of silk, gold, and silver that are fashionable among wealthy women. The bandeaux which some ladies employ to bind their bosoms are also frowned on; in the next world, the preachers say, these will be transformed into bands of fire.

The feminine ideal is a slender figure, blond hair, and fair skin—"white as snow on ice," says a poet. To achieve this ideal some women use ointments that are guaranteed to lighten complexions, but sometimes take the skin off along with the pigment.

One of the housewife's first chores in the morning is shopping for food, which must be done daily. In Troyes most of the food purveyors are clustered in the narrow streets that surround St.-Jean—the Rue du Domino, the

Rue des Croisettes (Little Crosses), the Cour de la Rencontre (Meeting Court). Many street names designate the trade practiced there—the Rue de la Corderie (Ropemakers), Rue de la Grande Tannerie and Rue de la Petite Tannerie, Rue de l'Orfàvrerie (Goldsmiths), Rue de l'Epicerie (Grocers). The Rue du Temple runs past the commandery of the Knights Templar.

Signs furnish a colorful punctuation to the rows of wooden houses—a bush for the vintner, three gilded pills for the apothecary, a white arm with stripes of red for the surgeon-barber, a unicorn for the goldsmith, a horse's head for the harness maker.

Shoppers must watch their step in the streets, which are full of unpleasant surprises. In the butchers' quarter slaughtering is performed on the spot, and blood dries in the sun amid piles of offal and swarms of flies. Outside the poulterers' shops geese, tied to the aprons of the stalls, honk and gabble. Chickens and ducks, their legs trussed, flounder on the ground, along with rabbits and hares.

The housewives pinching the fowl carry in their purses three kinds of coins. Two are of copper—oboles and half-oboles, the small change of the Middle Ages. The only coin of value is the silver penny, or *denier*. A fat capon costs six deniers,[2] an ordinary chicken four, a rabbit five, a large hare twelve.

Near the butchers' and poulterers' stalls are other food speciality shops. A pastry shop offers wafers at three deniers a pound. The spice-grocer displays a variety of wares. Vinegar comes in big jars at from two to five deniers. Most edible oils cost seven to nine deniers, although olive oil is double that price. Salt is cheap (five pounds for two deniers), pepper dear (four deniers an ounce), sugar even dearer. Even honey is expensive. Sweeteners appear on few medieval tables.

At the bakery, where an apprentice may be seen removing loaves from the oven with a long-handled wooden shovel, the prices of the different loaves are legally fixed. So are the weights, with variations permitted from year to year depending on the wheat crop. Bread is rather expensive this year. Some bakers cheat on quality or weight, and for this reason each baker must mark his bread with his own seal. A detected cheater ends up in the pillory with one of his fraudulent loaves hung around his neck.

The housewife is always on the lookout for poor quality or doubtful quantity—watered wine, milk or oil, bread with too much yeast, blown-out meat, stale fish reddened with pig's blood, cheese made to look richer by soaking it in broth. Dishonest tradesmen are the butt of numerous stories. A favorite: A man asked the sausage butcher for a discount because he had been a faithful customer for seven years. "Seven years!" exclaimed the butcher. "And you're still alive?"

Besides the food shops, there are the peddlers. About terce (nine o'clock) their cries augment the din of the streets. They sell fish, chicken, fresh and salt meat, garlic, honey, onions, fruit, eggs, leeks, and pasties filled with fruit, chopped ham, chicken or eel, seasoned with pepper, soft cheese and egg. "Good Champagne cheese! Good cheese of Brie!" cry the street vendors in Paris, and probably in Troyes as well. Wine and milk are also peddled in the street.

Marketing is only the first step in the preparation of food. All cooking is done over the open fire; there are no ovens in private houses. Food must be prepared and mixed by hand. Utensils are of iron, copper, pewter, earthenware—no steel or glass. There are no paper or paper products, no chocolate, coffee, tea, potatoes, rice, spaghetti, noodles, tomatoes, squash, corn, baking powder, baking soda, or gelatin. Citrus fruit is a rare delicacy.

Techniques for preserving food are limited. Fish are kept live or in pickling tanks, or salted and smoked; meat may be salted; winter vegetables can be stored in a cool cellar; some fruits, vegetables, and herbs are dried in the sun.

The dinner hour depends on the season and the trade of the household; one may dine as early as ten. Kitchen preparations begin early. Servants clean, mince, blanch, parboil, crush herbs in the mortar, fry and grill meat. To thicken sauces, bread crumbs ground with the pestle are used instead of flour. Recipes are characterized by a staggering complexity, except for roasts, which are turned on a spit over the fire. Vegetables must be blanched, rinsed and cooked for long periods in several changes of water; the mortar and strainer are in constant use; the lists of ingredients are endless. Menus in a prosperous household consist of a series of broths or brewets, thick soups, stews, roasts and fish dishes, followed by savories, fruit or pastries, spiced wine, and wafers. At feasts the last course is preceded by glazed and decorated *entremets* (eaten "between courses"). These are no trifles, but boars' heads, or swans roasted in their feathers, carried around on platters for all to admire.

Many tasks besides those of the kitchen occupy the housewife and her servants, of which even modest households have a few. City women in any case are better off than the peasant wives of the countryside, who must spin their own thread with the distaff and make their own cloth.

Among the daily tasks are making the beds, accomplished with the aid of a long stick to reach across the vast breadth of the master's bed. Covers and cushions must be shaken out and chamber pots emptied. Servants make up the kitchen fire in the morning, fill the water vat and the big iron kettle in the kitchen, sweep out the entrance and the hall, and occasionally lay fresh rushes.

There are laundresses in Troyes, but most households do their own laundry. From time to time, shirts, tablecloths, and bed linen are put in a wooden trough and soaked in a mixture of wood ashes and caustic soda, then pounded, rinsed and dried in the sun. Soft soap is also used, and is made at home by boiling caustic soda with animal fat. A much better hard soap is made in Spain from olive oil, but is too expensive for everyday use.

Furs and woolen clothes are periodically beaten, shaken, and scrutinized. A special cleaning fluid for furs and wool is made of wine, lye, fuller's earth (hydrous silicate of ammonia), and verjuice (pressed from green grapes). Grease stains are soaked in warm wine, or rubbed with fuller's earth, or with chicken feathers rinsed in hot water. Faded colors can be restored with a sponge soaked in diluted lye or verjuice. Furs hardened from dampness are sprinkled with wine and flour and allowed to dry, then rubbed back to their original softness.

Both city and country women cultivate gardens,[3] growing lettuce, sorrel, shallots, beets, scallions, and herbs. The herbs serve medicinal as well as cooking purposes—sage, parsley, fennel, dittany, basil, hyssop, rue, savory, coriander, mint, marjoram, mallow, agrimony, nightshade, borage. Flowers are planted indiscriminately with vegetables and herbs, and their blossoms are often used in cooking. Petals of lilies, lavender, peonies, and marigolds decorate stews; violets are minced with onions and lettuce as a salad, or cooked in broth; roses and primroses are stewed for dessert. Currant and raspberry bushes, pear, apple and medlar trees, and grapevines are also city garden favorites.

In the larger cities, garden space has been crowded out by housing. Now cities like Paris are clearing slum areas for use as city parks, like the Pré aux Clercs and the garden that Louis IX has created on one of the islands in the Seine.

Crusades and pilgrimages have introduced new plants, such as the oleander and the pomegranate. Legend will claim that St.-Louis brought the ranunculus to France from the Holy Land, and Thibaut the Songwriter the red rose of Provins, the town's emblem—although the rose that Thibaut brought was probably the pink Rose of Damascus, unusual in the Middle Ages in that it flowered more than once a season. Edmund of Lancaster, after marrying the widow of Thibaut's nephew, will adopt the rose of Provins as the emblem of his own house, so that the red rose of Lancaster, ex-Provins, will eventually help provide a romantic name for the bloody English dynastic war.

Monasteries, too, make their contributions to gardening, perpetuating strains of fruits and vegetables that might otherwise have been lost, or spreading new varieties and horticultural information when the monks go on pilgrimages.

To be a woman in the thirteenth century is much like being a woman in any age. Women are somewhat oppressed and exploited, as always, but as in any age, social status is the really important thing, and a burgher's wife is no serf. She is a person of dignity and worth, important in her family and respected in the community.

Unmarried women can own property, and in the absence of male heirs they can also inherit. Women of all classes have rights in property by law and custom. Women can sue and be sued, make wills, make contracts, even plead their own cases in court. Women have been known to appear as their husbands' attorneys. A "Portia" character is the heroine of a contemporary romance, *The Hard Creditor*.

Well-to-do women know how to read and write and

figure; some know a little Latin, or boast such ladylike accomplishments as embroidering and playing the lute. Girls receive instruction from private teachers, or board at convents. The convent of Notre-Dame-aux-Nonnains has a school for girls dating back to the sixth century. Universities are closed to women, but they are equally closed to men except those who are being trained for the clergy, law, or medicine. Among the landed gentry, women are better educated than men. In the romance *Galeran* a boy and girl brought up together are given typically different schooling—the girl learning to embroider, read, write, speak Latin, play the harp, and sing; the boy, to hawk, hunt, shoot, ride, and play chess.

Women work outside the home at an astonishing variety of crafts and professions. They may be teachers, midwives, laundresses, lacemakers, seamstresses, and even members of normally male trades and occupations[4]—weavers, fullers, barbers, carpenters, saddlers, tilers, and many others. Wives commonly work at their husbands' crafts, and when a man dies his widow carries on the trade. Daughters not infrequently learn their father's craft along with their brothers. In the countryside girls hire out as farm workers. The lady of the manor takes charge of the estate while her husband is off to war, Crusade, or pilgrimage, and wives run businesses while their husbands are away.

Women do suffer from an inequity in respect to wages, which are lower than men's for the same work. An English treatise on husbandry says, "If this is a manor where there is no dairy, it is always good to have a woman there at much less cost than a man."

Politically, women have no voice. They do not sit on the Town Council or in the courts, or serve as provosts or officials. Basically, this is because they do not bear arms. Yet women play political roles, often with distinction—Empress Matilda of England, Eleanor of Aquitaine, Queen Blanche of France, Countess Jeanne of Flanders, Blanche of Champagne, and many more. Countess Marie, wife of Henry the Generous, was asked to arbitrate claims between the churches of St.-Etienne and St.-Loup, and with her brother-in-law, William of the White Hands, archbishop of Reims, to decide important cases, including the seigneury of Vertus. In war, or at least sieges, women often play the heroine.

Women occupy positions of power and influence in the Church. The abbess of a convent such as Notre-Dame-aux-Nonnains[5] is invested with important executive responsibilities. Usually such posts are accorded to ladies of high rank, like Alix de Villehardouin, daughter of the marshal of Champagne. Abbesses are not afraid to assert their rights. A few years hence an abbess of Notre-Dame, Odette de Pougy, will defy the Pope's excommunication and lead a party of armed men to defend what she regards as the rights of her abbey. This establishment owes its extraordinary prestige to its ancient origins, which are believed to date from the third century. The abbess actually enjoys rights over the bishop of Troyes. When a new bishop is installed, he must lead a procession to the abbey, mounted on a palfrey that is handed over, saddle included, to the abbess's stable. Inside the convent, the bishop kneels and receives cross, mitre, and prayer book from the abbess's hands. He recites an oath: "I . . . bishop of Troyes, swear to observe the rights, franchises, liberties, and privileges of this convent of Notre-Dame-aux-Nonnains, with the help of God and his holy saints." The bishop spends the night in the convent and is given as a gift the bed in which he has slept, with all its furnishings. Only the next day does his installation as bishop take place in the cathedral.

Women achieve distinction outside the cloister, too. Marie de France is the most gifted woman poet of the Middle Ages, and "wise Héloise" the most noteworthy bluestocking, but there are many more. The contemporary scholar Albert the Great, debating whether the Virgin Mary knew the seven liberal arts, resolves the question affirmatively.

The cult of Mary serves to elevate the image of women and to counterbalance the misogyny of ascetic preachers who bestow such epithets as "man's confounder," "mad beast," "stinking rose," "sad paradise," "sweet venom," "luscious sin," and "bitter sweet," while lingering over the attractions of the temptresses. The chivalric ideal also glorifies women. The Church recognizes the wife to be subject to her husband, as Paul recommended, but as his companion, not as mere mistress or servant. Married people are expected to treat each other with respect, and many husbands and wives never call each other anything but Sir and Madam.

Wife-beating is common in an age when corporal punishment is the norm. But wives do not necessarily get the worst of it. A contemporary observer remarks that men rarely have the mastery of their wives, that nearly everywhere women dominate their husbands. One preacher complains that formerly wives were faithful to their husbands and peaceful as ewe lambs; now they are lionesses. Another tells the story of a storm at sea, when the sailors wished to throw into the sea anything that might overload the ship, and a certain husband handed over his wife, saying that there was no object of such intolerable weight. The expression "wearing the pants in the family" is already current, and henpecked husbands are a favorite theme of the *fabliaux*.

Perhaps the most important point to note about the medieval housewife, in contrast to women of earlier times, is that she has a purse. She goes shopping, she gives alms, she pays fees, she hires labor; she may, if the occasion arises, buy privileges and pay bribes.

She may do many other things with her money. Women make large gifts of land, money, and chattels to church institutions; found convents, monasteries, hospitals, orphanages, and asylums; buy benefices for their sons and places in convents for their daughters; engage in trading operations. They are denounced by priests for usury, pawnbroking, and price manipulations, and for their reckless expenditures for luxury goods. They may travel extensively, sometimes as far as the Holy Land.

A woman of means is always a person to reckon with.

Daughters of burghers, like daughters of knights, learn definite rules of conduct. A poet, Robert of Blois, has codified the behavior of women of the gentle class:

> *En route* to church or elsewhere, a lady must walk straight and not trot or run, or idle either. She must salute even the poor.
>
> She must let no one touch her on the breast except her husband. For that reason, she must not let anyone put a pin or a brooch on her bosom.
>
> No one should kiss her on the mouth except her husband. If she disobeys this injunction, neither loyalty, faith nor noble birth will avert the consequences.
>
> Women are criticized for the way they look at people, like a sparrowhawk ready to pounce on a swallow. Take care: glances are messengers of love; men are prompt to deceive themselves by them.
>
> If a man courts a lady, she must not boast of it. It is base to boast, and besides, if she takes a fancy later to love this person, the secret will be more difficult to keep.

A lady shuns the fashionable décolletage, a sign of shamelessness.

A lady does not accept gifts. For gifts which are given you in secret cost dear; one buys them with one's honor. There are, however, honest gifts which it is proper to thank people for.

Above all, a lady does not scold. Anger and high words are enough to distinguish a low woman from a lady. The man who injures you shames himself and not you; if it is a woman who scolds you, you will break her heart by refusing to answer her.

Women must not swear, drink too much or eat too much.

The lady who, when a great lord salutes her, remains silent with bowed head is badly brought up. A lady removes her hood before those whom she would honor. One may only remain with head bent when one has something to hide—if one has a yellow complexion, or is ugly. If you have an unattractive smile, however, hide it with your hand.

Ladies with pale complexions should dine early. Good wine colors the face. If your breath is bad, hold it in church when you receive the blessing.

Especially in church one must watch one's countenance, for one is in the public eye, which notes evil and good. One must kneel courteously, pray and not laugh or talk too much.

Rise at the moment of the Scripture, cross yourself at beginning and end. At the offering, hold yourself straight. Rise also, hands joined, at the elevation, then pray on your knees for all Christians. If you are ill or pregnant, you may read your psalter seated.

If you have a good voice, sing boldly. In the company of people who ask you, and by yourself for your own pleasure, sing; but do not abuse their patience, so that people will say, as they sometimes do, "Good singers are often a bore."

Cut your fingernails frequently, down to the quick, for cleanliness' sake. Cleanliness is better than beauty.

In passing other people's houses, refrain from glancing inside. To enter without knocking is indiscreet.

One must know how to eat—not to talk or laugh too much at table, not to pick out the best pieces, not to eat too much as a guest, not to criticize the food, to wipe one's mouth but not one's nose on the cloth.[6]

4.

Childbirth and Children

When they are washed of filth, they soon defile themselves again. When their mother washes and combs them, they kick and sprawl, and push with feet and hands, and resist with all their might. They always want to drink, unless they are out of bed, when they cry for meat. Always they cry, jangle and jape, except when they are asleep.

—BARTHOLOMEW ANGLICUS

The greatest hazard in the life of a woman of the thirteenth century is childbirth. If she survives the childbearing period, she stands a good chance of outliving her husband. There are no obstetrical instruments and no techniques for dealing with a breach presentation. Caesarian section is performed only when mother or child is dead, and then without antiseptics or anesthesia. If the pelvic opening is too small for the child's head, nothing can be done.

The baby's chances of survival are poorer than the mother's. Many die at birth, more during infancy. Birth defects are common, and generally attributed to supernatural causes. An eleventh-century king, Robert the Pious, was excommunicated for marrying a widow for whose child he had stood godfather. According to a chronicler, the pair was punished when their own child was born "with the head of a goose." Chastened Robert hastily put his queen away in a convent.

An old superstition holds that when twins are born the mother has had intercourse with two different men. In a popular romance, *Galeran*, the wife of a knight insults one of her husband's vassals by telling him that everyone knows twins are the product of two fathers. Two years later the lady has cause to repent her words when she herself gives birth to twin girls. Michael Scot, astrologer to Frederick II, asserts that multiple births are entirely normal and may run as high as seven: three boys, three girls, and the "middle cell"—a hermaphrodite.

Contemporary scientists agree that for a month each planet exerts its influence over the development of the child in the womb. Saturn bestows the virtue of discerning and reasoning, Jupiter magnanimity, Mars animosity and irascibility, the sun the power of learning, and so forth. When the influence of the stars is too strong, the child talks early, has discretion beyond his age, and dies young. Some say that if the hour of conception is known, the entire life of the child can be predicted. Michael Scot urges every woman to note the exact moment, to facilitate astrological forecasting. When his patron Frederick II married a third wife, sister of Henry III of England, he delayed consummation until the morning after the wedding, the moment astrology deemed favorable. Afterwards Frederick handed over his wife to the care of Saracen eunuchs and assured her that she was pregnant with a son, which information he also conveyed in a letter to the English king. Frederick's confidence was justified. The next year a son was born.

It is widely believed that the sex of a child can be foretold and even influenced. A drop of the mother's milk or blood may be dropped into pure spring water; if it sinks, the child will be a boy, if it floats, a girl. Or if a pregnant woman, asked to hold out her hand, extends the right, the child will be a boy; if the left, a girl. A woman who wants to have a boy is supposed to sleep on her right side.

When labor is imminent, the lying-in chamber is prepared for visiting and display—the best coverlets, fresh rushes on the floor, chairs and cushions. A cupboard exhibits the family's finest possessions—gold and silver cups, enamelware, ivory, richly bound books. Dishes of sugared almonds and candied fruits are set out for the guests.

Doctors do not attend women in childbirth. Men are excluded from the lying-in chamber. Midwives are therefore indispensable, so much so that when Louis IX decided to take his queen along on a Crusade, he also took a midwife, who assisted at two royal childbirths in the Orient.

During labor the midwife rubs her patient's belly with ointment to ease her travail and bring it to a quicker conclusion. She encourages the patient with comforting words. If the labor is difficult, sympathetic magic is invoked. The patient's hair is loosened and all the pins are removed. Servants open all the doors, drawers, and cupboards in the house and untie all the knots. Jasper is a gemstone credited with childbirth-assisting powers, as well as the powers of preventing conception, checking menstrual flow, and reducing sexual desire. The dried blood of a crane and its right foot are also useful in labor, and one authority recommends water in which a murderer has washed his hands. In extreme cases there are incantations of magical words, whispered in the patient's ear, but priests frown on this practice.

When the baby is born, the midwife ties the umbilical cord and cuts it at four fingers' length. She washes the baby and rubs him all over with salt, then gently cleanses his palate and gums with honey, to give him an appetite. She dries him with fine linen and wraps him so tightly in swaddling bands that he is almost completely immobilized and looks not unlike a little corpse in a winding sheet.

He is shown to his father and the rest of the family, then placed in the wooden cradle next to his mother's bed, in a dark corner where the light cannot injure his eyes. A servant rocks him, so that the fumes from the hot, moist humors of his body will mount to his brain and make him sleep. He remains securely bundled until he is old enough to sit up, lest his tender limbs be twisted out of shape. He is nursed, bathed, and changed every three hours, and rubbed with rose oil.

Well-to-do women rarely nurse their own children. The wet nurse is chosen with care, for all manner of qualities may be imbibed with her milk. She must be of good character, have no physical defects, and be neither too fat nor too thin. Above all, she must be healthy, for corrupt milk is blamed for many of the maladies that afflict infants. She must watch her diet—eat white bread, good meat, rice, lettuce, almonds and hazelnuts, and drink good wine. She must rest and sleep well and use moderation in bathing and in working. If her milk fails, she eats peas and beans and gruel boiled in milk. She avoids onions, garlic, vinegar and highly seasoned foods. If the doctor prescribes medicine for the baby, it is administered to the nurse. As the baby grows bigger, she will chew his meat for him. She is often the recipient of presents to sweeten her disposition and milk.

The baby is usually baptized the day he is born. Covered with a robe of silk and gold cloth, the little bundle is borne to church by one of his female relatives, while another holds the train of his mantle. The midwife carries the christening bonnet. Nurse, relatives, godparents, and friends follow. If the child is a boy, two godfathers and a godmother are chosen; if a girl, two godmothers and one godfather. The temptation to enlist as many important people as possible in the child's behalf led to naming so many godparents that the Church has now restricted the allotment to three, who are expected to give handsome presents.

The church door is decorated for the occasion, fresh straw spread on the floor, and the baptismal font covered with velvet and linen. The baby is undressed on a silk-cushioned table. The priest traces the sign of the cross on his forehead with holy oil, reciting the baptismal service. The godfather lifts him to the basin, and the priest plunges him into the water. The nurse dries and swaddles him, and the midwife ties on the christening cap to protect the holy oil on his forehead.

Birth records[1] are purely private—records kept by the parish, are three hundred years in the future. In a well-to-do family the father may write the baby's name and birth date in the Book of Hours, the family prayer book. If it is ever necessary to establish age or family origin in a court of law, the oral testimony of the midwife, godparents, and priest will be taken down and recorded by a notary.

When the mother recovers from her confinement, she is "churched." Until this ceremony has taken place she is considered impure and may not make bread, serve food, or have contact with holy water. If a mother is churched on Friday, she will become barren. A day when a wedding has taken place in the church also threatens bad luck.

On an appropriate day for the ceremony the mother puts on her wedding gown and, accompanied by family and friends, enters the church carrying a lighted candle. The priest meets her at the door, makes the sign of the cross, sprinkles her with holy water, and recites a psalm. Holding one end of his stole, she follows him into the nave, while he says, "Enter the temple of God, adore the Son of the holy Virgin Mary, who has given you the blessing of motherhood." If a mother dies in childbirth, this same ceremony takes place, with the midwife or a friend acting as proxy.

Leaving the church, the mother keeps her eyes straight in front of her, for if she sees someone known for his evil character, or with a defect, the baby will be similarly afflicted. But if her glance lights on a little boy, it is a happy omen—her next child will be a boy.

The celebration is topped off with a feast for godparents, relatives, and friends.

From swaddling bands, the infant graduates directly to adult dress. He is subject to fairly strict discipline, often physical, but is indulged in games and play. His mother may hide and watch while he searches for her, then, just as he begins to cry, leap out and hug him. If he bumps himself on a bench, she beats the bench until the child feels avenged.

Children play with tops, horseshoes, and marbles. They stagger about on stilts. Girls have dolls of baked clay or wood. Adults and children alike engage in outdoor games such as prisoner's base, bowling, blindman's buff. Sports are popular too—swimming, wrestling, and early forms of football and tennis; the latter is played without a racket but with a covering for the hand. All classes enjoy cock fighting. In winter, people tie on their feet skates made of horses' shinbones, and propel themselves on the ice with a pole shod with iron. Boys joust with the pole as they shoot past each other.

Young and old play dice, chess, and checkers. Chess is in great vogue. Some people own magnificent boards, mounted on trestles, with heavy pieces carved out of ivory— the bishop with his mitre, the knight fighting a dragon,

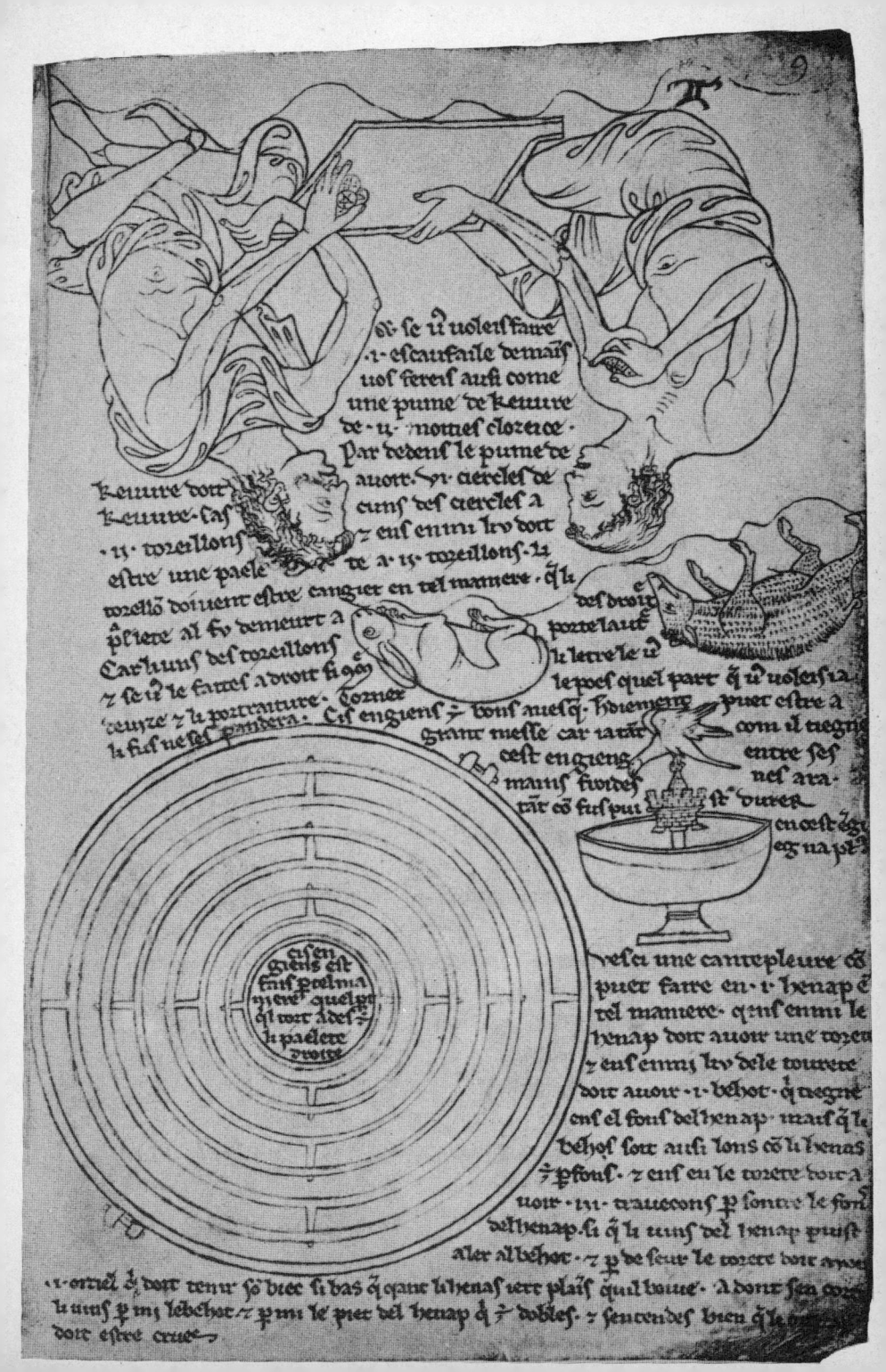

Se il uoles faire
.i. escaufaile de mais
uos sereis ausi come
une pume de keuure
de .ii. moties clorence
Par dedens le pume de
auoir. .vi. cierceles de
cuns des cierceles a
eus enmi lev doit
estre une paele
de a .ii. torellons. li
torello doiuent estre cangier en tel maniere. qil

keuure doit
keuure las
.ii. torellons
estre une paele

pliere al tu demeurt a
Car luns des torellons
z se il le faites adroit si qil
ceuze z li portraiture. Cis enguiens z tous nuele.

des droit
porte laut
li letre le u
le poes quel part q il uoles la
grant nesle car iarte
cest enguiens
mains surdes
tant cõ sus pui

puer estre a
com il uiegnia
entre ses
nes ara
st uures

en cest eg
eg na pt

uesi une cantepleure cõ
puer faire en .i. henap e
tel maniere. qil enmi le
henap doit auoir une tore
z eus enmi lev dele torere
doit auoir .i. behot. qi uiegne
ens el fons del henap. mais qil
behos soit ausi lons cõ li henas
z psous. z eus eu le torere doir a
auoir .iii. traueçons p sontre le fon
del henap. si qil cuns del henap puist
aler al behot. z p de seur le torere doit ape

cis
engiens est
fais par mai
nere quelqil
soit adest z
li paelere
droite

.i. ortiel q doit tenir so biec si bas q qant li henas sert plais quil uaine. Adont sen co
li tuns p mi lebehot z pmi le pier del henap q z dobles. z sentendes bien q le o
doit estre crue

king and queen in ceremonial robes and crowns. The game has recently evolved into its permanent form; until the twelfth century the two principal pieces on either side were two kings, or a king and his minister, who followed him step by step. But the minister was turned into a "dame" without at first changing his obedient course of play. Then the dame became queen and was left free to maneuver in all directions.

The Church condemns games of all forms—parlor games, playacting, dancing, cards, dice, and even physical sports, particularly at the universities. Games flourish, nevertheless, even at the court of pious St.-Louis, as the Troyen knight-chronicler Joinville observes. On shipboard during his Crusade, the king, in mourning for his brother Robert of Artois, lost his temper when he found his other brother, the count of Anjou, playing backgammon with Gautier de Nemours. The king seized dice and boards and flung them into the sea, scolding his brother for gambling at such a moment. "My lord Gautier," observes Joinville, "came off best, for he tipped all the money on the table into his lap."

Parlor games are played, too, such as those described in Adam de la Halle's *Jeu de Robin et de Marion*. In "St.-Cosme" one player represents the saint and the others bring him offerings, which they must present without laughing. Whoever falls victim to his grimaces must pay a forfeit, and become St.-Cosme himself. In another game, "The King Who Does Not Lie," a king or queen chosen by lot and crowned with straw asks questions of each player, being required in return to answer a question from each. The questions and replies of the peasant characters in *Robin* are ingenuous: "Tell me, Gautier, were you ever jealous?" "Yes, sire, the other day when a dog scratched at my sweetheart's door; I thought it was a man." "Tell us,

Dice players, from the notebook of thirteenth-century engineer Villard de Honnecourt. Dice, chess, and checkers were favorite recreations of the Middle Ages.

Huart, what do you like to eat most?" "Sire, a good rump of pork, heavy and fat, with a strong sauce of garlic and nuts."

There is no children's literature in the sense of stories written solely for children. But folk tales, passed down through the centuries in many versions, are the greatest single source of popular entertainment for adults and children alike. One that cannot fail to delight is the story of the shepherd and the king's daughter:

Once there was a king who always told the truth, and who was angry when he heard the people at his court going about calling each other liars. One day he said that no one was to say, "You're a liar," anymore, and to set the example, if anyone heard him say, "You're a liar," he would give him the hand of his daughter.

A young shepherd decided to try his luck. One night after supper, as he sometimes liked to do, the king came to the kitchen and listened to the songs and tales of the servants. When his turn came, the shepherd began this story: "I used to be an apprentice at my father's mill, and I carried the flour on an ass. One day I loaded him too heavily, and he broke right in two."

"Poor creature," the king said.

"So I cut a hazelnut stick from a tree, and I joined the two pieces of the donkey and stuck the piece of wood from front to rear to hold it together. The donkey set out again and carried the flour to my clients. What do you think of that, sire?"

"That's a pretty tall tale," the king said. "But continue."

"The next morning I was surprised to see that the stick had grown, and there were leaves, and even hazelnuts on it, and the branches went on growing and grew until they reached the sky. I climbed up the hazelnut tree, and I climbed and I climbed and pretty soon I reached the moon."

"That's pretty steep, but go on."

"There were some old women winnowing oats. When I wanted to go back to earth, the donkey had gone off with the hazelnut tree, so I had to tie the oat beards together to make a rope to go back down."

"That's very steep," the king said. "But go on."

"Unluckily my rope was short, so that I fell on a cliff so hard that my head was driven into the stone up to my shoulders. I tried to get loose, but my body got separated from my head, which was still stuck in the stone. I ran to the miller and got an iron bar to get it out."

"Steeper and steeper," said the king. "But continue."

"When I came back an enormous wolf wanted to get my head out of the rock to eat it, but I gave him a blow with the iron bar so that a letter was forced out of his behind!"

"Very steep indeed!" cried the king. "But what did the letter say?"

"The letter said, sire, that your father was a miller's apprentice at my grandfather's house."

"You're a liar!" cried the king indignantly.

"Well, king, I have won," said the shepherd. And that's how the shepherd got the king's daughter!

5.

Weddings and Funerals

*In the great hall there was much merry-making,
each one contributing what he could to the entertainment: one jumps, another tumbles, another does
magic; there is story-telling, singing, whistling,
playing on the harp, the rote, the fiddle, the flute
and pipe, singing and dancing. At the wedding that
day everything was done which can give joy. Not a
wicket or a gate was left closed; but the exits and
entrances all stood ajar, so that no one, poor or rich,
was turned away.*

—CHRÉTIEN DE TROYES in *Eric et Enide*

Marriage in the thirteenth century normally unites people of the same class. But social mobility is present here as in all times. Marriages joining prosperous burgher families with the petty nobility are not uncommon. Marriage is also an avenue for an artisan to make his fortune; an alliance with a rich widow may mean a house in town, a stock of clothing belonging to the late husband, furniture, silver, and real estate.

Arranged marriages are the rule, but the Church emphasizes consent. Its preachers heap scorn on marriages based exclusively on financial considerations. "One might as well publish the banns of Lord Such-and-Such with the purse of Madame So-and-So, and on the day of the wedding

68

lead to the church not the fiancée but her money or her cows," says the sharp-tongued Paris preacher Jacques de Vitry. By Church law, a bride must be at least twelve, a bridegroom fourteen. Consanguinity is taboo; bride and groom cannot be related in the fourth degree (until the Fourth Lateran Council in 1215 it was the seventh). The expression of the free accord of the two parties is the most important feature of the marriage ritual.

Marriages are recognized between slaves, between freemen and serfs, between Catholics and heretics, or Catholics and excommunicants, but not between Christians and heathens, since the latter have not been baptized. Until the Fourth Lateran Council, marriage between an adulterer who became free to marry and his fellow-sinner was prohibited, as was marriage between an abductor and a victim he later set free; now both are permitted.

Divorce (annulment) is rare. It is only permitted on the grounds that the union has broken one of the Church's three laws on marriage—age, consent, and consanguinity. The intricacies of consanguinity sometimes provide a loophole toward annulment for the rich and powerful, but even they cannot easily get away with fraudulent claims. King Philip Augustus ran afoul of the Church when he sought to get rid of his Danish wife, and finally had to take her back.

Marriages, at least those of the wealthy classes, have a legal as well as religious basis, with a contract drawn up by the notary specifying the bride's dowry. The son and daughter of wealthy burghers may start life with a house, one or two small farm properties, some cash, and the rent from a house in town. The contract may also specify what property will be the bride's after her husband's death; if it does not, she automatically inherits one-third of his worldly goods.

After the contract is drawn up, the next step is the betrothal, a religious ceremony of a solemnity approaching that of marriage itself. In fact, the similarity of the vows exchanged to those of the marriage ceremony gives rise to an awkward difficulty that results in many suits in the ecclesiastical courts. The Church emphasizes the distinction between these "words of the future" spoken at the betrothal and the "words of the present" that will be said at the wedding, but sometimes couples consider themselves married when they are no more than betrothed, converting an engagement into a clandestine marriage, which one party may later find easy to dissolve.

The priest asks the prospective groom, "Do you promise that you will take this woman to wife, if the Holy Church consents?" He addresses the girl similarly. The couple exchange rings, and the banns are published on three successive Sundays. Weddings cannot take place during Advent and the twelve days of Christmas, or during Lent, or between Ascension Sunday and the week of Pentecost.

On the day of the wedding, the bride's mother and sisters and some of her friends help her to dress. There is no special bridal costume. She simply wears her best clothes: her finest linen chemise; her best silk tunic, trimmed with fur, perhaps with a velvet surcoat over it, embroidered with gold thread; and a mantle edged with gold lace. On her head a small veil is held by a narrow gold band; on her feet are shoes of fine leather, worked with gold.

The groom is also dressed in his best. As they ride to church, a little troop of *jongleurs* precedes them, playing on flute, viol, harp, and bagpipe. Behind ride parents and relatives and the other wedding guests. All along the way crowds gather to watch. In the square in front of the church everyone dismounts, and the priest steps out under the portico, carrying an open book and also the wedding ring.

He interrogates the couple: Are they of age? Do they swear that they are not within the forbidden degree of consanguinity? Do their parents consent? Have the banns been published? Finally, do they themselves both freely consent? Taking each other's right hand they repeat their vows.

The priest delivers a short homily. A typical example, by Henri of Provins, dwells on religious education of children, domestic peace, and mutual fidelity. Henri observes that at the moment of the Flood, the Lord by preference saved married creatures; that if the blessed Virgin, the Queen of Paradise, had not been married God would not have been born from her womb; and that conjugal life represents a model of felicity in this world.

The priest blesses the ring; the groom takes it and slips it in turn on each of three fingers of the bride's left hand, saying, "In the Name of the Father, and of the Son, and of the Holy Ghost." Finally he fits it onto her third finger, saying, "With this ring I thee wed."

Alms are distributed by the bride and groom to the poor who have collected outside the portico, and the wedding party enters the church. At this point, some ten years before in Dijon, a moneylender met with disaster at his wedding when one of the sculptures on the portico—a stone figure of a usurer in a Last Judgment scene—fell and struck him a fatal blow on the head with its purse. His relatives and friends obtained permission to demolish the other sculptures on the portico.[1]

By their exchange of promises, the young couple are married. After the nuptial mass, the groom receives the Kiss of Peace from the priest and transmits it to his bride. They leave the church, remount their horses, and the procession returns to the bride's home, again led by the little troop of minstrels.

A wedding feast in a wealthy burgher's household is gargantuan, with wine by the barrel, legs of beef, mutton, veal and venison, capons, ducklings, chicken, rabbits, wafers from the wafer maker, spices, confections, oranges, apples, cheese, dozens of eggs, perhaps a boar's head or a swan in its plumage. An array of extra servants is hired for the day— porters, cooks, waiters, carvers, stewards, a sergeant to guard the door, a chaplet maker to prepare garlands.

Jongleurs[2] accompany the successive courses with music, and as soon as the spiced wine, wafers, and fruit are served the entertainment begins. It starts off with handsprings, tumbles, and other acrobatics. Imitations of bird calls, sleight-of-hand tricks, and a juggling act are likely to be on the program. Interspersed are singers who accompany themselves on two musical inventions of the Middle Ages: the six-stringed, pear-shaped lute, which is plucked, or the five-stringed viol, the first bowed instrument. Both are tuned in fourths and fifths, the accompaniment following the tune either in unison or at intervals of an octave or a fifth, sometimes with a drone note (a repeated tone with unchanging pitch) in the bass.

The professional entertainment over, tables are dismantled and guests join hands to dance and sing carols, accompanied by lute and viol, or perhaps by a tabor-pipe and tabor—a small flute played with the left hand and a light tambourine-like drum played with the right; sometimes the tabor is fastened to the player's shoulder and he uses his own head as a drumstick.

At suppertime the tables are set up again, for more food, more wine, more music. At Vespers the priest arrives, and the guests accompany the young couple to their house. The priest blesses the new hearth, the chamber, and the nuptial bed, and gives his blessing again to bride and groom. The bride's mother has taken care to search the bed to make sure that no ill-wisher has secreted anything there that may impede conjugal relations, such as two halves of an acorn or granulated beans.

The celebration is usually over in the morning, but a really big wedding can go on for days. One such wedding, described in a romance called *Flamenca*, lasted "several weeks." The streets were decorated with tapestries, spices burned in all the squares of the town; "five hundred sets of clothes, of purple decorated with gold leaf, a thousand lances, a thousand shields, a thousand swords, a thousand hauberks and a thousand chargers" were prepared as gifts for the wedding guests. The wedding cortege was "several leagues long." "Two hundred jongleurs" fiddled while the guests danced, and story tellers recounted the tales of "Priam, Helen, Ulysses, Hector, Achilles, Dido and Aeneas, Lavinia, Polynices, Tydee and Eteocles, Alexander, Cadmus, Jason, Dedalus and Icarus, Narcissus, Pluto and Orpheus, Hero and Leander, David and Goliath, Samson and Delilah, Julius Caesar, the Round Table, Charlemagne and Oliver of Verdun." The festivities were "as delightful as Paradise."

Like marriage, death has its ritual. For a well-to-do burgher the most important task in preparation for departure from this world is the disposition of his property. The Church strongly advises not only making a will in plenty of time, but giving in advance the endowments that will speed the donor through purgatory. The preacher Henri of Provins tells the story of a man dining at the house of a friend, who sends a servant to light his way home so that he will not stumble and fall in the mud. If the servant carries the lantern behind the guest's back, says Henri, it will not prevent him from stumbling or falling. Thus it is with alms: If you keep them to distribute after your death, your lantern will be carried behind your back. Henri to the contrary notwithstanding, many burghers like to hang on to their wealth till the last possible moment.

That moment is extreme unction, after which the Church considers a man as good as dead. A sick man who recovers after receiving it must fast perpetually, go barefoot, and never again have intercourse with his wife. In some places he cannot even amend his will.

A dying man in particular fear of hell, because he is pious or guilty, may express his penitence by having himself laid on the ground on a hair cloth sprinkled with ashes. Louis IX, given up by the doctors, adopted this practice and discoursed so eloquently on the insubstantiality of this world's wealth and power that he drew tears from his audience—and then recovered to go on a Crusade. Prince Henry of England, son of Henry II, after tying a rope around his neck and having himself dragged to his bed of ashes, where gravestones were placed at his head and feet, also recovered.

When a burgher dies, a public crier is hired to announce his death and the hour and place of burial. The doors of the house and of the death chamber are draped with black serge. Two monks from the abbey wash the body with perfumed water, anoint it with balsam and ointment, and encase it in a linen shroud; then they sew it in a deerskin and deposit it in a wooden coffin. Draped in a black pall, the coffin is placed on a bier consisting of two poles with wooden cross-pieces and taken to the church, attended by a cortege of clergy and black-clad mourners, the widow and family making loud and visible lament. The bier halts outside the chancel gates (if the dead man is a priest, the body is laid out within the chancel), and the Mourning Office is said—the "Dirge," from *Dirige*, the first word of the first antiphon. When the mass is over, the priest removes his chasuble, censes the body and sprinkles it with holy water, says the Lord's Prayer, in which all join; then he pronounces the Absolutions, a series of prayers and antiphons of forgiveness and deliverance from judgment.

As the cortege proceeds to the church burial grounds, monks from the abbey lead the way with crosses, sacred books and thuribles, and mourners follow with candles. The latter are numerous, for the poor can earn alms by carrying candles in a rich man's funeral procession. When the place of burial is reached, the priest makes the sign of the cross over the grave, sprinkles it with holy water, and digs a shallow trench in the shape of the cross. The real grave-digging is then done to the accompaniment of psalms. The wooden coffin is lowered, the final collect for forgiveness said, the grave filled in, and a flat tombstone laid. (Those who cannot afford coffins rent one, and the remains are buried without the coffin.)

The procession returns to the church, singing the Seven Penitential Psalms. For a time the tomb will be lighted with candles and a funeral lamp. In a few years the bones may be lifted out of the grave and stacked, so that the space can be used again.

6.

Small Business

And he looks at the whole town
Filled with many fair people;
The moneychangers' tables covered with
    gold and silver
And with coins;
He sees the squares and the streets
Filled with good workmen
Plying their various trades:
One making helmets, one hauberks,
Another saddles, another shields,
Another bridles, and another spurs,
Still another furbishes swords,
Some full cloth, others dye it,
Others comb it, others shear it;
Others melt gold and silver,
Making rich and beautiful things,
Cups, goblets, écuelles,
And jewels with enamel inlay,
Rings, belts, clasps;
One might well believe
That the city held a fair all year round,
It was full of so many fine things,
Of pepper, wax and scarlet dye,
Of black and gray velvet
And of all kinds of merchandise.

> —CHRÉTIEN DE TROYES I
> in *Perceval, le Conte du Graal*

Almost every craftsman in Troyes is simultaneously a merchant. The typical master craftsman alternately manufactures a product and waits on trade in his small shop, which is also his house. Sometimes he belongs to a guild, although in Troyes only a fraction of the hundred and twenty guilds of Paris[1] are represented. Many crafts stand in no need of protective federation or have too few members to form a guild.

Each shop on the city street is essentially a stall, with a pair of horizontal shutters that open upward and downward, top and bottom. The upper shutter, opening upward, is supported by two posts that convert it into an awning; the lower shutter drops to rest on two short legs and acts as a display counter. At night the shutters are closed and bolted from within. Inside the shop master and apprentice and a male relative or two, or the master's wife, work at the craft.

In a tailor's shop, the tailor sits inside, cutting and sewing in clear view of the public, an arrangement that simultaneously permits the customer to inspect the work and the tailor to display his skill. When the buying public arrives—even if it is only a single housewife—tailors, hatmakers, shoemakers and the rest desert their benches and hurry outside, metamorphosing into salesmen who are so aggressive that they must be restrained by guild rules—for example, from addressing a customer who has stopped at a neighbor's stall.

Related crafts tend to congregate, often giving their name to a street. Crafts also give their names to craftsmen— Thomas le Potier ("Potter"), Richarte le Barbier ("Barber"), Benoît le Peletier ("Skinner"), Henri Taillebois ("Woodman"), Jehan Taille-Fer ("Smith"). With the rise of the towns, surnames are becoming important; the tax collector must be able to draw up a list. But neither in the case of the

Medieval shop front, sketched in Brittany by Viollet-le-Duc, nineteenth-century architect. The horizontal shutter was raised when the shop was opened to form an awning over the merchandise.

man nor the street is the name a reliable guide to the occupation. Just as a grocer's son may be a chandler, so the Street of the Grocers may be populated by leather merchants and shoemakers.

Not far from the helmetmakers, armorers, and swordmakers one may be sure to find the smiths, who not only produce horseshoes and other finished hardware for retail sale, but supply the armorers with their wrought iron and steel. Iron ore is obtained almost entirely from alluvial deposits—"bog iron"—and only rarely by digging. Though coal is mined in England, Scotland, the Saar, Liège, Aix-la-Chapelle, Anjou, and other districts, iron ore is smelted almost exclusively by charcoal. A pit is dug on a windy hilltop, drains inserted to allow the molten iron to be drawn off, and charcoal and ore layered in the hole, which is sealed at the top with earth. The advantage of this method is that the iron drawn off has some carbon in it; in other words, it is steel of a sort. Medieval metallurgists do not really understand how this happens. This "mild steel" is taken in lumps to the smithy.

The blacksmith's furnace is table-high, with a back and a hood, and like those of the smelters, burns charcoal. The smith's apprentice plies a pair of leather bellows while the mith turns the glowing bloom with a long pair of tongs. When it is sufficiently heated, the two men drag it out of the furnace to the floor, where they break off a chunk and take it to the anvil, which is mounted on an oak stump. They pound, then return the chunk to the fire, then back to the anvil for more pounding, then back to the fire. Hour after hour the two swing their heavy hammers in rhythmic alternation, their energy slowly converting the intractable metal mass. This metal may vary considerably in character, depending on the accident of carbon-mixing at the smelter.

If the smith is fabricating wire, the next step will be to draw a piece of the hot metal through a hole with pincers. Several such drawings, each time through a smaller hole in a plate, accomplished with patience and much labor, produce a wire of the correct diameter, which is re-tempered and cut into short lengths. These are sold to the armorer up the street, who pounds them around a bar into links, the basis of chain mail.

The sages believe iron is a derivative of quicksilver (mercury) and brimstone (sulfur). The smith and the armorer know only that the material they get from the smelter sometimes is too soft to make good weapons or good chain mail, in which case they consign it to peaceful uses—plowshares, nails, bolts, wheel rims, cooking utensils. Other craftsmen who use the products of the forge include cutlers, nail makers, pin makers, tinkers, and needlemakers. But the great use of iron, the one that ennobles the crafts of smith and armorer, is for war, either real or tournament-style.

There are also metalworkers on a more refined plane: goldsmiths and silversmiths. Since the twelfth century those of Troyes have enjoyed a wide reputation. The beautifully worked decoration of the tomb of Henry the Generous and the silver statue of the same count are justly famous. Gold-smiths are the aristocrats of handicraft, though not all are rich. Some goldsmiths scrape along working alone, making and selling silver ornaments, with hardly a thread of gold to their name. But most have an apprentice and a small store of gold, and fabricate an occasional gold paternoster or silver cup. The most prosperous have well equipped shops with two workbenches, a small furnace, an array of little anvils of varying sizes, a supply of gold, and two or three apprentices. One holds the workpiece on the anvil while the master hammers it to the desired shape and thickness, wielding his small hammer with incredible speed. Gold's value lies not merely in its rarity and its glitter but in its wonderful malleability. It is said that a goldsmith can reduce gold leaf by hammering to a thickness of one ten-

Sculptors at work, as shown in Chartres Cathedral window. Medieval sculpture, much of high quality, was created by men trained as stonemasons. Often the Master of the Works doubled as sculptor.

Merchant furriers. The furrier displays a cloak to a customer, while his apprentice stands behind him ready to hand out additional furs from the stock. The picture is the signature of the St. James window at Chartres, donated by the wealthy furriers' guild.

thousandth of an inch. Thin gold leaf embellishes the pages of the illuminated manuscripts over which monks and copyists labor.

Hours of labor, tens of thousands of blows, with the final passage of the hammer effacing the hammer marks themselves—these are the ingredients of goldsmithing, a craft of infinite patience and considerable artistry.

But the bulk of even a prosperous goldsmith's work is in silver, the second softest metal. Sometimes a smith makes a whole series of identical paternosters or ornaments. To do this he first creates a mold or die of hardwood or copper and transfers the shape and design to successive pieces of silver by hammering. For repair jobs he keeps on hand a quantity of gold and silver wire, made in the same way the blacksmith makes his iron wire.

As the armorer depends on the smith, the shoemaker depends on the tanner, though he prefers to have his shop at a distance from his supplier's operation. The numerous tanners of Troyes occupy two streets southeast of the church of St.-Jean. Hide-curing, either by tanning or the ancient alternative method of tawing, creates a pungent atmosphere. Masters and apprentices may be seen outdoors, scraping away hair and epidermis from the skins over a "beam" (a horizontal section of treetrunk) with a blunt-edged concave tool. The flesh adhering to the underside is scraped off with a sharp concave blade. Next the hide is softened by rubbing it with cold poultry or pigeon dung, or warm dog dung, then soaked in mildly acid liquid produced by fermenting bran, to wash off the traces of lime left by the dung.

For extra soft leather—shoe uppers, coverings of coffers, scabbards, bagpipes, bellows—the leather is returned to the beam to be shaved down with a two-handled currier's knife. Then it goes to the pit, which is filled and drained with a

succession of liquid baths. The first is old and mellow, the last fresh and green, their flavor imparted by oak bark, oak galls, acacia pods, and other sources of tannin. In the final stages the hides lie flat in the pit of liquid for several weeks, with crushed bark between the layers. The whole process of tanning takes months—usually, in fact, over a year. A new, quicker process, employing hot water, will appear later in the century, taking as little as ten days.

Tanning an oxhide is a laborious process, but it multiplies the skin's value. Whitened oxhide and horsehide are even more expensive.

Footwear is insubstantial—little better than slippers. Ladies of fashion wear goatskin leather, or cordwain (from "cordovan," a fine leather originally made by the Moors of Cordova), even less sturdy than ordinary cowhide.

The shoemaker is not only a skilled craftsman, but a merchant of some status, capable of acquiring modest wealth. A shoemaker of Troyes named Pantaléon has given his son Jacques an education in the Church. Jacques is today a canon at Lyons, soon will be bishop of Verdun, and will eventually become Pope Urban IV.

Besides shoemakers, hatmakers, candlestick makers, and other craftsmen, there are the practitioners of the service trades: food purveyors, oil merchants, pastrycooks, wine sellers, and beer sellers. In addition there is the wine crier, who is also an inspector. Each morning he goes into the first tavern he can find that has not yet hired a crier for the day; the tavern keeper must accept him. He oversees the drawing of the wine, or draws it himself, and tastes. Then, furnished with a cup and a leather flagon stoppered with a bit of hemp, he goes out to cry the wine and offer samples of it to the public. Before setting out he may ask those in the tavern how much the tavern keeper charged them, in order

Cartwright and cooper, two skilled workers. This Chartres Cathedral window shows the cartwright finishing a wheel while the cooper fits a hoop to a barrel—one of the inventions of the Middle Ages.

to check on the prices. Customers are served directly from the barrel; glass bottles are almost nonexistent.

There are some fifty vintages in thirteenth-century France. Among the favorites are Marly, Beaune, Epernay, Montpellier, Narbonne, Sancerre, Carcassonne, Auxerre, Soissons, Orléans, and, most highly regarded, Pierrefitte. Burgundy is already famous and northern Champagne produces excellent wine, though not the sparkling variety with which the province will centuries later become identified. Cider is unknown except in Normandy, and outsiders who have tasted it consider it to be a curse God has visited on the Normans. One observant chronicler reports that the French prefer white wine, the Burgundians red, the Germans "aromatic wines," and the English beer.

Another trade closely associated with the taverns is prostitution. The girls of the Champagne Fair cities are famous throughout Europe. When the fair is on, servant girls, laundresses, tradeswomen, and many others find a profitable sideline. Child labor being the rule, prostitution begins at an early age.

Taverns are the chief setting for another vice—gaming. The dicemakers' guild has strict laws against making fraudulent dice, which nevertheless find their way into the hands of professional sharpers. The fine for making such dice is heavy, so the sharpers pay a high price for them. Poor light in the taverns facilitates trickery.

Others engaged in service trades include the coal sellers, hay merchants, barbers, furniture menders, dish menders, and clothes menders—these latter three being the leading itinerants, whose peculiar rhymed gibberish echoes daily through the streets.

An ancient trade of the countryside, recently urbanized, is that of the miller. The numerous mills of Troyes are owned by the count, the bishop, the abbeys, the hospital, and various other proprietors. Most are situated on canals, with a few on the Seine below the city, mounted on floating hulls, the wheel over the side and the millstones seated on a cupola-shaped platform amidships. Sacks of grain are brought by boat to the miller, who pours the grain into the funnel over an opening in the upper stone. The current turns the wheel, which activates the stone, and the milled flour trickles into a sack beneath the platform.

Both millers and mills have other functions besides grinding grain. In slack periods the millers fish or spear eels. Mill wheels furnish power for a growing variety of businesses, notably tanning and fulling. The old undershot wheel, pushed lazily around by the current flowing against the lower paddles, is being supplanted by the overshot wheel, which is turned by water flowing over the top. Either type of wheel can be used when a weir or dam is constructed that creates a narrow, rapid current. The power of this current can be multiplied by guiding it to the mid-point of a waterwheel, so that the wheel's turn starts underneath, or by guiding it to the top of the wheel, so that the wheel's turn starts at the top. Although water mills are important, old-fashioned mills worked by horses and cattle still hold their own, because animals can work in all weather, whereas river and millrace currents may freeze in winter or dry up in summer.

From time to time the horse market is held in the Corterie-aux-Chevaux, near the Porte de la Madeleine. Nervous colts, sedate palfreys, powerful chargers, mares with foals trotting at their heels, broad-shouldered oxen, pack-asses and pack-mules, pigs, hogs, cows, chickens, ducks, and geese noisily crowd the market place. Knights, ladies, burghers and peasants bargain, argue, examine animals, turn back horses' lips, feel coats and muscles, and now and then mount a palfrey or a charger.

Only nobles and rich burghers ride horses; everyone else rides donkeys or walks. A pregnant lady or wounded knight may be carried in a litter (carriages are far in the future). The knights who come to the horse mart sometimes take prospective mounts outside the city walls to try out. Often there are races, with the noisy assistance of the boys and young men.

The saddlemakers display their work at the market, and it is worthy of display. Bows of saddles are wooden, often ornamented with plates of ivory, hammered metal, or elaborately painted leather, with semiprecious stones soldered into the surface of the pommel and cantle. The saddlecloth is richly embroidered. Sidesaddles are manufactured for ladies, but not all ladies use them.

Farm implements, fashioned by the city's blacksmiths, are on display too. These include sickles for harvesting grain, long-handled scythes with lateral grips added for efficient haymaking, sharp-bladed felling axes. Wooden spades have iron cutting edges. There are also farm machines —many-toothed harrows and wheeled plows, with coulter, plowshare and mouldboard for turning the earth to left or right.

The development of heavier breeds of horses has greatly augmented their value. They bring much higher prices than a mule or an ordinary draft horse. If Julius Caesar could wander through the horse market of Troyes, he would be startled far less by the wheeled plow and the new, heavily padded, rigid horse collar than by the size of the horses. Neither the Romans nor their foes ever rode anything like these. The Parthians and Byzantine Greeks began the development of the big warhorse, now completed in this area of northern France and Flanders. It is no accident that this is *par excellence* the region of feudal chivalry.

Guilds have two kinds of regulations. One has to do with external affairs, with what might be called the commercial side of the guild; the other deals with internal matters, such as wages, duration and conditions of apprenticeship, welfare, and obligations to the guild.

Every guild recognizes its stake in protecting the public, for since the guild restricts competition, it has an obligation to guarantee standards of quality. On being invested, the officers of the bakers' guild solemnly swear that they will "guard the guild" carefully and loyally, and that in appraising bread they will spare neither relatives nor friends, nor condemn anyone wrongly through hatred or ill-feeling. Officers of other guilds swear similar oaths. Guild legislation on the quality of merchandise is painstakingly detailed. Precise quantities and types of raw materials are specified and supervision follows through all the stages of manufacture and sale. Ale must have no constituents except grain, hops, and water. The beadmaker must discard beads less than perfectly round. Butchers are not to mix tallow with lard or sell the flesh of dogs, cats, or horses. Makers of bone handles are forbidden to trim them with silver lest they pass them off for ivory. Knife handles may not be covered with silk, brass, or pewter for the same reason. If a tailor spoils a piece of cloth by faulty cutting, he has to make restitution to the customer and pay a fine besides. Chandlers must use four pounds of tallow for each quarter-pound of wick, and wax tapers are not to be adulterated with lard. A tailor may not mend old clothes, for that function belongs solely to the old-clothes mender, who in turn must not make new clothes. Sometimes the old-clothes mender does such a good job that the result looks like new; therefore, to keep the distinction visible, the mender is enjoined from pressing, folding, and hanging his products like new garments.

In most guilds inspection is no sham formality. Visits are made unexpectedly, scales checked, substandard goods confiscated on the spot, either to be destroyed or to be given to the poor, while the culprit pays a fine commensurate with the value of the merchandise. The jeweler found using colored glass and the spice dealer guilty of purveying false merchandise pay the highest fines.

Combinations to fix prices or to seek a monopoly on materials are forbidden. Retailers cannot buy eggs, cheese, and other produce from farmers except at the Friday and Saturday markets, and even here they cannot buy until the farmer is actually in the marketplace with his wagon or pack animal. They cannot buy from him on consignment, or arrange in advance to take his produce. These restrictions are all designed to prevent monopoly of food in time of famine, a threat never far distant. Unhappily, guild regulations and town ordinances alike frequently go unobserved.

The second kind of guild regulation, governing its internal affairs, often merely codifies ancient customs, such as observance of holidays, early closing on Saturdays during Lent and during the "short days" of the year.

The membership of most guilds is divided simply into masters and apprentices. A middle grade, the valet or journeyman, has been introduced in a few crafts where business demands more labor but masters do not want more competition. In most guilds a master is permitted only a single apprentice, or perhaps two. Grain merchants, ale brewers, goldsmiths, greengrocers, shoemakers, and some others are allowed more, and all masters are given great freedom in hiring relatives—as many sons. brothers, even nephews as they wish. Guild regulations reflect the nature of industry, which is small scale and familial.

Guilds often provide members with baptismal gifts when their children are born, help ill and destitute members, pay something toward hospital and funeral expenses, and do a little charitable work. This mutual-aid aspect of the craft guild goes far back. A guild that does not provide benevolent services usually has a "brotherhood," an auxiliary that may be the original form of the association. Weavers, furriers, bakers, and many other crafts have brotherhoods, each under an appropriate patron saint: St. Catherine for the wheelwrights, because she was broken on the wheel; St. Sebastian for the needlemakers, because he was martyred by arrows; St. Mary Magdalen for the perfumers, because she poured oil on Jesus' feet; St.-Barbe ("beard") for the brushmakers; St.-Cloud ("nail") for the nailmakers; St. Clare ("clear") for the mirrormakers.

The contract between master and apprentice (regardless of whether they belong to a guild) is sometimes written, sometimes simply "sworn on the relics"—all medieval oaths are taken on sacred relics. The master undertakes to feed, lodge, clothe, and shoe his apprentice and "to treat him honorably as the son of a goodman." Sometimes the apprentice receives a stipend—a small one. Sometimes the master also undertakes to educate the apprentice. Often he needs employees who can read and write and add and subtract. Twice a week the apprentice may go to the notary to learn his letters.

An apprentice's day is long and hard. His situation depends very largely on the personality and condition of his master. A kind master is a blessing; perhaps an even greater blessing is a prosperous master. A kind mistress may be important too. Since the apprentice's labor is not restricted to the trade and he may be called on to do any kind of household chore, many apprentices find themselves more tyrannized by mistresses than by masters. Guilds often specify in their regulations that an apprentice should not be beaten by the master's wife.

Apprenticeship varies in duration, usually from four years to twelve; five years is common. The length of service is often related to the size of the initiation fee, as in the case of weavers, whose craft can be quickly learned and yet is remunerative. A weaver's apprentice may become a master in four years by paying four pounds (livres), in five years by paying three pounds, in six years by paying one pound, in seven years without any payment. Brasswire makers require twelve years, or ten years plus a fee of twenty shillings (sous). Goldsmiths undertake a ten-year apprenticeship.

An apprentice has five obligations to fulfill. First, he must supply a certificate to the officers of the guild, stating that he is "prudent and loyal." Second, he must demonstrate that he knows the craft. In some guilds the emerging apprentice must produce a "masterpiece." An apprentice hatmaker fashions a hat, a cake baker bakes cakes. Third, the apprentice must show that he has enough capital to go into business. Sometimes his capital is his tools, sometimes he needs cash. Fourth, he must swear on the saints' relics to uphold the guild's law and customs, which the officers read aloud to him, explaining and clarifying as they go. Finally, he pays a fee, which goes not to the guild but to the prince— in Troyes the count of Champagne—for guilds "belong" to the sovereign. In 1160 Louis VII sold five of his Paris guilds (the leatherworkers, pursemakers, baldric makers, shoe repairmen and dockworkers) to the widow of a wealthy burgher, who thereafter collected the dues formerly owed the king.

On paying his fee, the apprentice becomes a member of the corporation, the inner body of the guild, that consists of the masters alone, or the masters and journeymen. His rise in status calls for a celebration—a round of drinks at the tavern, or possibly a dinner. Or he may merely pay five or ten sous to the corporation treasury.

An apprentice's ambition may even soar beyond acquiring the status of a master. He may dream of some day being an officer of the corporation. Officers are elected by the masters, or by the masters and journeymen, and the election is ratified by the count's provost.

Married apprentices are not unknown, and occasionally a master may even provide his apprentice with an allowance for taking his meals outside the master's house. But such cases are the exception.

A craft may make a man modestly rich. Of course it may also make him stoop-shouldered, but this is a hazard of any trade. A man repeats the same motion with hammer, with maul, with saw, with shears, with needle, with loom, ten, twelve, fourteen hours at a stretch, day in and day out, transmitting the energy of his hand, arm and shoulder into chalice, statue, vestment or article of furniture. Forty years of such effort can leave him bent and crooked. His servile forefathers, however, ended their days not only crippled and deformed by their labors but with nothing to show for it.

In the old *cité* near the Abbey of St.-Loup is one of the crowded town's most crowded districts. This is the Broceaux-Juifs, the old ghetto of Troyes. Its streets are hardly distinguishable from the rest of the old quarter, except for the Mezuzah (a small parchment scroll inscribed with Old Testament writings) on every doorpost. The men, women and children on the streets do not look very different from their Christian neighbors, except that on the breast of each is sewn a yellow circle, or wheel. They speak perfectly good French, though they use Hebrew characters in writing. Jews make their living, like Christians, by manufacture and trade—as goldsmiths and leatherworkers, tanners and glass-blowers, weavers and dyers. In the south of France they practice viticulture, though agriculture generally is closed to them, as are many avenues of commerce. Some enlightened princes, like Louis IX of France and Edward I of England, favor abolishing the Jewish disabilities, even while Louis' zeal for the Christian religion causes him to burn copies of the Talmud.

Many Jews lend money, mostly on a small scale, against pledges. A dozen are wealthy and even own land outside town. Some devote their lives to scholarship. The ghetto of Troyes, which had one of the earliest Jewish schools in northwest Europe, has been the home of several of the most famous Jewish scholars of the Middle Ages, such as Salomon ben Isaac (Rashi) and his grandson Jacob ben Meir, who presided over a major synod in Troyes in the previous century. The most important member of the community in the thirteenth century is the wealthy Jacob of Troyes, who holds the title "Master of the Jews." He is in effect mayor of the ghetto, which is a separate, privileged community, a foreign colony, not unlike the Christian merchants' colonies in the Levant, or the colonies of Italians and other nationalities in London. Jews do not belong to the commune and do not participate in the town government. A legal case involving a Christian and a Jew must be taken to the count's court, where the testimony of a Christian against a Jew, or of a Jew against a Christian, must be corroborated by a coreligionist. A Jewish merchant receives full protection against thieves. If he is robbed in another principality, on the road to Troyes, the count demands restitution as forcefully as for a Christian merchant.

The same is true of other sovereigns. The Pope has threatened excommunication in defense of Roman Jewish bankers. When a Jewish merchant from Aragon was robbed by Castilian bandits, the king of Aragon promised to repay him at the expense of Castilian merchants unless the king of Castile made good the loss.

Princely punctilio about the rights of Jewish merchants and bankers is securely anchored in self-interest. But princely self-interest is a capricious force. The chief threat to Jewish life comes not from popular outbursts, which are rare, but from official edicts. A prince who needs money is tempted to lose his tolerance, listen to a charge (or cause one to be made), and order expulsion of all Jews from his territory. Expulsion automatically involves confiscation of goods.[2] It also, almost as automatically, involves an increment to the sovereign at some later date when the Jews are graciously permitted to reenter the territory. Seventy years ago, at the time of the Third Crusade, the Jews of Troyes suffered expulsion, as did Jews in many other places. The synagogue in the old ghetto was taken over by Christians and converted to a church, St.-Frobert. A second synagogue in the new commercial quarter west of the *cité* suffered a similar fate, and became St.-Pantaléon. The street next to it remains, and will remain through the centuries, the Rue de la Synagogue.

Even the emotionally charged accusation of ritual murder is usually a pretext for a fine rather than capital punishment. An alleged ritual murder in London in 1244 resulted in an exorbitant fine—60,000 marks, levied against the Jewish community. Frederick II, king of Sicily and emperor of Germany, recently heard an indictment against the Jews of the town of Fulda. The scientific-minded emperor ordered an investigation, interrogating converted Jews from England. Concluding that there was no basis for the ancient charge, Frederick forbade further accusations. However, he did not neglect to collect a fine from the Jews of Fulda for breach of the peace. The Pope (Innocent IV) has also discredited the ritual murder superstition, which nonetheless persists among the ignorant masses.

Jewish conversion to Christianity is rare, but not unknown. Sometimes special protection is extended to converts not only against reprisals by Jews and insults by Christians, but against loss of property. More often, however, a converting Jew faces a considerable bill from his Christian prince, who does not wish to sacrifice the Jewish taxes without compensation. There are many other ways a prince may make money from his Jews. Henry III, present king of England, has recently mortgaged his Jews to his brother, Richard of Cornwall.

Forcible conversion is forbidden, as is interference with celebration of Jewish rites. However, the terms in which the prohibition is couched indicate that Christians are less tolerant than one could wish. "During the celebration of their festivals," Pope Innocent III ruled, "no one shall disturb them by beating them with clubs or by throwing stones at them." It is also expressly forbidden to extort money from the Jews by threatening to exhume the bodies of their dead from the Jewish cemetery.

Yet despite the suspicion and hostility with which the Broce-aux-Juifs is hedged around, contacts between Christians and Jews are numerous and not necessarily uncongenial. Jews have often served as bankers to the counts and have farmed tolls and taxes. The erudite Count Henry the Generous, the present count's grandfather, is said to have consulted Jewish scholars on textual problems of the Old Testament. Jewish and Christian merchants and moneymen often embark on joint ventures. That many Jews of Troyes prosper is demonstrated by the fine houses along the Rue de Vieille Rome, south of the ancient donjon.

If the thirteenth century is not the best time to be a European Jew, neither is it the worst.

7.

Big Business

Buy stingily and sell dear,
And practice usury and fraud.

— RUTEBEUF OF TROYES

Feudal dues, guild regulations, princely prerogatives and ecclesiastical dicta notwithstanding, the western European businessman of the thirteenth century makes money—often a great deal. There are two main avenues to fortune, the cloth trade and banking. Very commonly the two are combined by a single entrepreneur.

The typical capitalist of Troyes conducts his typically many-sided business from the ground floor of his house in one of the better streets on the outskirts of the fair quarter. There are two rooms on this floor. In front is the workroom where the apprentice puts in his long hours. It is likely to be piled with a variety of merchandise—skins, furs, silks, utensils, copper wire, iron tools, paper, parchment—whatever the merchant happens to be dealing in. But the most important item is fairly certain to be wool, which is raw, semi-finished or finished.

In the rear is the counting room, where the merchant and perhaps his eldest son do their office work. Light is poor. A prominent piece of office equipment is the calculating board, a table marked out with horizontal lines on which bone counters are manipulated. The bottom line represents units, the next not tens but twenties—because in the universal money of account, twenty shillings (sous) equals one pound (livre). Vertical lines assist in positioning the counters.

Records are kept on wax tablets. Parchment, a seal, half a dozen quills, ink, and ribbon or cord supply the tools for correspondence. When a merchant writes a letter, he closes it with his seal affixed to a ribbon or cord. Most business letters are written in French, but sometimes correspondence is in Latin, and occasionally in Italian, or even a more exotic tongue, in which case the assistance of a professional scribe may be required. A couple of tables, three or four hard chairs or stools, a chest or two, and a few candles nearly complete the inventory of office furnishings.

But there is one more piece of furniture, the most important. The merchant's strongbox is bound with iron and fastened with a large iron lock. In it he keeps his working capital. Though cash is less important in business life than it was a hundred years ago, a prosperous merchant still has a tidy hoard of silver-copper-zinc deniers (pennies),[1] along with a stack of parchment pledges. The livre (pound) and sou (shilling), though used to count with throughout Europe, do not yet actually exist as coins. The only important coin circulating in any volume is the penny, which comes in a remarkable variety of sizes and alloys. About five-eighths of an inch in diameter, and at its best about one-third fine silver, it will suffice to hire a workman for three or four hours. It varies capriciously because a large number of princes and bishops enjoy the right of coinage. Mints being expensive to operate, they require profit margins, and the temptation is strong to widen this margin by increasing the copper content of the coins. The *denier de Provins* (Provins penny), minted at Troyes' sister city, is universally respected for its reliable content of thirty per cent fine silver. But some lords take a shortsighted view and profit from debasements. However, even those who debase the currency are very jealous of the privilege, and tampering with coinage by subjects is attended everywhere by the most ferocious legal penalties.

Though the pounds-shillings-pence ratio (one to twenty to twelve) may seem clumsy, merchants have no difficulty with it. Lately a big new silver coin has been minted in Italy. Called a *grosso* (groat),[2] it has the value of twelve pennies, thereby converting the imaginary shilling for the first time into a reality. But the grosso circulates very little outside Italy, where business is bigger than in the West.

Troyen merchants invest their pennies in many things, but above all in wool. Some wool is grown locally, but the best comes from abroad, especially from England. A poet uses the metaphor "carrying wool to England" in the sense of "carrying coals to Newcastle." Long-wooled flocks roam the grasslands and fens of the Cotswolds and Lincolnshire; short-wooled animals, the hills and moors of the Welsh and Scottish borders and the downlands of Shropshire and Herefordshire. The flocks belonging to monasteries, such as those of Tintern Abbey, are especially famous. Most of the English wool feeds the looms of Flanders, but some finds its way to France and Champagne. Merchants of Troyes also buy Burgundian wool, nearly as good as English. Buying in quantity, a merchant gets a much better price than could an individual weaver. He then in turn supplies weavers, specifying the kind of weave he wants. In theory he sells raw wool to individual weavers and buys finished wool back, but since he usually buys from the same weavers, a wool merchant actually operates a factory scattered through town.

If the wool market is strong, as it usually is, the weavers are able to buy bread to feed the wives and children who crowd their upper-story tenement dwellings and who help spin and weave. But if the cloth market drops, as a result perhaps of a war which severs trade routes, merchants naturally turn their attention and capital elsewhere, and weavers' families beg in front of the church doors.

The weavers' guild is the first to include a number of "valets" or "journeymen." By 1250 the towns of Flanders have many of these. Finished with their apprenticeship, the journeymen are not yet permitted to become masters, yet their labor is needed by cloth merchants. Even in good times they are subject to the caprices of the market and their employers. Every Monday morning they gather in the squares and before the churches, where the masters hire labor for the week. On Saturday night, after a week's dawn-to-dusk work, the journeyman is paid off and must again look for work on Monday morning.

Five years ago something incredible happened in Douai, one of the richest Flemish cloth towns. The weavers got together and refused to work. The outraged cloth merchants crushed this insurrectionary movement, and every burgher trusts that workingmen will never do anything of the kind again.

A merchant may enter into a long-term contract with one of the great English abbeys to take all the shearings of the abbey for a period of years, often seven. He pays a cash sum in advance, and agrees to a fixed annual payment for the duration of the contract. The contract is drawn by a notary, first in rough draft, then with care on parchment in three copies, one for each of the parties and one for his own files, which acquire the force of legal records.

When a wool consignment from England is delivered to

a merchant of Troyes, it is first given preliminary treatment at his house. An apprentice removes damaged wool and sorts the good wool into three grades—fine, medium, and coarse. Next it must be washed in lye to remove grease, and spread on boards in the sun to dry. Forceps in hand, the hardworking apprentice gets on his hands and knees to remove bits of soil and other particles. If they cannot be picked out, he clips them with small shears. The wool of carcass sheep is kept separate; it is an offense to mix it with live shearings.

When the wool has been washed and dried, it must be laboriously beaten, combed, and carded. Then the merchant consigns it to the weaver, whose wife spins it into yarn with a distaff and spindle. The warp thread, stronger than the woof, must be sized and wound and sorted into the required number of threads of a certain length, and the woof thread must be wound onto the bobbin to be inserted in the shuttle. Although spinning is still done in ancient fashion, looms have advanced well beyond Roman models. The weaver sits in a high-backed chair with his feet on the treadles, tossing his shuttle of wool back and forth between the rising and falling heddles, which raise and lower the warp threads.

The material that comes from the weaver's loom is not finished cloth. It must be taken to the fuller, who soaks and shrinks the fabric, and rubs it with fuller's earth, not only to clean it but to give it body and help it take dye. The soaking is done in a trough, the fuller and his assistants trampling the mixture in their bare feet (whence another word for fuller— "walker"—the English surnames Fuller and Walker denoting the same trade). This process also hardens the material. When the cloth has been soaked, it is hung to dry on an upright wooden frame called a tenter, fastened by tenter-hooks placed along parallel bars which can be adjusted so that the cloth is stretched to the right length and breadth. This task is often undertaken by women. Then the cloth is finished by raising the nap with teasels while it is still damp and by shearing it when dry with great flat shears, three or four feet long. The finest cloth is shorn and reshorn a number of times. Finally it is brushed, pressed, and folded.

Dyeing may take place at any stage in the manufacture. Sometimes the cloth is already dyed in the yarn stage, or even in its original raw form, whence the expression "dyed in the wool." Sometimes it is sold as undyed cloth, especially to the *Arte di Calimala*, the clothfinishing industry of Florence. Sometimes dyeing is the last step in the process. The dyer heats his tub over a fire and, turning the cloth with long poles, soaks it in water colored with woad (blue), madder (red), or other dyes, tempered by wood ashes. One can tell a dyer anywhere by the color under his nails. He dyes not only cloth, but sometimes other products, such as wooden crucifixes and ornaments.

Besides wool, the merchant may deal occasionally in three other textiles. One is linen, woven from flax, a vegetable fiber grown widely throughout Europe. Another is silk, imported from the East for hundreds of years, but now a major industry in Italy, Sicily, and Spain. The third is cotton, originally imported from India, but introduced into Spain by the Moors and manufactured in France, Italy, and Flanders.

Wool is the beginning, rather than the end, of a Troyen wool merchant's business. When he sells cloth at the fair to the Italians, he may buy spices from the Far East, wines from Burgundy, or metal from Germany. Some merchandise he can resell immediately to customers pledged in advance. Some he must break down into small lots. Some he may warehouse and hold for a rising market. Some, such as wood and metal, he sends out for finishing.

He is likely to invest part of his profits in real estate. He can rent houses in the city, perhaps to his own weaver families, and outside the city he may buy forest land, which cannot fail to rise in value, and in the meantime can be farmed for timber. He may acquire fishing rights in a stream or pond, operating as a fishing landlord and dividing the catch with his fisherman tenants.

Almost inevitably, whether he wants to or not, the successful merchant turns moneylender. People who want to borrow money go where the money is. In mid-thirteenth century the ancient monopoly of the Jews has become a large-scale business from which most of the Jewish lenders have been elbowed aside. The Italians are the biggest bankers today, but businessmen of northwest Europe give them increasing competition. Moneychangers tend naturally to become moneylenders. The men of Cahors, in southern France, who have long made a specialty of money-changing, are among the most prominent pawnbrokers. Their knowledgeability in coinage makes them also expert at evaluating silver plate and jewelry. The word "Cahorsin" has joined "Jew" and "Lombard" as a synonym for money-lender.

All moneylenders are resented—even Christian knights. The Templars, originally a band of Crusaders from Champagne who swore an oath at Solomon's Temple to devote their lives to defending Jerusalem, are celebrated as much for their financial as for their military prowess. Their commanderies, which stand in most of the important towns of northwest Europe, including Troyes, are usually square stone buildings looking like a cross between a blockhouse and a bank.

But if moneylenders are resented, they are also respected. So prestigious is the profession of moneychanger that instead of the master paying his apprentice or even supporting him, he demands and gets a payment from the apprentice's father for the lad's education. The following clause appears in a contract between a moneychanger and an apprentice's father in Marseille in 1248: ". . . and if it should happen, which God forbid, that the said William should cause you any loss I promise to reimburse you by this agreement, believing in your unsupported word . . ."

Moneylenders run risks, so interest rates are high. The Church officially condemns all interest as usurious, but churchmen nevertheless borrow, and lend, too.

The highest rates are charged by the Jews, who run the greatest risks, partly because their political position leaves them vulnerable to the connivance of their debtors with the authorities, and partly because they draw the worst borrowers—those who have trouble borrowing anywhere else. Like the Cahorsin, the Jewish moneylending business is largely pawnbroking. To become a pawnbroker in Troyes one must purchase a "table," a license from the count.

Nevertheless a moneylender, Christian or Jewish, has a growing power behind him, and it is much easier to collect a debt in 1250 than it was a hundred years earlier. Generally a debtor who fails to meet his obligations may expect to have his goods seized and handed over to the creditor. If they are insufficient to meet the debt he will be imprisoned or banished from the city, the latter punishment being more effective from the creditor's point of view, since it gives the debtor a chance to raise money. By an old custom a defaulted debt is an obligation of the debtor's commune. It is to the advantage of both sovereign and citizens to have their town enjoy a reputation of security for businessmen.

Noblemen are the greatest borrowers. Count Henry II of Champagne borrowed from ten bankers to equip himself for the Third Crusade, and ultimately he left the debt to be paid by his successor. The present count, Thibaut IV, borrowed large sums in his youth and refused to pay up. The bankers, some of whom were Italian and one a Jew, appealed to the Pope, who excommunicated the count and placed the whole of Champagne under interdict; no church services could be celebrated till the debt was paid. Not long after, spendthrift Thibaut got himself into another such jam. This time he went even further; he seized one of his creditors, an Italian banker named Ilperni, threw him into prison, frightened him, and extracted twelve hundred livres from him. The Pope, furious, threatened fresh excommunication and interdict, and rash Thibaut only escaped by promising to go on Crusade. At this very moment Thibaut owes two thousand livres to the monks of St.-Denis in Paris, who hold the gold cross from his chapel of St.-Etienne-de-Troyes as a pledge.

Lending and credit are intimately connected with the Champagne Fairs. Promises to pay are often dated from one fair to the next, or extended in installments over the next several fairs. Discounting is often done on such promises to pay; that is, a merchant may sell such a promise at something less than its face value if he needs immediate cash.

House "rent" is a form of interest. The householder borrows money to build or buy his house, agreeing to pay a certain rate of interest, usually eight to ten per cent. He may never pay anything on the principal of the loan, for which the lender always has the security of the house. The house may pass through several generations of such "rent paying."

Besides feudal lords, businessmen, and ordinary citizens, towns themselves often borrow, offering "life rents" in the form of annual or quarterly payments during the life of the lender. Sometimes the obligation is made for two lives, the lender's and his heir's. To combat fraud, towns offer prizes for news of the death of a rent holder.

The successful bourgeois entrepreneur stirs considerable envy. He is reputed to have acquired his wealth, the amount of which is generally exaggerated, by sharp practice rather than by hard work. The mystery by which capital grows is not understood by those who do not possess it. Neither are the worries of the businessman whose capital is committed to the hazards of a baron's whim, a flock's health, the stormy seas, or the chance of war.

The silver of commerce has in everyone's eyes, even in those of the merchants themselves, something of the diabolical. "He owes a fine candle to God, one may believe, who has remained honest in commerce without scorning the poor and without hating religion," says a popular proverb. And a writer describes a character: "After having passed most of his life in innocence, he became a merchant."

Nevertheless, the poets do not accord the merchants the kind of contempt they heap on peasants. Even the trouvères, spokesmen of chivalry, show a grudging respect for these townsmen, who not infrequently cross the line dividing their class from the nobility. A wealthy burgher may be knighted for his financial services to a great lord. Renier Accore, for example, a Florentine merchant who became a citizen of Provins, did business with the great nobles of Champagne, and became a knight and the Seigneur de Gouaix. Many burghers have seen their sons knighted. Some of the trouvères themselves are burghers, such as Adam de la Halle, whose graceful verses to his equally non-noble wife are widely quoted, and Gilbert de Barneville, who compares his mistress to the Northern Star.

Patents of nobility are hardly necessary. Universally accorded the title of "Sire," the wealthy merchants may be said to possess their own rank of nobility. Such officials of the count's service as Sire Doré ("Golden"), who married a noble Genoese lady and was Keeper of the Fair in 1225, and Sire Herbert Putemonnaie ("Badmoney"), financial agent of the count, need not genuflect to knights or petty barons. A son of a fishmonger, Sire Girard Meletaire, served as provost of Troyes in 1219, chamberlain to the count in 1230, and was its first mayor in 1231. Another burgher, Pierre Legendre, was bailiff of Provins in 1228, mayor of Troyes in 1232, and Keeper of the Fair in 1225 and 1228. His daughter married a wealthy Italian, Nicholas of Cremona, whose family handled transalpine affairs for the count.

If the breach between wealthy townsmen and the poor is indisputably widening, that between wealthy townsmen and the lordly aristocracy of the countryside is narrowing.

8.

The Doctor

Requesting a urinal, Renard had Noble the Lion fill it, then held it up to the light and examined it to distinguish the effect of the divers humors in the King's body. Then he pronounced, "Sire, you have an ague fever, but I have the remedy for it . . ."

—ROMAN DE RENARD

In a city the size of Troyes there are fewer than half a dozen licensed doctors,[1] not counting the numerous midwives, barbers, monks, and outright quacks who practice medicine or some branch of it. The trained physician is an aristocrat of professionals, enjoying high status and excellent fees. His practice is naturally confined to the better class, as the medical texts and treatises make clear.

One such treatise recommends interrogating the servant who has come to fetch the doctor, so that "if you can learn nothing from examining the patient, you still may astonish him with your knowledge of the case." At the patient's house the well advised doctor conducts himself with a certain ceremony. In the sick room he bows, seats himself, and drawing a sand-glass from his bag takes the patient's pulse. He requests a sample of urine, which he sniffs and tastes for sugar. In case of a gross infection he examines the urine for sediment. He inquires about the patient's diet and stool, and then delivers a discourse on the disease. The stomach, he may explain, is a cauldron in which food is cooked. If it is filled too full, it will boil over and the food remain uncooked. The liver supplies the heat for this interior furnace. The humors must be kept in balance—phlegm, blood, bile and black bile, which are respectively cold and moist, hot and moist, hot and dry, and cold and dry. Fevers are tertian, quartan, daily, hectic, and pestilential. Which kind is present can be determined by the pattern of recurrence, whether every third day, or every fourth, and whether it grows more severe. Recovery depends on many things, including the phases of the moon and the position of the constellations.

On quitting the sick chamber, the doctor may assure the patient that recovery will soon come with God's help; but with the family, he cannily adopts a graver tone, implying that he did not wish to alarm the sufferer, but that it is a lucky thing that science was called in. He may leave a prescription of herbs and drugs, and recommend diet—perhaps chicken broth, the milk of pulverized almonds, or barley water mixed with figs, honey, and licorice.

Often the doctor is invited to dine with the family. He accepts, without seeming too eager. During the course of the meal he may entertain the table with accounts of illnesses and wounds he has cured, but he makes sure to send a servant two or three times to ask the patient how he fares, thus reassuring him that he has not been forgotten.

If the thirteenth-century doctor's science is questionable by the standards of a later age, it is nevertheless an advance over the past. In the earlier Middle Ages abbeys and monasteries were the repositories of medical knowledge. The principal effect of their regime was to repeal Hippocrates' law that illness is a natural phenomenon and to make it appear to be a punishment from on high. This view is not dead in the thirteenth century, and even doctors pay it lip service, but the secular practitioner represents a distinct move toward the rational understanding of illness.

He also represents a move toward commercialization. The same medical text that tells him how to treat a patient gives precise instructions on bill collecting: "When the patient is nearly well, address the head of the family, or the sick man's nearest relative, thus: God Almighty having deigned by our aid to restore him whom you asked us to visit, we pray that He will maintain his health, and that you will now give us an honorable dismissal. Should any other member of your family desire our aid, we should, in grateful remembrance of our former dealings with you, leave all else and hurry to serve him." This formula, devised at the world's first and most famous medical school, that of Salerno, is hard to improve on. The fees which doctors charge are scaled to the patient's wealth and status. A rich man's illness may be valued at ten livres or more; kings have been charged a hundred. Setting a broken or dislocated limb is a matter of several sous or even a livre. Popular spite attributes a proverb to the medical profession: "Take while the patient is in pain."

A second text offers more hints for the general practitioner. "When you go to a patient, always try to do something new every day, lest they say you are good at nothing but books." And even more cogently: "If you unfortunately visit a patient and find him dead, and they ask you why you came, say you knew he would die that night, but want to know at what hour he died."

One acerbic writer asserts that the wily physician tells one person that the patient will recover, another that he will succumb, thus assuring his reputation in at least one quarter. "If the patient has the good fortune to survive," he con-

cludes, "he does so in spite of the bungling doctor, but if he is fated to perish, he is killed with full rites."

Skeptical barbs notwithstanding, the profession attracts many of the ablest young men of the age. Besides Salerno, there is an almost equally respected school at Montpellier, where Arab and Jewish scholars from Spain mix with Provençals, Frenchmen, Italians, and others. Paris and Montpellier have the only two medical schools in northwest Europe, though there are now several in Italy. After a preliminary three-year course, the prospective physician takes a five-year course, followed by a year's internship with an experienced practitioner. He is then allowed to take a formal examination, upon successfully completing which he receives from the faculty a license to practice. Since the universities are highly ecclesiastical in makeup, the license is given in the name of the Pope, and is conferred by the bishop in a ceremony in church.

But the Church's control is nominal. The real shortcoming in medical education is its subservience not to the saints but to astrology and numerology. Constellations and planets are believed to preside over different parts of the body. Numerology provides complicated guides for the course of an illness. The body is believed to have four "humors" and three "spirits," all of which must be checked by examination of the urine and stool and by feeling the pulse, then adjusted by bloodletting, from the side of the body opposite the site of the disease.

All these ideas are derived from the Greeks, and they go to make up an anatomy and physiology as simple and logical as an arithmetic problem.

Medical textbooks[2] are few and precious. Most of the Greek writings have arrived in the West by a circuitous route, first translated into Arabic, then from Arabic into

Apothecary at work, crushing herbs in a mortar (from Chartres Cathedral window). Herbs had a dual function, as seasoning and as medicine.

Latin. The translators who undertake the latter task are often teams of Jewish and Christian scribes working in Spain; the Jewish scholars render the Arabic roughly into Latin, and the Christians polish this version into scholarly language. How many errata and variations creep into a Greek work on its journey to Montpellier and Paris may be imagined.

Their knowledge of Arabic has placed Jewish physicians in the forefront of medicine, and their services are frequently called for by princes and great lords. One of their principal specialties is diseases of the eye. Even a rigorous enforcer of restrictions on Jews like Alphonse de Poitiers, brother of St.-Louis, will consult a Jewish specialist about an eye malady. Like the Arab physicians, Jewish doctors are moving toward a fully rational therapy, yet all medicine—Christian, Arab, and Jewish—is still bound up with astrology, numerology, and magic.

With these aids and his own common sense, the medieval doctor battles valiantly against a variety of ailments. Skin diseases are very widespread in an age when rough wool is often worn next to the skin; when bathing, at least among the masses, is infrequent; and laundry hard to do. Defects of diet—the scarcity of fresh fruit and vegetables—create a dangerous scorbutic tendency in the whole population, and, in the cities especially, insufficient sanitary arrangements facilitate the spread of infection and contagion. In winter dwellings are cold and drafty. Pneumonia is a great killer. Typhoid is common, as are many types of heart and circulatory disease.

But the most frequent demand for medical aid is for treatment of wounds and injuries. Here the medieval surgeon achieves his best success, even showing some understanding of the problem of infection. He applies such medicaments as sterile white of egg to piercing and cutting wounds. A contemporary Italian, Friar Theodoric of Lucca, son of a Crusading surgeon, recommends wine, which of course contains alcohol, and cautions against the complicated salves and nostrums in fashion with some doctors. Surgical instruments include scissors, speculum, razor, scalpel, needle and lancet.

A variety of surgical operations are performed for such disorders as cataracts and hernias; lithotomy (removal of stones from the kidney or gall bladder) and trepanning are also practiced. None of these operations promises well for the subject.

Occasionally the agony of the surgical patient may be relieved by some form of narcosis. Theodoric of Lucca speaks of sponges drenched with opium, and mandrake, dried, then soaked in hot water and inhaled. Bartholomew Anglicus expatiates on the value of mandrake as an anesthetic: "Those who take a portion of it will sleep for four hours and feel neither iron nor fire." However, he adds: "A good leech [physician] does not desist from cutting or burning because of the weeping of the patient."

Bloodletting, that long-popular health measure, is commonly done by barbers, some of whom have recently abandoned the shave and haircut to devote themselves exclusively to surgery. Many also specialize in pulling teeth. Owing to poor diet, teeth are a chronic health problem, more because of bad gums than cavities. Wealthy patients have been known to pay as much as five livres for an extraction, while barbers get as much as fifteen sous for a bleeding. The lower classes are spared these luxuries.

Mental illness is widespread. Birth injuries often leave brain damage. Collective mental disorders, such as St. Vitus' Dance, are notorious, though the most famous outbreak of this "dancing mania" will not appear until the fourteenth century. Joining hands, the victims dance in wild delirium until they fall exhausted, foaming at the mouth. This communal fit is treated either by swaddling the victims like babies, to prevent them from injuring themselves and others, or by exorcism.

The mentally ill are rarely confined, though they are sometimes tied to the rood screen in church, so that they may be improved by attending mass. Or the sign of the cross is shaved into the hair of their heads. They are invariably numbered among the armies of pilgrims at the shrines—along with the spastics, the paralytics, the scrofulous, and the very numerous cripples—at Rome, Mont-Saint-Michel, Roc Amadour, Compostella, and on the road to Jerusalem.

In this pathetic troop one never sees the most pitiful of all the medieval sick—the victims of leprosy. This very widespread disease, attended by its frightful disfigurement, has inspired terror in the clergy as well as the laity.

There are two thousand leper colonies in France, including several in the neighborhood of Troyes. A famous one, the Leproserie des Deux Eaux, was founded in the eleventh century by Count Hugo on the eve of his departure for the First Crusade. Before the leper is committed to the enclosure, his isolation is sanctified by a special church ritual. The unfortunate victim is brought to the tribunal of the diocesan official and examined by surgeons. The "separation" is pronounced the following Sunday. The unhappy man, dressed in a shroud, is carried to the church on a litter by four priests singing the psalm, "Libera me." Inside the church the litter is set down at a safe distance from the congregation. The service of the dead is read. Then, again singing the psalm, the clergy carry the leper out of the church, through the streets, out of town, to the leper colony. He is given a pair of castanets, a pair of gloves, and a bread basket. After the singing of the "De profundis" the priest intones, "Sis mortuus mundo, vivens iterum Deo" (Be thou dead to this world, living again to God), concluding, "I forbid you ever to enter a church or a monastery, a mill, a bakery, a market, or any place where there is an assemblage of people. I forbid you to quit your house without your leper's costume and castanets. I forbid you to bathe yourself or your possessions in stream or fountain or spring. I forbid you to have commerce with any woman except her whom you have married in the Holy Church. I forbid you if anyone speaks to you on the road to answer till you have placed yourself below the wind." Then everyone leaves the poor victim condemned to a living death.

The disease is believed to be transmitted not only by touch but by breath. With all the care taken to isolate lepers, from time to time rumors lead to panic and lynching.

Cruel though medieval treatment of leprosy is, it represents a step forward in the history of medicine: recognition of the problem of contagion. Ironically, leprosy (Hansen's disease) is only slightly contagious, and the frightening disfigurement results not from the disease itself but from loss of sensation in nerve endings and consequent wearing away of tissue. But medieval medicine accurately guesses that diseases are transmitted by contact or through the air.

A still more important contribution of medieval medicine is the hospital, a wholly new idea. Hospitals, like monasteries and abbeys, are favorite recipients of Christian charity. The Hôtel-Dieu-le-Comte in Troyes was founded by Count Henry the Generous some seventy-five years ago, and has continued to profit by gifts not only from the count's successors but from others as well. One lady bequeathed the revenue of seven chambers of a house facing the public baths. Another gave a carpenter and his family, who were her serfs. A burgher gave a stall in Money-changer's Place at the fair. Another gave a fisherman, his family and all his possessions, and his fishing rights in the Seine. Still another endowed the hospital with three garments, worth thirteen sous apiece, and six pairs of shoes a year. A vintner gave income from his vineyards to buy earthenware bowls and cups for the sick and wine to celebrate mass. Other rents, revenues, fees, and taxes from fairs, mills, vineyards, bakeries, farms, and fisheries have poured in.

Counts and popes have accorded this hospital, like many others, their blessing and protection. Eight priests, of whom one is prior and master of the house, staff the hospital, assisted by as many nuns as are needed. When a patient is admitted, he confesses and takes communion, his feet and body are washed, and he is given hospital clothes and food. If his disease is considered contagious, he is isolated—an advance in medicine in itself. The critically ill are also isolated, for intensive care. Upon recovery, indigent patients are furnished with clothes. The hospital does not receive women in childbirth, because their cries may disturb other patients; nor does it take foundlings, the blind, the crippled, and victims of plague (or leprosy), who would swamp the hospital. Responsibility for the care of these unfortunates falls on the parish churches.

The regimen of the hospital is strict and simple, with emphasis on common sense. In fact, there remains a considerable fund of common sense in medieval man's attitude toward health. Many sound health rules are contained in aphorisms and verses, one of the most famous compendiums of which is known as the Health Rule of Salerno. It is said to have been inspired by Robert of Normandy, wounded in the First Crusade, during his stay at the famous medical center. Written in Latin verse, it contained these recommendations, given here in the Elizabethan translation of Sir John Harington:

> A King that cannot rule him his diet
> Will hardly rule his realm in peace and quiet.
>
> For healthy men may cheese be wholesome food,
> But for the weak and sickly 'tis not good.
>
> Use three doctors still, first Dr. Quiet,
> Next Dr. Merry-man and Dr. Diet . . .
>
> Wine, Women, Baths, by art of nature warme,
> Us'd or abus'd do men much good or harme.
>
> Some live to drinke new wine not fully fin'd,
> But for your health we wish that you drink none,
> For such to dangerous fluxes are inclin'd,
> Besides the lees of wine doe breed the stone.
> But such by our consent shall drink alone.
> For water and small biere we make no question
> Are enemies to health and good digestion;
> And Horace in a verse of his rehearses,
> That water-drinkers never make good verses.

9.

The Church

*I know you need a short sermon and a long table.
May it please God not to make the time of the mass
last too long for you.*

—*An Easter sermon by* ROBERT DE SORBON

C hurches in the thirteenth century are places where people go not only to pray or visit the shrines of saints, but for secular purposes, because churches are often the only large public buildings in town. Business life often centers around a town's principal church. In Troyes the fairs crowd the precincts of St.-Jean and St.-Rémi. In Provins the stalls of the moneychangers are set up in front of St.-Ayoul. In many towns churches are used for town meetings, guild meetings, and town council sessions.

Everywhere the church is a familiar, friendly place. It is not, however, particularly comfortable. There are no benches or pews.[1] Some worshippers bring stools and cushions, some kneel on the straw-covered floor. The building is chilly, even in mild weather, and in the winter many of the congregation come armed with handwarmers —hollow metal spheres holding hot coals.

A bell signals the start of service. The congregation stands as the procession of priests, choir, and clerks enters singing a hymn. The melody of Gregorian chant, seeming to wander at will, actually follows strict rules in mode, rhythmic pattern, phrasing, accent, and relationship of words to music. The group sings in unison, or sometimes in an antiphon between choir and cantor or between two halves of the choir. A momentous change is just taking place, however—the birth of polyphonic music. Out of a part of the chant in which the melody is accompanied by a sustained note in the tenor, music for more than one voice part is developing. First the tenor, from a single note of indefinite length, becomes a separate melody with its own rhythm; then another voice is added; and out of this grows a "motet," a sort of little fugue. Another important innovation is the beginning of modern notation, with rhythm indicated as well as pitch.

The singers may be accompanied by a "portative organ," which looks like the fruit of a union between an accordion and a full-sized organ. It is suspended from the player's neck; he operates the bellows on the back of the instrument with his left hand and the keyboard with his right. Some churches have standard organs, powerful, clumsy, and generally out of tune. The one constructed at Winchester in 980, with four hundred pipes and two manuals, produced a noise so great that everyone "stopped with his hand his gaping ears, being in no wise able to draw near and hear the sound." Instrumental keys, introduced in the twelfth century, are so heavy and stiff that they must be played with the clenched fist. Organs have a range of three octaves, and are the first instruments to become entirely chromatic.

The Gregorian liturgy, having triumphed over several rivals, is in use throughout western Europe. In almost any church in France, England, Germany, Italy, or Spain the service is celebrated exactly as it is in Troyes. The congregation stands, kneels, and sits in accordance with the ritual;

otherwise, however, it takes little active part in the service.

Few present understand Latin, but sermons are delivered in the vernacular, except when the audience is clerical. The sermon usually lasts half an hour, measured by the water clock on the altar. The priest mounts the pulpit and begins by making the sign of the cross, then gives his *thema* or text in a short Latin passage from the Gospels, which he translates for the benefit of the congregation. This he follows with a rhetorical introduction explaining his unfitness to discuss the subject (the sentiments are humble but the language is flowery) and with an invocation to the divine spirit. Then he develops his text.

Frequently he runs over the time limit in order to get in his "example." This indispensable part of the program consists of a story, illustrative of the sermon's text, told with dramatic flair. For a sermon on the Christian virtues, a popular example goes like this:[2]

A merchant is returning from the fair, where he has sold all his merchandise and gained a large sum of money. Pausing in a city —such as Amiens or Troyes—he finds himself before a church, and goes into the chapel to pray to the Mother of God, Holy Mary, putting his purse beside him on the ground. When he rises, he forgets the purse and goes away without it.

A burgher of the city is also accustomed to visit the chapel and pray before the blessed Mother of God Our Lord, Holy Mary. He finds the purse and sees that it is sealed and locked. What is he to do? If he lets it be known that he has found it, people will cry that they have lost it. He decides to keep the purse and advertise for its owner, and he writes out a notice in big letters, saying that whoever has lost anything should come to him, and posts it on the door of his house.

When the merchant has gone a good distance, he realizes that his purse is missing. Alas, all is lost! He returns to the chapel, but the purse is gone. The priest, questioned, knows nothing about it.

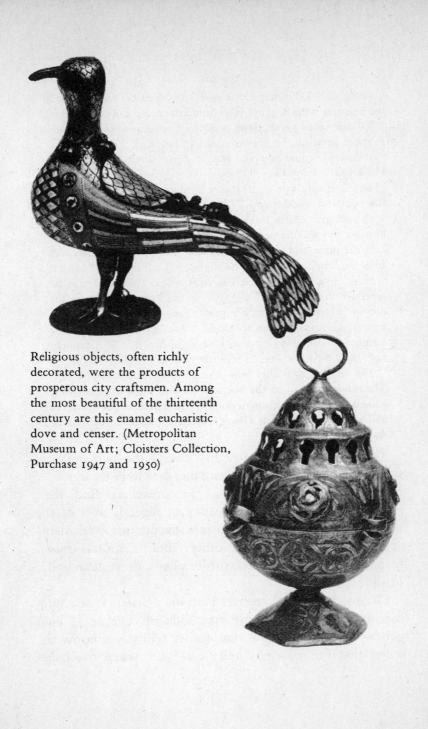

Religious objects, often richly
decorated, were the products of
prosperous city craftsmen. Among
the most beautiful of the thirteenth
century are this enamel eucharistic
dove and censer. (Metropolitan
Museum of Art; Cloisters Collection,
Purchase 1947 and 1950)

Coming out of the chapel, the merchant finds the notice, enters the house, sees the burgher who found the purse and says to him, "Tell me who wrote those words on your door." And the burgher pretends he knows nothing but says, "Good friend, many people come here and put up signs. What do you want? Have you lost anything?" "Lost anything!" cries the merchant. "I have lost a treasure so great that it cannot be counted." "What have you lost, good friend?" "I lost a purse full of money, sealed with such and such a seal and such and such a lock." Then the burgher sees that the merchant is telling the truth, so he shows him the purse and returns it to him. And when the merchant finds the burgher so honest, he thinks, "Good sir God, I am not worthy of such a treasure as I have amassed. This burgher is far worthier than I." "Sir," he says to the burgher, "surely the money belongs to you rather than to me, and I will give it to you, and commend you to God." "Ah, my friend," says the burgher, "take your money; I haven't earned it." "Certainly not," says the merchant, "I will not take it." And he leaves.

The burgher runs after him crying, "Stop thief! Stop thief!" The neighbors take up the hue and cry and catch the merchant, and ask, "What has this man done?" "He has stolen my poverty and my honesty, which I have carefully preserved up to this moment."

The congregation thoroughly enjoys the performance, with its moral, which the priest takes care to point out.

Besides homely anecdotes, the preachers find their examples in extracts from history or legend, lives of the saints, Bible stories, contemporary events, personal memories, fables from Aesop or other fabulists, morals drawn from bestiaries or from accounts of plants, the human body, or the stars.

Oratorical devices[3] are not beneath a priest. If attention lags during the sermon, he may suddenly exclaim, "That person who is sleeping in the corner will never know the secret that I'm going to tell you!" Or when the ladies become restive during a sermon on the wickedness of women, he may address them: "Shall I speak of the good woman? I will tell you about that old lady there who has fallen asleep. For Heaven's sake, if someone has a pin, wake her up; people who sleep during the sermon somehow manage to stay awake at table."

The sermon is followed by the Creed, the Offertory, and the celebration of communion, which has been preceded by the Kiss of Peace. The priest kisses the Gospel, which is kissed in turn by every member of the congregation. Those who receive the sacrament come forward and stand before the altar with hands outstretched, palms touching, one knee bent slightly forward; they do not kneel. The priest celebrates communion in front of the altar with his back to the people—a recent innovation.

Communion over, the service nears its end, and the priest asks prayers for certain persons: for the Church, for Count Thibaut, his peace and prosperity, for the bishop and other priests, for the Holy Land and its defenders, for the dead, some of whom he mentions by name. He may even lower his voice and ask a blessing for an unlucky priest who has been disciplined. Everyone kneels and the prayers are recited together, with several *Paters* and *Aves*. Then the priest pronounces his final blessing, and the service is over.

Like the Christian service, worship in the synagogue retains an age-old universal form. The Almemar (the platform from which the Scriptures are read), and the ark containing the sacred scrolls stand in the center of the paved floor. Wax candles illuminate the interior. Tallow, though permitted for private use, is forbidden in the synagogue.

Services are read twice daily, in late afternoon and again in the evening. Behavior is casual, compared with that of a

Christian congregation. Children are noisy, adults wander
in and out. A Takkanah (edict) imposes a heavy fine for
striking one's neighbor in the synagogue. Jewish services are
well attended, though workers who must rise at sunup are
excused except on the Sabbath. The form of service is
identical throughout northern France. The ancient custom
by which men of the congregation read successive portions
of the Scriptures has been modified, and the Reader per-
forms this task, either alone or with various individuals who
are called up. Sermons are delivered only on festivals, when
the whole congregation sings the Hallel (Psalms 113–118),
which is possibly what provoked a famous complaint by
Pope Innocent III against excessive noise emanating from
synagogues.

One of the features of the Christian religion which has
given worship a distinctive character is the taste for inter-
cessory saints. Though prayers to a saint may be said at home
as well as in church, their effect is believed to be greatly
enhanced by the presence of part of the saint's mortal
remains. This conviction dates from the martyrdom of the
early Christians. Bones and other physical fragments of men
stoned, burned, and tortured were reverently rescued and
preserved.

Saints and martyrs multiplied, and their relics multiplied
even more rapidly. Churches were built on the tombs of
martyrs. Princes and bishops went to extraordinary lengths
to acquire relics. Constantinople became the center of a
vast commerce, owing to its favorable position near the
scenes of the Old and New Testaments. St. Helena, mother
of Constantine, is said to have found the three crosses of
Calvary and identified the True Cross by touching a dead
man with it and bringing him to life. So precious was this

Reliquary chest. Sometimes reliquaries were made in the shape of
the bone fragments they contained—an arm to contain an ulna, a
head to contain a piece of skull. (Metropolitan Museum of Art,
Gift of George Blumenthal, 1941.)

relic that it was cut into bits and bestowed, traded, and sold all over Europe (to such effect that Calvin later counted enough pieces of it "to make a full load for a good ship").

The capture of Jerusalem in 1099 brought a flood of relics—Judas' pieces of silver, one of the Biblical sower's wheat seeds, two heads of St. John the Baptist ("Was this saint then bicephalous?" acidly demanded Guibert of Nogent), and hundreds of other items. But this was a trickle compared to the torrent loosed by the capture of Constantinople in 1204. Bishop Garnier de Traînel, who served as chaplain of the Latin army, brought back many treasures to Troyes, among them a silver arm encompassing a relic of St. James the Greater; the skull of St. Philip the Apostle, incased in a reliquary decorated with a gold crown studded with precious stones; and several pieces of the True Cross, enclosed in a Byzantine cross of gilded silver set with five fine emeralds. The Crown of Thorns, pawned by the new Latin emperor to the Venetians, was eventually purchased by St.-Louis, who built the Sainte-Chapelle to receive it, apparently regarding it as superior in authenticity to the two other Crowns of Thorns that Paris already possessed. Other relics aroused skepticism even in a religious age: one of Christ's baby teeth (How did anyone think to save it? wondered Guibert of Nogent), pieces of stone tablets on which God was said to have written the Ten Commandments, and the "authentic relic" of the Lord's circumcision, claimed by a number of churches.

Despite cavils, the cult of relics is at its zenith in the middle of the thirteenth century. Every church has its treasures. Besides the relics brought back by Garnier de Traînel, the cathedral treasury of Troyes displays the basin in which Christ washed the disciples' feet; the surplice of St. Thomas of Canterbury, on which traces of his brains are

Virgin worship, as popular with city burghers as with
the knights and peasants of the countryside, was at its
height in the thirteenth century, when the newly
founded Dominicans popularized the "hail Mary."
Statue above is from the Strasbourg Cathedral.
(Metropolitan Museum of Art, Cloisters Collection,
Purchase 1947)

visible, and a foot of St. Margaret. The treasury of Sens contains a drop of blood and a bit of the garment of St. Clement and one of Judas' thirty pieces of silver. The church of Ste.-Croix at Provins has an arm of St. Lawrence and a fragment of the True Cross, given by Count Thibaut on his return from a Crusade in 1241. Sometimes relics are preserved in gold and enamel boxes, ornamented with jewels; sometimes they are fitted into a more artfully contrived reliquary—an arm-bone encased in a sculptured arm of brass, enamel and gold, or a piece of skull fitted neatly into a lifelike representation of a saint's head in silver and brass.

The number of saints is large and indeterminate. In early Christian times cults were local, and inquiries into qualifications for sainthood were usually instituted by the bishop of the diocese in which the candidate lived. Not until the tenth century did the Pope come to play an important part in canonization, and in the twelfth, Alexander III established once and for all the principle that no person, however holy his reputation, could be venerated as a saint without direct papal authorization. In the thirteenth century the process of canonization is undergoing its final development.[4] Petition must be made to the Pope, who appoints two or more commissioners as his representatives. They set up a court of inquiry, examine witnesses, and fill the role of devil's advocate as well as of defendant and judge. The petitioners choose a proctor who marshals witnesses and expedites the suit if there is a delay. A record of the proceedings is kept, put into "public form" by a notary, and presented to the papal Curia, where canonization is finally granted or denied. The successful candidate is placed in the martyrology, but in 1250 church calendars still present wide local variations.

Despite the popularity of such regional patrons as St.-Loup, one saint stands far above all others in appeal. The prayers of Christians are directed more often to the Virgin Mary than to all the rest together. Virgin worship goes back to the fourth century, when controversies over the nature of Christ brought the need for a new intercessor between God and man. In the thirteenth century this worship is at its height. The monastic orders find in the Virgin an ascetic ideal. The Carmelites celebrate Our Lady of Carmel, the Franciscans have instituted the Feast of the Presentation, the Dominicans have popularized the Hail Mary. Works of Marian theology and devotion by St.-Bernard and St.-Bonaventure have been translated into the popular tongue and are widely read.

Many a burgher seeks the intercession of saints by visiting their relics, either to effect a cure or to do penance for a sin. One may make a pilgrimage to the new cathedral at Chartres and follow the "Chartres mile" on one's knees—a labyrinth of concentric circles in the middle of the nave. Or the pilgrim may journey to Roc Amadour, where he strips to his shirt, binds himself in chains, and climbs the hundred and twenty-six steps to the Chapel of Our Lady on his knees. There a priest recites prayers of purification and removes the chains, presenting him with a certificate and a lead medallion with the image of the Virgin. Henry II, St. Dominic, St.-Louis, Blanche of Castille and thousands of others, famous and obscure, have climbed those steps.

Some burghers possess lead medallions from half a dozen pilgrimages, either the result of persistent attempts to cure an affliction, or exceptional piety—or perhaps a fondness for travel. Chaucer's pilgrims were not the first to enjoy their trip.

If there are saints to pray to, there are also devils to fear.

Every corner of hell is minutely described by the priests and depicted on church portals. People are often possessed by devils, which must be exorcised by the priest. Belief in demons is older than the Church, which has certified their existence (Thomas Aquinas cites the authority of the saints and of the Christian faith.) Thoughts of hell and purgatory give Christians moments of apprehension and even terror, and influence some decisions, especially in the realm of charity. But though merchants are aware that the Bible does not recommend laying up riches as a means of gaining the kingdom of Heaven, they go right on laying them up.

In the cosmos of the thirteenth century many mysteries are unsolved and, failing other hypotheses, must be explained by supernatural means. Yet the outlook of the burghers of Troyes is not devoid of skepticism and common sense. Though the Roman Church is at the pinnacle of its prestige, there is a strong current of resistance to its authority. The weapons of excommunication and interdict are not as effective as they used to be, partly through overuse. The late Bishop Hervée, quarreling with Thibaut the Song-writer over prerogatives, threatened the count with excommunication so frequently that the Pope felt constrained to caution the embattled prelate. And even the Pope's own edict did not prevent Dandolo, the elderly Doge of Venice, and his fellow Crusaders from capturing the Christian city of Zara and dividing the spoils.

The cities, with their notorious worldliness, are widely blamed by the Church for the spread of skepticism and something worse—heresy. A powerful, subversive religious underground has stirred upheaval throughout Europe. Several heretical movements varying from moderate to lunatic-fringe have been suppressed, but one, the most dangerous of all, continues to alarm all right-thinking

people. Albigensianism, or Catharism, originally brought
to the West from Bulgaria by weavers and cloth merchants
and fostered, as the Church complains, by the new inde-
pendence and skepticism of the cities, has been the object
of a vigorous crusade, lasting thirty-four years, with a ten-
year interval of truce. Many of its practitioners have gone
into hiding, and the Inquisition, placed in the hands of the
new mendicant orders, is busy ferreting out suspects everywhere.

The orthodox majority hates and fears the heretics, whose
doctrines are shocking enough without being exaggerated,
as they naturally are. Cathars deny the Redemption and
the Incarnation. Some claim that Christ's entry into the
world was made by way of Mary's ear. They scoff at the
Old Testament and take stock in neither hell nor purgatory,
maintaining that this world is hell enough. They reject the
cross, which they consider as a merely material object. Their
conviction that marriage is evil, because procreation em-
beds souls deeper in the material world, has given an
especially dubious reputation to the Cathars, who are
believed to have originated in Bulgaria—hence the latter-
day connotation in French and English of the word *bougre*,
originally meaning Bulgar.

Parties of Dominican and Franciscan inquisitors journey
from town to town inviting heretics to reform and Christians to inform. Heretics who confess and repent may get off
with a penance, which sometimes takes the form of a
saffron-colored cross sewed on breast and back. Whipping
and imprisonment may be employed, though not torture—
as yet. A guilty and unrepentant heretic may be "delivered
to the secular arm" to be burned. Verdict is pronounced and
sentence executed in the town square, and the ashes are cast
into the nearest river.

The heresy hunters visited Champagne in the 1230s, their activities reaching a frightful climax in 1239, on the eve of Count Thibaut's departure for the Holy Land. An old woman of Provins, Gille, called "the Abbess," who had been in prison since 1234 awaiting sentence for heresy, bought her own release by disclosing the names of other heretics to the notorious inquisitor Robert le Bougre, an ex-Cathar turned Dominican. At Mont-Aimé, some fifty miles north of Troyes, one hundred and eighty-three men and women were burned in the presence of a huge throng of spectators. When the fires were lit, the Cathar leader raised his voice and gave his fellow-martyrs absolution, nobly explaining that he alone would be damned because there was no one to absolve him.

10.

The Cathedral

Nothing doing in the workyard, for the moment
I'm out of money.

—FROM THE ACCOUNTS OF A
FOURTEENTH-CENTURY CATHEDRAL

The Cathedral of St.-Pierre and St.-Paul has experienced many vicissitudes through the centuries that it has been the church of the bishop of Troyes. From small beginnings as a chapel, occupying the site of the present choir, it grew slowly into a ninth-century basilica of sufficient size and dignity to serve as the scene for a council of Pope John VIII.

Fourteen years later the Vikings burned St.-Pierre to the ground; Bishop Milon restored it in the following century. In the new cathedral St.-Bernard preached to a capacity crowd in 1147 and cured many sick, including a servant of the bishop, an artisan, and an epileptic girl. Milon's work was destroyed by the Great Fire of 1188, after which Bishop Hervée undertook to rebuild the church, using the new engineering technique which a later day will call Gothic. At the time of Hervée's death, in 1223, the sanctuary and the seven chapels of the apse were nearly finished. His successor, Bishop Robert, continued the work; it is proceeding today under Bishop Nicholas de Brie and will go on for the next three centuries, stopping and starting as money comes in.

In Italy churches and cathedrals are often projects of communes; in northwest Europe the lead is more frequently taken by the bishop or abbot. Abbot Suger of St.-Denis led his carpenters into the forest to choose timber for his beams and personally ascertained "with geometric and arithmetical instruments" that the new choir aligned with the old nave. At Troyes the bishop is invariably the moving force in the endless task of construction and reconstruction.

Cathedrals are usually built on the crypts of their predecessors. The new cathedral of St.-Pierre is being constructed on the site of the old, but the larger apse, with its radiating chapels, requires more room, so Hervée negotiated a trade with a fisherman who owned the strip between the crumbling Roman wall and the branch of the Seine that marks the eastern limits of the old city. The wall was dismantled, and the chevet of the new cathedral now extends beyond it.

As work on a cathedral halts, resumes, progresses, halts again, several master builders may be in charge at different periods, which among other things leads to stylistic alterations and inconsistencies. Also, during these changes, the names of the masters[1] tend to get lost. None of St.-Pierre's early builders are known by name, though they were without doubt prominent men in their own lifetime. The cathedral builder, in fact, is one of the outstanding figures of the Middle Ages. If vanished records swallow the names of many, enough information survives to supply evidence of the kind of men they were. Many insured the durability of their fame by inscribing their signatures on their works. Carved into the soffit of the topmost window facing the New Tower of Chartres is the name "Harman" and the date "1164." On the roof of St. Mary's, Beverley, can be

read the message: "Hal Carpenter made this rowfe."
Names are signed in the labyrinth on the floor of the nave
at Amiens: Robert de Luzarches, Thomas de Cormont, and
Renard de Cormont; and at Reims: Jean d'Orbais, Jean le
Loup, Gaucher de Reims, and Bernard de Soissons. Tombs
bear the names of many builders. One at Reims is dedicated
to Master Hugues Libergier, "who began this church in the
year of the Incarnation 12 . . ."—the precise date obscured
by the footsteps of seven hundred years. Documents record
the names of many others, such as Pierre de Montreuil, one
of the best-known men of his time, who in 1248 completed
the Sainte-Chapelle in Paris in the amazing time of thirty-
three months—showing what a Gothic engineer could do
when the money did not run out. The brilliant Villard de
Honnecourt perpetuated his name and fame by leaving a
large parchment sketchbook filled with drawings, plans,
and elevations which is one of the priceless documents of
the thirteenth century.

The names of builders are well known to prospective
employers. William of Sens was hired in 1174 to rebuild
Canterbury Cathedral on the strength of his reputation as
the builder of the Cathedral of Sens. Builders are well paid,
with a liberal daily stipend supplemented by a clothing
allowance, a food allowance, fodder for their horses, a fur-
trimmed robe, and often special privileges, such as freedom
from taxes for life. Typically rising from the ranks of the
masons, they are remarkably versatile. Not only do they
habitually combine the functions of engineer and architect,
but some are adept sculptors and painters, or even poets.
They are expert at every kind of construction—castles,
walls, bridges, secular buildings. One architect, John of
Gloucester, not only supervised the works at Westminster
Abbey, but undertook at Westminster Palace to repair a

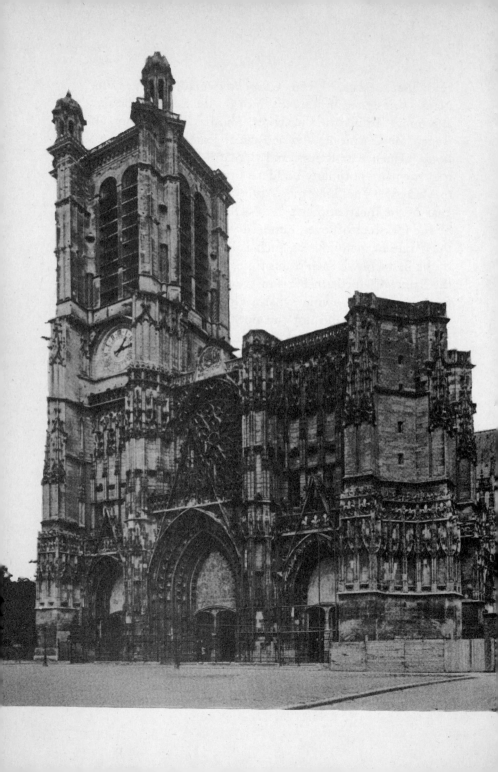

chimney and a conduit supplying water to the king's lavatory, and to build a drain to carry off refuse of the kitchen to the Thames, "which conduit the king ordered to be made on account of the stink of the dirty water which was carried through his halls which was wont to affect the health of the people frequenting them."

The builders' plans[2] are skilfully drafted on parchment, to explain their intentions to bishop and chapter: ground plans for each part of the nave, choir and transepts, sketches of portals with sculpture indicated, scale drawings of bays and ambulatories, variant possibilities for roofing and drainage. Accomplished mathematicians, especially strong in geometry, they determine proportions by supplementing measurements in feet and inches with modules, based on squares, equilateral triangles, and other regular polygons. This knowledge is so esoteric that it remains a professional secret.

The master builder is not only well paid but highly respected, as are the master masons. A preacher cannot restrain his indignation in describing the lordly status of these elite commoners: "In great buildings the master-in-chief orders his men about but rarely or never lends his own hand to the work; and yet he is paid much more than all the others . . . The master masons, with walking sticks and gloves, say, 'Cut here,' and 'Cut there,' but they do no work themselves."

The master builder is the general of a skilled, and consequently expensive, army of workers. Pilgrims and other faithful sometimes contribute voluntary labor, usually in the transport department. Occasionally a long line of penitents hitch themselves to a wagonload of stone, doing the work of oxen. On the whole, oxen do the work better. A more efficacious form of volunteer labor is the peasant with ox

Cathedral of St.-Pierre, Troyes. Begun in the early thirteenth century, its construction, like that of most cathedrals, was interrupted for long periods by lack of funds, and was not finally completed until the sixteenth century. (Touring-Club de France)

The flying buttress, a key element in the revolutionary Gothic system of construction, drawn by Villard de Honnecourt at Reims Cathedral.

and wagon who receives an indulgence from the bishop in return for his help. Even so, moving a large quantity of stone a long distance overland is a serious problem. Troyes imports some of its stone from Tonnerre, only twenty-five miles south, but without a connection by water. The stone quintuples in cost on the journey. Water transport is much cheaper. The marble for the columns of the great abbey church at Cluny was moved ten times as far, down the Durance from the Alps and up the Rhône. When they can, bishops cannibalize pagan monuments, as at Reims, where an early archbishop obtained permission from Louis the Pious to dismantle the Roman ramparts so that he could build the old Romanesque cathedral.

But a convenient quarry is even better than an old Roman wall. Suger's discovery of the quarry at Pontoise was regarded as miraculous. The bishops of Troyes have a quarry which is worked by masons from the cathedral work gang.

Never do volunteers figure as an important element of the labor force. They cannot dress stone, or set it in courses, or make mortar and tile, or lay lead roofs and gutters, or construct arch ribs, or sculpture stone, or carve wood, or fabricate stained glass, or assemble it into windows. Cathedral labor is necessarily professional.

In the terminology of construction workers of a later day, the masons are "boomers." They go where the job is, living in barracks in the cathedral yard, collecting their pay, saving it if they are prudent, spending it on drink and girls if they are not. Many own their own valuable tools, which are passed from father to son. Others depend on tools supplied by the employer, who is normally responsible for repair and maintenance. Keeping soft iron points and edges sharp is a problem. Besides picks, hammers, wedges and points, basic to stone dressing, masons need hatchets, trowels, spades, hoes, buckets and sieves for mortar, and lines for laying out walls.

Masons are free men, skilled at their profession, capable of rising in the world. There are several categories with varying wage rates: plasterers and mortarers, stonecutters, master masons, and unskilled laborers. They usually spend their first years in the quarry, learning to cut stone. A mason in the quarry may be paid twenty-four deniers a week plus his meals and lodging, though in winter his wage is automatically cut to match the shorter working day. A summer wage may reach thirty deniers. There is plenty of work for an expert mason; from eight to ten churches a year are going up in France alone.

On a summer day, the workyard before a cathedral hums with activity. Masons are clustered in twos and threes. One man hammers while a comrade holds the point to the stone, cutting a voussoir, one of the wedge-shaped stones that form the ribs of an arch. Most difficult to fashion is the keystone, whose projections must fit into cuts made in the four rib stones that meet it, to pin the vault securely at the top. Some workers are dressing stone blocks for the exterior masonry. The Master of the Works, or one of his aides, may construct wooden "molds" against which the stone blocks are measured to insure uniformity and accuracy. A master mason marks each finished block with a number, to facilitate assembly of the great jigsaw puzzle. Some men are at work on more delicate pieces, sections of pier capitals or portal frieze borders. Some are busy making mortar with buckets, sieves, hoes, and trowels. They have the valuable assistance of a recent invention—the wheelbarrow. Two blacksmiths are sharpening tools, one turning the grindstone as the other hones the cutting edge of a hatchet. One shed shelters a forge where the iron clamps[3] and dowels are wrought. Another is the carpenters' shack, near which is the pit where the heavy beams for the timbering are sawed by the big two-handed pit saw. The plumbers also have their shed, where they fashion lead fittings for eaves and gutters.

An exceptionally skilled craftsman at work in the yard may be the bell founder, really a brass founder, who makes brass pots, washbasins, and mortars when there are no bells to be cast. He has a large pit dug, and in it he constructs a mold with a clay core which supports a wax model of the bell, in turn encased in a clay "cope." The mold will be dried by kindling a fire in the brickwork of the core, which will at the same time melt the wax, leaving a space to be filled in with bell metal. This is a mixture of copper and tin. Experience has shown that the best proportion is thirteen parts copper to four of tin; a higher percentage of tin improves the tone of the bell but makes the metal brittle. The bell is "long-waisted"[4] (longer in proportion to its diameter than bells in later centuries). It will be rung with a simple lever; later bells will be operated with a half wheel, three-quarter wheel, and finally a complete wheel. The founder casts his bells so that they will have a "virgin ring" and will need no further tuning. Tuning is a laborious and noisy process of chipping around the inside of a bell.

When the metal is poured and the bell mounted, the bishop baptizes it as if it were a child, with salt, water, and holy oil. He prays that when it is sounded faith and charity may abound among men, that all the devices of the devil— hail, lightning, winds—may be rendered vain by its ringing, and all unseasonable weather be softened.

The bell founder signs his work with the mark of a shield with three bells, a pot and a mortar, and sometimes with an inscription such as "Iohannes Sleyt Me Fecit" or "Iohannes De Stafforde Fecit Me in Honore Beate Marie," or a bit of bell ringer's verse: "I to the church the living call, and to the grave do summon all," or "Sometimes joy and sometimes sorrow, marriage today and death tomorrow."

Dominating the scene is the great incomplete shell of the cathedral itself. The rising wall is covered with scaffolding fashioned of rough-hewn poles lashed together in trusses, with the diagonals cinched by tourniquets. Inside the walls a giant crane stands on a platform, its long arm reaching over the wall, dangling a line to the ground. When the line is secured around a building stone, word is passed from the ground outside via the men on the scaffold to the crane operator inside. The "engine" is started—a yoke of oxen harnessed to walk in a circle around the crane platform, winding the line on a windlass. The driver commands, the whip snaps, the oxen shove, the windlass turns, the line moves, the block rises, till it reaches the scaffold where the men are waiting. Cries go back and forth over the wall, the "engine" is halted, the men on the scaffold grasp the block, maneuver it in, call for another lift of a foot or so, then for a back-off to lower the stone in place, and amid shouts, commands and perhaps a few curses, the block is securely bedded in the prepared mortar course. Smaller stones are lifted by a lighter windlass, which is turned by a crank— another invention of the Middle Ages.

Most of the masonry work consists of old, long-practiced technique. The Romans maneuvered bigger blocks into position than any that medieval masons tackle. On the Pont du Gard there are stones eleven feet in length. But medieval masons are steadily improving their ability to handle large masses of stone. In the bases of piers, monoliths weighing as much as two tons are sometimes used. The Romans habitually built without mortar, dressing their stones accurately enough so that walls and arches stood simply by their own weight. Some builders are beginning to essay this, but by and large medieval masonry relies on mortar.

Thirteenth-century timbering is also less daring than Roman. The entrance to the choir at present is a veritable maze of heavy crisscrossing timbers supporting the work in progress on the first bay of the choir vault.[5] The rough-hewn timbers stand in a network of Xs and Vs, supporting a rude ogival arch of timber on which the stone ribs are laid. The timber arch does not meet the stone accurately at all points, and where it fails to do so, chips or blocks are driven into the interstice.

In the early Middle Ages, the problem of fireproofing a church was reduced to the question of how to support a masonry vault with something less expensive than a thick wall. Roman engineers actually had a solution, the groined vault, contrived by making two of their ordinary semi-circular "barrel vaults" intersect. The weight of the resulting structure was distributed to the corners, permitting it to be supported by piers, and so providing architectural advantages. But the groined vault, though used by the Romans in the Baths of Caracalla and by some builders since, presents a difficulty. The variously-shaped stone blocks must be meticulously cut; in other words, they are expensive.

When medieval engineers found another way to mount a vault on piers they opened the door to Gothic architecture.[6] The Romans, acquainted with the pointed arch, found as little use for it as had the Greeks or Persians. It was French engineers of the twelfth century who made the discovery that two pointed arches, intersecting overhead at right angles, created an exceptionally strong stone skeleton, which could rest solidly on four piers. The stones were easy

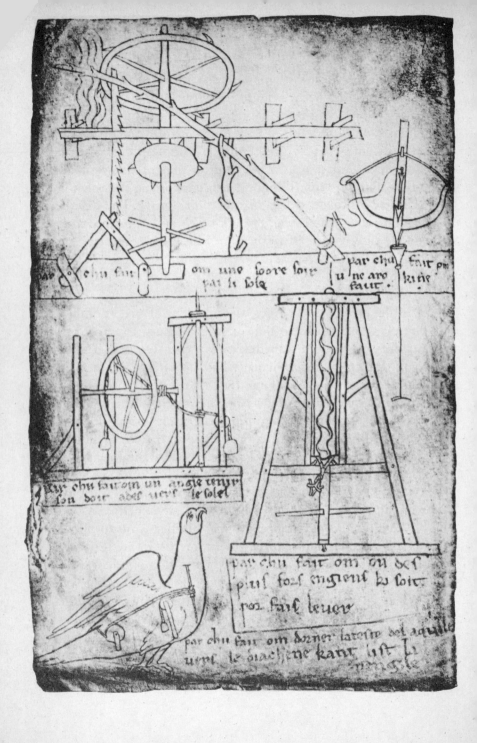

par ꝯ chu fait · om une boore soir u ne aro kine par chu fait om
pai li sole fait ·

par chu toutoin un angle uir
en doit aber uers le solel

par chu fait om ou des
pius fort engiens la soir
pos fail leuer

par chu fait om drner latorir del aquile
uert le diachene kant list li
mangile

to cut and the spaces between could be filled with no exceptional skill on the part of the mason. And once mounted on its piers, the new vault could be raised to astonishing heights at moderate cost. The higher the vault, the more room for windows, and the better illuminated the church. A problem remained. As the vault rose, the piers required reinforcement to contain the thrust from the ribs, which threatened to topple them outward.

At first this difficulty was met by buttressing, that is, by giving an extra thickness to the exterior wall at the point where the rib connected. But this made it impossible to put side aisles in the church. The spectacular answer to the problem was the flying buttress, a beam of masonry that arched airily over the low roof of the side aisle to meet the point where the rib supporting the main vault connected with the top of the pier.

By 1250 the intricate combination of piers, ribs, and flying buttresses has become an established, functioning system, one which would have opened the eyes of Roman engineers.

Medieval builders have a better theoretical grasp of structural relationships than had their Roman predecessors, who often used unnecessarily heavy underpinnings. But there is still no such thing as theoretical calculation of stress, or even accurate measurement. Gothic churches are full of small errors of alignment, and sometimes a vault crashes. But with or without a grounding in theory, the new technology usually works, and works so well that though originally conceived in a spirit of economy, it has had a history similar to that of many other engineering advances. It has opened such social and aesthetic possibilities that in the end it has raised the cost of church construction. A hundred years ago the nave of one of the first Gothic cathedrals, at

Medieval machinery, sketched by Villard de Honnecourt: top, mechanical saw for splitting beams; upper right, crossbow with sighting device; middle, hoisting machines; lower left, a mechanical eagle.

Noyon, soared to a height of eighty-five feet. Notre-Dame-de-Paris then rose to a hundred and fifteen feet, Reims to a hundred and twenty-five, Amiens to a hundred and forty, and Beauvais, just started, is aiming at over a hundred and fifty. Spires above the bell towers reach much higher, that of Rouen ultimately holding the championship at four hundred and ninety-five feet, higher than the Great Pyramid.

It is no accident that the development of Gothic architecture coincides with growing affluence. The bishop of Troyes could not have undertaken the new Cathedral of St.-Pierre two hundred years ago, not merely for want of engineering technique but for wait of cash.

Money to pay for a cathedral comes from a number of sources. Added to the steadily growing revenues of the chapter and its dependencies are the profits from indulgences, which are the bishop's monopoly. Many an avaricious baron has made peace with God by a handsome gift to a cathedral building fund. Deathbed bequests[7] are an especially fruitful source. The Church has campaigned long and shrewdly in favor of wills. Relics, which are part of the reason for building a cathedral, help raise money long before its completion. They attract pilgrims to the site, and since they are portable, they can be sent on mission to the surrounding countryside. Those of Laon journeyed as far south as Tours and north and west to England, where they visited Canterbury, Winchester, Christchurch, Salisbury, Wilton, Exeter, Bristol, Barnstable, and Taunton, performing miracles all along the way.

Even with all the resources of guilty consciences and psychological cures few cathedrals would be completed without the assistance of an entirely different factor: civic pride. The cathedral belongs to the town as well as to the bishop and is often used for secular purposes, such as town meetings. The burghers can be counted on to give it financial support, not merely through private contributions by the wealthy, but through corporate contributions by the guilds. Proud, devout, and affluent, the guilds compete with each other and with the great lords and prelates in endowing the pictures in glass of Bible stories and lives of the saints which are the chief glory of the cathedral, and which represent no less than half its total cost. For at least one cathedral, Chartres, we have precise figures: of one hundred and two windows, forty-four were donated by princes and other secular lords, sixteen by bishops and other ecclesiastics, and forty-two by the town guilds, who signed their identities with panels representing their crafts.

Windows are not all installed at once. A cathedral's glass may be incomplete a hundred or two hundred years after the masonry is begun. The installation of a window in the clerestory of the choir is an event. The mosaic of colored glass is passed up from hand to hand and eased onto the projecting dowels of a horizontal iron saddle bar, the ends of which are buried in the masonry. A second narrow bar with openings that match the dowels fits parallel to the first bar and is fastened to it with pins. Together these bars, and the vertical stanchions, hold the glass in place and brace it against wind pressure.

Glass is not manufactured at the site of the cathedral, nor indeed even inside the city. The glassmakers locate their hut in a nearby forest, which supplies fuel and raw materials. Glassmaking is a very ancient art, and "stained" (colored) glass is at least several centuries old, but not until recently has it been in great demand. The new technology and the new affluence have created this major industry.

The glassmaking process, brought to the West by the Venetians, has changed little through the ages—two parts ash (beechwood for best results) to one part sand in the mixture, a hot fire in a stone furnace, blowing and cutting. Blowing is done with a six-foot-long tube, creating a bubble of glass in the form of a long cylinder closed at one end and nearly closed at the other. The cylinder is cut along its length with a white-hot iron, reheated, and opened along the seam into a sheet. The result is a piece of glass of uneven thickness, full of irregularities—bubbles, waves, lines—not very clear, of a pale greenish color. Medieval glassmakers, like their predecessors, cannot turn out a good transparent, colorless pane. One consequence has been that glass never had much appeal as material for the small windows of the Romanesque buildings.

The vast Gothic window spaces have changed the situation. Imperfections in the glass are unimportant, as coloring becomes not only acceptable but desirable. Colors, apart from the indeterminate green of "natural" glass, have always been readily obtainable by adding something to the basic mixture—cobalt for blue, manganese for purple, copper for red. As the big new church windows came into fashion the glaziers took to cutting up sheets of colored glass and leading bits together to make a design. Almost at once the idea occurred of making the designs not merely geometric but pictorial, and the art of stained glass was born. Art begets artists, and the function of assembling the pieces of glass into pictures that the sun turned into miracles of radiant color devolved on those who were skilled at it.

The cathedral windows are made from glass manufactured in the hut in the forest, but are designed and assembled in a studio near the cathedral, under the direction of the master glazier. His craft demands special knowledge (often transmitted from father to son), exceptional skill, and long experience. Like the master builder and the masons, the window maker and the workmen he commands are itinerants, moving from town to town and church to church.

The master glazier oversees every part of the operations of his shop, but one function that he reserves for himself alone is that of drawing the picture. First he produces a small scale-drawing of the whole window on parchment, coloring in the segments. Then he draws a cartoon the size of the panel on which he is working, not on parchment, but on the wooden surface of an enormous bench or table of white ash. A panel is sketched on the table in the form of a diagram in black and white, indicating by numbers and letters which colors are to be used in each tiny section. As the big panes made by the glaziers are cut roughly to size with a hot iron under the master's eye, each piece is laid in its correct position on the table. It does not quite fit. Using a notched tool called a grozing iron, a workman dextrously nibbles the piece's edges to precision.

A visitor watching the workmen fashion the legend of St. Nicholas, or the story of the Wise and Foolish Virgins, for St.-Pierre's windows would scarcely be able to make out any picture at all. The work table is a jigsaw confusion of oddly-shaped segments, with only here and there a recognizable fragment: a purple demon, or the white and yellow robes of the virgins.

Variations in the thickness of the glass produce colors that vary in intensity. In windows of the twelfth century this accident was used to artistic effect in the alternation of light and dark segments. But the men working on St.-Pierre's glass do not take time to sort it out; the thirteenth century's booming market has eliminated this subtlety of workman-ship. Even so, the effects achieved are astounding, and will in centuries to come be attributed by legend to a secret process known only to medieval glaziers. In reality the master glazier has no secrets.[8] He carefully paints the lines in the drapery of the garments, the features of the faces, and decorative details; then he supervises the firing of the segments in the kiln and sees that they are assembled properly. The assembly is accomplished by means of doubly-grooved lead cames bent to follow the shape of the glass segments. The cames are soldered to each other at their intersections and sealed with putty, to keep out the rain. Lead is the source of another aesthetic accident: it keeps the colors from radiating into each other when the sunlight strikes.

The finished panel is wrapped in cloth and carried to the cathedral. Measurements do not always prove exact. If the panel turns out to be too large, it is cut down. If it is too small, it is built up with a border. As it is fastened into place, the glazier sees it against the light for the first time. Until that moment of truth he must rely on past experience and observation of other windows for his effects.

Once the panel is made, the design is rubbed off the table and vanishes forever. Occasionally a design may be copied on parchment and used elsewhere, but this is rare. The master glazier is not aiming at immortality or even fame, though he is agreeably aware that his name is well known among glassmakers, masons, prelates, and even the general public. Yet he puts something into his work that is not merely talent and knowledge. Neither is it religious zeal. It is pride, and he can find ample justification for it in religion, for the priests say that God was a craftsman who looked on his work and found it good.

Although he is aware of the dazzling brilliance of his windows when they are in place, as the builder is of the soaring majesty of his completed masonry, neither of them regards his work as art, or himself as an artist. They are not necessary geniuses, but all of them are intelligent men with expert skill, standing historically at the end of a remarkable series of accidents—the cross-rib vault, which led to the flying buttress and the expansion of window space, and the imperfect glazing techniques that dictated colored glass.

Thirteenth-century bishops are delighted with the technology that gives them their incomparable cathedrals. Interestingly enough, clerical opinion in the past was not always so favorable. St.-Bernard[9] wrote angrily to William, abbot of St.-Thierry, about the great Cluniac churches: "Why this excessive height, this enormous length, this unnecessary width, these sumptuous ornaments and curious paintings that draw the eyes and distract the attention from meditation? . . . We, the monks, who have forsaken ordinary life and who have renounced the riches and ostentation of the world . . . in whom do we hope to awaken devotion with these ornaments? . . . One could spend a whole day gaping instead of meditating on God. What ineptitude, and what expense!"

But St.-Bernard is dead, and even his Cistercians have grown less puritanical. Few object today to the new style. Besides, St.-Bernard notwithstanding, the cathedrals' success in creating an atmosphere of mystery and awe is of incontestable value to religion. No man, burgher or baron, can enter a Gothic cathedral without experiencing a sense of human insignificance in the presence of such majesty.

11.

School and Scholars

He would dispense his instructions to his hearers gradually, in a manner commensurate with their powers of assimilation. . . . In view of the fact that exercise both strengthens and sharpens the mind, Bernard would bend every effort to bring his students to imitate what they were hearing. In some cases he would rely on exhortation, in others he would resort to punishments, such as flogging. . . .

—JOHN OF SALISBURY, *describing the teaching methods of Bernard of Chartres, twelfth century*

Along with workmen, housewives, priests, cows, horses, and pigs, the stream of morning traffic includes a scattering of boys with close-cropped hair, carrying hand-copied Latin grammars under their arms. They are on their way to school. As they trudge along, kicking stones and horse manure and calling greetings to each other, they are only faintly conscious of the novelty of their position.

There are no public schools in Troyes. But having taken primary instruction from a parish priest, these boys are now enrolled in the cathedral school. They are the elite of the city's youth—mostly the sons of the well-to-do. To their inherited station in life they are adding the advantage of education, and they are placing themselves permanently above the level of weavers, peasants, and ignorant tradesmen.

The cathedral school was not originally conceived as a secondary school. Founded in the seventh century by Bishop Ragnegisile, it remained for centuries merely a training school, turning out clerks for the diocese. The bishop himself did the teaching. Today's boys still wear the tonsure, as a sign of what is called "a disposition toward an order." The chancellor of the cathedral teaches theology and confers teaching licenses, but most of the instruction is in the hands of the schoolmaster and his assistant canons, who teach a distinctly secular course.

In the schoolroom the pupils sit on the floor, all ages together. Instruction is predominantly oral and in Latin, though beginners are allowed to lapse into the vernacular. The schoolmaster lectures, and students take notes on oblong wooden tablets coated with black or green wax, using a stylus of bone, ivory, or metal. The whitish scratches it makes can be erased by rubbing with its rounded end. The scholars soon acquire a Latin shorthand: *Sic hic e fal sm qd ad simlr a e pducible a do, g a e et silr hic, a n e g a n e pducible a do* means *Sicut hic est fallacia secundum quid ad simpliciter, A est producibile a Deo, ergo A est. Et similiter hic, A non est, ergo A non est producibile a Deo* ("Thus here is the second fallacy, which is simply, A is created by God, therefore A exists; and similarly this, A does not exist, therefore A is not created by God"). In drill, pupils repeat in chorus after the teacher and go on repeating an exercise until they have learned it by heart. Since books have to be copied by hand and writing materials are expensive, memory and oral exercises are indispensable.

The schoolmaster reads aloud, explaining and underlining as he goes, pointing out figures of speech, rhetorical devices, well-chosen words, adjectives that suit the nouns they modify, metaphors that give speech a beyond-the-ordinary meaning. Though discipline may be mild, the attention of the students does not wander, for each of them must recite tomorrow part of what he has heard today.

The lecture, the main teaching session of the day, takes place in the early afternoon. Following it, there is a period of free discussion, then drill, and finally a lesson chosen for moral and religious edification, closing with the Sixth Penitential Psalm and the Lord's Prayer. The next morning is devoted to the "repetition," recalling and committing to writing things learned the previous day. At this time the pupils are also required to imitate the Latin masters they are studying by writing compositions of their own, in verse and prose. They are expected to commit to memory every day a selection from Ovid or Vergil, or another Latin author. These will be helpful in writing letters or compositions, which are traditionally crammed with quotations.

A letter from Gerald of Wales to the archbishop of Canterbury quotes in five pages three times from the Book of Wisdom, twice from St. Jerome, once each from Proverbs, Psalms, Vergil, and Ovid, and seven times from Horace. A letter written by Nicolas of Clairvaux[1] to the bishop of Auxerre, whose see was renowned for its wines, runs:

> In the words of the Gospel, *they have no more wine.* (John 2:3). Do not send me *the wine of sorrow* (Psalm 59:5), but *the wine which rejoices the heart of man* (Psalm 103:15), whose color is excellent, the savor very fine, and whose *agreeable odor* (Exodus 29:18) testifies to its quality. It is in these three elements that it manifests its perfection, and *the cord with three strands does not easily break* (Eccl. 4:12).
>
> The wines of our region are turbid and do not come from those plants which grow in your region in a state of blessedness; their

juice has not passed *from one nation to another, and from one kingdom to another people* (Psalm 104:13) . . . . Send separately to the abbot and to me; *the Jews do not deal with the Samaritans* (John 4:9).

Theoretically, the curriculum consists of the "seven liberal arts."[2] But schools rarely teach all seven of the arts, and the emphasis is very unequal. These "arts" are "liberal" because their purpose is not moneymaking and because they are worthy of a free man. There are seven mainly because people are fond of the number seven, one of the keys to a numerologically ordered universe. In the sixth century Boethius divided the liberal arts into the *trivium* and *quadrivium* ("three roads" and "four roads"). The trivium comprises the literary subjects: grammar, rhetoric, and logic; the quadrivium the scientific: arithmetic, geometry, astronomy, and music.

The bishops' schools of the sixth to ninth centuries offered little more than what was indispensable for clerks—Latin, enough arithmetic and astronomy for the computation of Easter and other movable feasts, and music for the chant. Monastic schools taught a similar curriculum. Like the episcopal schools, they were internal—that is, they trained their own personnel. When they occasionally received children of princes and nobles, it was rather as pages than as regular pupils. Parish priests, too, trained their own successors.

After Charlemagne's time the bishops' schools began to expand and to take outside pupils, boys from the town and boarding scholars. Gradually they came to eclipse the monastic schools. This urbanization and secularization created an educational revolution during the eleventh century. In the hundred years that followed, the cathedral schools became international centers of adult scholarship as well as training schools for the diocesan clergy. The

emphasis was on grammar and rhetoric, with theology, philosophy, and canon law as added disciplines. The most famous school was at Chartres, where, under the direction of the great schoolmaster Bernard (not to be confused with St.-Bernard of Clairvaux) there was a revival of classical literary humanism.

Now, in the thirteenth century, the function of higher education has been largely absorbed by the universities. Where universities are within easy reach, the cathedral schools restrict themselves chiefly to grammar, rhetoric and the rudiments of logic. In remote districts, cathedral schools teach a curriculum similar to that of the universities.

The grammar of the cathedral school embraces not only linguistics but writing, spelling, composition, speech, and general literature, including poetry and history. Pupils must master the elements of Latin by memorizing the *Ars Minor* of Donatus, a fourth-century authority. Ten pages of question-and-answer supply a knowledge of the eight parts of speech. From this the student proceeds to the same author's *Ars Grammatica*, and then to Priscian's *Grammatical Commentary*, a sixth-century work. Donatus and Priscian wrote for pupils to whom Latin was a native language, and are not ideally suited for northwest Europe in 1250. Two new manuals in verse are beginning to replace them, Alexander of Villedieu's *Doctrinale*[3] and the *Grecismus* of Eberhard of Bethune (so-called because it includes some Greek etymology).

Twelfth- and thirteenth-century writers have developed an extraordinary fondness for versifying, and almost every species of literary production appears at one time or another in verse. Historical chronicles are often written in verse. There are verse formularies for letter writing. Sermons sometimes lapse into poetry or rhythmic prose. There is a

"Music," one of the Seven Liberal Arts, is among the sculptured figures of the Royal Portal of Chartres Cathedral. She holds a psaltery in her lap, has a vielle, an early version of the violin, beside her, and plays a set of bells.

versified Bible (the *Aurora* of Peter Riga). Even legal documents are sometimes rhymed.

In grammar, the student is exposed to a series of authors, pagan and Christian, with little critical evaluation or regard for chronological order. Anything written in a book has a certain sacredness, all the established authors are authorities, and all are timeless, from Aesop to Horace. Some, like the late Roman elegiac poet Maximianus, are surprisingly profane and even erotic, but they are nevertheless studied for their rhetorical artifices. Sometimes the pagan spirit of Roman poetry arouses qualms. Guibert of Nogent confesses in his autobiography that early in his monastic life he took up verse making and even fell into "certain obscene words and composed brief writings, worthless and immodest, in fact bereft of all decency," before abandoning this shocking practice in favor of commentaries on the Scriptures. St.-Bernard himself wrote verse in his youth at Cîteaux, and was guilty of great proficiency. By the end of the twelfth century, verse writing was forbidden to members of the austere Cistercian order, but many abbots and bishops continue to write love poetry.

All the scholars observe that grammar helps in understanding the Holy Scriptures. The Bible, they point out, is rich in figures of speech, and a study of the literary art assists in appreciating it. Like St. Jerome, they compare secular learning to a heathen slave girl; the Hebrew who wishes to marry her must cut her hair and nails; similarly, the Christian who loves secular learning must purify it from all errors so that it will be worthy to serve God.

The authors who are so revered fulfill many needs. They dispense information about everything from medicine to history. Ovid is prized for his moral sayings. Collections of "sentences," or apothegms containing wise saws from the writings of antique and medieval authors, are popular.

After grammar comes rhetoric, the second of the arts in the trivium, literally the "craft of speech." In democratic Athens and Rome speechmaking was a major element in public life. In the Middle Ages political oratory has little place, and judicial rhetoric is only beginning to reappear with the revival of Roman law. Yet students practice both these forms of eloquence as school exercises. Of more practical use is the course in letter writing.

Logic, or dialectic, the third subject of the trivium, teaches clear thinking. It leans heavily on Aristotle. Disputation is a teaching method and a pastime. On examination and speech day at a cathedral school, the students may hold competitions in syllogisms, fictitious arguments, harangues, and epigrams.

The scientific part of the curriculum, the quadrivium, is not much influenced by the Greek science that scholars and translators are bringing in from the Moslem world. The pupil at the cathedral school absorbs relatively little true scientific knowledge. He may be given a smattering of natural history from the popular encyclopedias of the Dark Ages, based on Pliny and other Roman sources. He may learn, for example, that ostriches eat iron, that elephants fear only dragons and mice, that hyenas change their sex at will, that weasels conceive by the ear and deliver by the mouth.

The most popular subject in the quadrivium is astronomy, a mixture of science and astrology. Arithmetic involves, as earlier, the *computus*, a body of rules for determining the date of movable feasts. The scholar may also learn the use of the abacus, the computer of the ancient and medieval world. He learns something of the properties of numbers, especially ratio and proportion, and the propositions (without the proofs) of Euclid's first book of geometry. As part of his geometry course he may acquire some rudiments of geography, studying a map of the world[4] that shows the circular earth composed of three continents equal in size— Asia, Africa, and Europe—separated by narrow bands of water. East is at the top, Jerusalem at the center. In various places on the map one may marvel at dragons, sirens, men with dogs' heads, men with feet turned backward, men with umbrella feet with which they protect themselves from the sun while lying down. It is not a map for finding one's way, but for illustration and edification. More practical and less picturesque maps exist—mariners' charts produced by sailors armed with the newly introduced compass and astrolabe, accurately delineating coastlines, capes, bays, and shallows, and locating ports of call and places for watering and victualing so that a navigator can find them easily. But the schoolboy and his teachers know nothing of such maps.

The science of the thirteenth century, in fact, resides mainly outside the schools. Furriers, trappers, hunters, and poachers could correct much of the natural history in the encyclopedias. The craftsmen who are building the cathedral know geology, engineering, geometry, arithmetic, and mineralogy, and have an intimate acquaintance with nature. The capitals of their piers are decorated with leaves of plantain, ivy and oak, arum, ranunculus, fern, clover, coladine, hepatica, columbine, cress, parsley, strawberry, snapdragon, and broom—all observed with care and re-created with precision. The notebook of the great architect-engineer Villard de Honnecourt is filled not only with columns and vaults, but with animal and even insect life—a lobster, parrots, a snail's shell, a fly, a dragonfly, a grasshopper, not to mention a bear, a lion, a cat, and a swan. Even the gargoyles with which the cathedral workers give an aesthetic justification to their drainspouts reveal a command of animal anatomy.

Many of the businessmen fathers of the cathedral school-boys are aware of a truly remarkable new piece of learning, a historic advance in the most basic of all sciences, mathematics. Introduced into western Europe from Moslem North Africa, not by a scholar, but by an Italian business-man, it is nothing less than the use of Arabic numbers. Leonard Fibonacci, a Pisan, has written a treatise called *Liber Abaci* popularizing the new system and summarizing the arithmetical knowledge of the Arabs. The numerals (actually Indian in origin) are spreading through the Italian business community. The key to the Hindu-Arabic system is the zero, which permits the position of the digit to indicate its value as unit, ten, hundred, or thousand. Rapid and accurate computation can be done, something difficult with clumsy Roman numbers. The businessmen of Troyes still prefer their calculating boards, but they are familiar with the new notation through their contacts with Italian businessmen and moneychangers at the fairs.

The cathedral school offers no French grammar, composition, or literature, no languages except Latin—not even Greek. It teaches no history, except a bit incidentally in the grammar course, and no science, except a little natural science that emerges from a study of the "authors." Music is taught only as a theoretical science. There are no courses in social science, physical education, or art.

The use of Latin throughout the schools gives a wide currency to ideas and makes sources of culture accessible to everyone, even though students probably never learn to read it as proficiently as their native French, English, or

German. Latin is a cultural catalyst, but it is also an impediment to self-expression and communication.

There is no university in Troyes, which is not surprising, since there are only five in northwest Europe[5]—at Paris, Orléans, Angers, Oxford, and Cambridge. There are three more in the south of France, eleven in Italy, three in Spain. Of these twenty-two, the two oldest, at Bologna and Paris, are by far the most important. Their precise origins are lost in the twelfth century, but they are true archetypes, for the Greeks and Romans had no universities.

A bright alumnus of the cathedral school at Troyes who wishes to continue his education may journey to Paris, only a hundred miles away. If he does, he will join some two or three thousand young men in the Latin Quarter, who every morning grope their way out of their lodgings to join the crowd of clerical gowns and tonsured heads hurrying to the Street of the Straw, so-named from the floor covering on which students sit all morning. At noon the scholars break for dinner, meeting again in the afternoon for another lecture or a disputation. When the day is over they may turn to studying or copying by candlelight, or, since all forms of athletics, and even chess, are prohibited, to gaming, drinking, and whoring. Although scholars usually enter the university at fourteen or fifteen, their private lives are almost entirely unsupervised. There are no university buildings.[6] Classes are held in the masters' houses. Student lodgings, schools, and brothels are cheek by jowl, and sometimes masters and students conduct disputations on the second floor, whores and pimps on the first.

The favorite sport of university students is fighting—with each other, with the townspeople, with the provost's guard. Some of their riots make history, for the University of Paris is by 1250 an institution of formidable stature. A democratic anomaly in the heart of a feudal monarchy, it enjoys remarkable power and prestige and extraordinary privileges. Though it has a charter from the king of France, it is thoroughly international, with some of its most celebrated scholars from Italy, Germany, and England. Pope Innocent III was a master at Paris; Thomas Aquinas is studying there in 1250.

Though the University of Paris is famous for its faculty of theology,[7] the learning it transmits to most of its students is more secular than that of the cathedral schools. Aristotle is the supreme text and master. After six years' study a student may face the examiners, and if he passes receive a license to teach. Ultimately he may take orders and become a church official, or a scholarly luminary at this or another university. He may go on to study medicine or law, both lucrative and prestigious professions. He may become a copyist. Or he may enter the service of some prince or baron. For a young burgher of Troyes, the count of Champagne's service is most attractive. He can rise to become bailiff, or keeper of the Fair, with splendid emoluments, not to mention opportunities for graft. Education pays, in the thirteenth as in other centuries.

12.

Books and Authors

Sire cuens, j'ai vielé
Devant vous en vostre ostel,
Si ne m'avez rien doné
Ne mes gages aquité:
*   C'est vilanie!*
[Sir count, I have played the
viol before you in your house, and
you have given me nought, nor paid my
expenses: 'Tis villainy!]

—COLIN MUSET

A number of students in the twelfth century followed none of the conventional paths. Instead they undertook the footloose and precarious existence of wandering scholars, drifting from one school or one patron to another, passing their days in taverns, living by their wits. Some of them, the so-called "Goliards," contributed to the world's literature a stock of Latin verse of a new kind—lyric, frankly pagan, satirical, and irreverent.

But many of the poets who have created a literary revival in the past century and a half write in the vernacular, especially in one of two varieties of French—Provençal or northern. An important center for the latter is Troyes. Count Henry the Generous and his bluestocking countess, Marie, daughter of Louis VII of France and Eleanor of

Aquitaine, patronized a number of poets, of whom the most famous was Chrétien de Troyes. Chrétien's verse tales of the Round Table not only are of high literary merit, but serve as the chief source of all Arthurian romances.

Another sort of Champenois literary production came out of the Fourth Crusade. Geoffroi de Villehardouin, marshal of Champagne and native of the neighborhood of Troyes, helped sack Constantinople and afterwards wrote an account of his adventures whose naive vigor and honesty won him a niche in literature as well as history. Neither a clerk nor a poet, but a plain soldier, Geoffroi wrote in vernacular prose, and so won the distinction of creating the very first masterpiece in French prose.

The present count of Champagne, Thibaut IV, is a poet. Guarded through his minority by his capable mother, Blanche of Navarre, Thibaut grew up to marry, one after the other, a Hapsburg, a Beaujeu, and a Bourbon princess, by whom he had eight children. To these children he added four more, products of his numerous love affairs. But the enduring passion of his life was a chaste one, owing to the inaccessibility of its object, the queen of France. This lady, Blanche of Castile, wife and widow of Louis VIII and mother of Louis IX (St.-Louis), was a dozen years Thibaut's senior. Nevertheless Thibaut's penchant for Blanche was such that he was suspected of poisoning her husband when the king died suddenly. The injustice of the accusation provoked Thibaut to join a couple of baronial trouble-makers, Hugo of La Marche and Peter of Brittany, in a sort of antiroyal civil war. When on sober second thought Thibaut changed his mind, Hugo and Peter turned their spite against him and invaded Champagne, setting haystacks and hovels ablaze. Stopped by the walls of Troyes, they were forced to turn around and go home when a relieving force arrived, sent by Queen Blanche.

Partly as a result of the war, Thibaut was constrained to sell three of his cities—Blois, Chartres and Sancerre—to the king of France. At the last moment he felt a reluctance to hand over Blois, cradle of his ·dynasty, and carried stubbornness to the point of courting a royal invasion. But forty-six-year-old Blanche of Castile dissuaded thirty-three-year-old Thibaut in an interview of which the dialogue was recorded, or at least reported, by a chronicler:

> *Blanche:* Pardieu, Count Thibaut, you ought to have remembered the kindness shown you by the king my son, who came to your aid, to save your land from the barons of France when they would have set fire to it all and laid it in ashes.
>
> *Thibaut* (overcome by the queen's beauty and virtue): By my faith, madame, my heart and my body and all my land is at your command, and there is nothing which to please you I would not readily do; and against you or yours, please God, I will never go.

Thibaut's fancy for Blanche needed sublimation. Sage counselors recommended a study of canzonets for the viol, as a result of which Thibaut soon began turning out "the most beautiful canzonets anyone had ever heard" (a judgment in which a later day concurs). The verses of Thibaut the Songwriter were sung by trouvères and jongleurs throughout Europe. A favorite:

> Las! Si j'avois pouvoir d'oublier
> Sa beauté, sa beauté, son bien dire,
> Et son très-doux, très-doux regarder,
> Finirois mon martyre.
>
> Mais las! mon coeur je n'en puis ôter,
>   Et grand affolage
>   M'est d'espérer:
>   Mais tel servage
>   Donne courage
>   A tout endurer.

Et puis, comment, comment oublier
Sa beauté, sa beauté, son bien dire,
Et son très-doux, très-doux regarder?
    Mieux aime mon martyre.

[Could I forget her gentle grace,
Her glance, her beauty's sum,
Her voice from memory efface,
I'd end my martyrdom.

Her image from my heart I cannot tear;
    To hope is vain;
    I would despair,
    But such a strain
    Gives strength the pain
Of servitude to bear.

Then how forget her gentle grace,
Her glance, her beauty's sum,
Her voice from memory efface?
I'll love my martyrdom.]

Thibaut is a prince; Chrétien de Troyes was (probably) a clerk; Geoffroi de Villehardouin was a noble. But there is another native Troyen writer, in 1250 just embarking on his career, who is a plain burgher. "Rutebeuf" (Rough-ox) he calls himself, and his verses have little in common with the polished elegance of Chrétien or the tender passion of Thibaut. Rutebeuf describes real life—mostly his own.

Dieus m'a fait compagnon à Job,
Qu'il m'a tolu à un seul cop
    Quanques j'avoie.
De l'ueil destre, dont mieus veoie,
Ne voi je pas aler la voie
    Ne moi conduire . . .

Car je n'i voi pas mon gaain.
Or n'ai je pas quanques je ain,

C'est mes domages.
Ne sai se ç'a fait mes outrages;
Or devendrai sobres et sages
         Après le fait,
Et me garderai de forfait.
Mais ce que vaut? Ce est ja fait;
         Tart sui meüs,
A tart me sui aperceüs
Quant je sui en mes las cheüs.
         C'est premier an
Me gart cil Dieus en mon droit san
Qui pour nous ot paine et ahan,
         Et me gart l'ame.

Or a d'enfant geü ma fame;
Mes chevaus a brisié la jame
         A une lice;
Or veut de l'argent ma norrice
Qui me destraint et me pelice
         Pour l'enfant paistre,
Ou il revendra braire en l'estre . . .

[God has made me a companion for Job,
Taking away at a single blow,
All that I had.
With my right eye, once my best,
I can't see the street ahead,
Or find my way . . .

I can't earn a living,
I enjoy no pleasures,
That's my trouble.
I don't know if my vices are to blame;
Now I'm becoming sober and wise,
After the fact,
And will keep from doing wrong,
But what good is that? It's done now.
I'm too late.
I discovered too late
That I was falling into a trap.

It's the first of the year.
May God who suffered pain for us
Keep me healthy.
Now my wife has had a child;
My horse has broken his leg
On a fence,
Now my nurse is asking for money,
She's taking everything I've got
For the child's keep,
Otherwise he'll come back home to yell . . .]

Thibaut and Rutebeuf are not only widely sung and recited, but published. By 1250 books are multiplying spectacularly, even though every single book must be copied by hand. During the Dark Ages book copying took refuge in the monasteries, but now it is back in town. Schools and universities supply a market for textbooks, and copyists are therefore often located in the neighborhood of the cathedral or university, but they do more than copy texts. They also serve as secretaries, both for the illiterate and for those who want a particularly fine handwriting in their correspondence.

A copyist sits in a chair with extended arms across which his writing board is placed, with the sheets of parchment held in place by a deerskin thong. His implements include a razor or sharp knife for scraping, a pumice, an awl, a long narrow parchment ruler, and a boar's tooth for polishing. He works near the fire, or keeps a basin of coals handy to dry the ink, which is held in an oxhorn into which he dips a well-seasoned quill. The oxhorn fits into a round hole in the writing board, with a cover.

The copyist begins by scraping the parchment clean of scales and incrustations, smoothing it with the pumice, and marking out lines and columns with ruler and awl. Then he sets to work. Some of his productions may be ornate works of art—Latin psalters or French romances, in gold, silver, and purple ink, with initials overlaid with gold leaf. Bound in ivory and metal covers mounted on wood, these elaborate volumes are fabulously expensive. By far the greater number of books consist of plain, legibly written sheets bound in plain wooden boards, perhaps with untooled leather glued over for extra protection. Students often bind several books together under the same covers. Even these cheaper books are expensive, owing not only to the cost of parchment but to the enormous labor involved in their production. It takes about fifteen months to copy the Bible. Books are valuable pieces of property, often pawned, and rented out as well as sold. Students are the chief renters. When a student rents a book he usually does so in order to copy it. He pays rent by the *pecia*—sixteen columns of sixty-two lines, each with thirty-two letters, renting for a penny or halfpenny. An industrious student can create his own library, but it is a work of long night watches. Across the bottom of the last page of many a book is written *Explicit, Deo Gratias* ("Finished, thank God"). Some students end with a more jocular flourish: "May the writer continue to copy, and drink good wine"; "The book finished, may the master be given a fat goose"; "May the writer be given a good cow and a horse"; "For his pen's labor, may the copyist be given a beautiful girl"; "Let the writer be given a cow and a beautiful girl."

Books are kept not on open shelves but in locked chests. Students who borrow are cautioned not to scratch grooves in the margin with their fingernails or to use straws from the lecture floor as placemards. A Jewish ethical treatise warns that a man must not express his anger by pounding on a book or by hitting people with it. The angry teacher must not hit the bad student with a book, nor should the student use a book to ward off blows.

Book cover, thirteenth century. The more elaborate
productions of medieval copyists were usually bound in
ivory and metal covers mounted on wood; sometimes, as
in this example, they were decorated with champlevé
enamel. But most books were bound in utilitarian wooden
boards, sometimes covered with leather. (Metropolitan
Museum of Art, Gift of J. Pierpont Morgan, 1917)

Despite the cost, books enjoy a wide circulation. An opponent of Abélard noted that "his books cross the sea, pass the Alps . . . are carried through kingdom and province." Normal, or legitimate, book circulation is reinforced by a black market. Many scholars borrow books and surreptitiously copy them. John of Salisbury lent a book to a friend at Canterbury, and later referred to him as "that thief at Canterbury who got hold of the *Policraticus* and would not let it go until he had made a copy." St.-Bernard wrote a would-be borrower, "As regards the book you ask for . . . there is a certain friend of ours who has kept it a long time now, with the same eagerness you show. You shall have it as soon as possible, but although you may read it, I do not allow you to copy it. I did not give you leave to copy the other one I lent you, although you did so."

Copyists are not always accurate. Authors sometimes conclude their books with the injunction: "I adjure you who shall transcribe this book, by our Lord Jesus Christ and by His Glorious coming, Who will come to judge the quick and the dead, that you compare what you transcribe and diligently correct it by the copy from which you transcribe it, and this adjuration also, and insert it in your copy."

Works are seldom composed on parchment. Authors usually write on wax tablets and have their productions copied by scribes. If the work is written in the vernacular, it may be dictated to a scribe, who writes first on wax and copies over on parchment.

Even the most luxurious of the illuminated manuscripts show minor defects. The illuminator does not always leave space for the picture caption, which must be crowded in somehow, often impinging on the text. Against such a contingency, the captions may be lettered in red. Sometimes the illuminator leaves space for a caption which the copyist overlooks. Blank sections of columns—most books are lettered in double column—show where a copyist finished his assigned section in less space than had been allowed. Now and then words skipped by a careless copyist are inserted in the margin. Sometimes the artist turns such an error into a joke. A verse omitted from the text is added at the top of the page, and the figure of a scribe in the margin tugs at a rope tied to the first letter of the misplaced line, while a second man leans out from the proper space on the page, ready to receive the rope and pull the line into place.

The style of lettering has undergone an important series of changes through the Middle Ages. At the end of the Roman period, Roman square capitals developed into the more casual "rustic" style, out of which slowly grew a small-letter alphabet. The "Caroline minuscule," evolved during Charlemagne's reign at Alcuin's school at Tours, crowned this achievement with an alphabet that clearly differentiated between capitals and small letters, not only in size but in form. At the present moment a new, more elaborate style is sweeping northern Europe: Gothic or black-letter, with stiff, narrow angular letters executed with heavy lines that look black on the page.

Many kinds of books are available from thirteenth-century booksellers,[1] and wealthy individuals, as well as universities, are acquiring libraries.[2] Among the Latin classics there are the antique poets and the more recent didactic poets, the new scientific writings and translations, books of law, such as Justinian's *Code* and *Digest* and the *Decretum* of Gratian; medical books—Galen and Hippocrates, works of theology and philosophy, "vocabularies" (dictionaries of important terms), books of "sentences" (aphorisms), chronicles, encyclopedias, and compilations.

But these weighty volumes in Latin are getting serious

Sicut sagitte in manu potentis: ita filii
excussorum.

Beatus uir qui impleuit desiderium
suum ex ipsis: non confundetur cum
loquetur inimicis suis in porta.

Beati omnes qui timent dominum:
qui ambulant in uiis eius.

Labores manuum tuarum quia man-
ducabis: beatus es et bene tibi erit.

Uxor tua sicut uitis habundans: in
lateribus domus tue.

Ecce sic benedicetur homo: qui timet
dominum.

Benedicat tibi dominus ex syon: ut
uideas bona ierusalem omnibus diebus
uite tue.

Et uideas filios filiorum tuorum: pacem
sup israel.

Sepe expugnauerunt me a iuuentute

Filii tui sicut nouelle oliuar: in circuitu men-
se tue.

competition in French. More and more people want something to read, or especially something to read aloud—and can afford to pay for it. Saints' lives, biographies, *dits* (poems on such everyday subjects as the cries of Paris street peddlers), paraphrases of the stories of antique writers, moralizing poems—all these are popular. The rather tedious *Roman de la Rose* is in great vogue—an allegory by Guillaume de Lorris in which a Lover strives to win his Lady, encouraged and frustrated by various personifications, such as Welcome, Shame, Danger, Reason, Pity. Many works are written more to amuse than correct—such as the *Bible of Guiot*, by a jongleur from Provins, or the *Lamentations of Matthew*.

A series of verse tales known as the *Roman de Renard* has been popular through the twelfth and thirteenth centuries, not only in France, but in Flanders and Rhenish Germany. They are copied over and over by scribes and clerks, in numerous variations. The main characters are Renard the fox, Ysengrin the wolf, Tybert the cat, and King Noble the lion. In a favorite Renard story the fox, stealing chickens from a monastery farmyard, looks into a well and, seeing his own reflection, takes it for his wife Hermeline. Climbing into one of the two buckets that serve the well, he descends, to find nothing but water and stones at the bottom. He struggles in vain to escape. Meanwhile Ysengrin the wolf happens on the well, looks in, and sees his reflection, which he takes for his own wife, Lady Hersent, with Renard at her side. Renard tells him that he is dead, and the well is Paradise. If Ysengrin will confess his sins and climb into the other bucket, he can also achieve the celestial realm, where there are barns full of cows and sheep and goats, and yards full of fat chickens and geese, and woods abounding in game. When Ysengrin jumps into the bucket at the top, he

Manuscript copyists employed ingenious and sometimes humorous devices to correct omissions. A page from an illuminated Book of Hours shows a figure hauling an omitted line into place. (Walters Art Gallery, Baltimore)

descends while clever Renard ascends and escapes. In the morning when the monks come to draw water, they pull the wolf out and beat him. There is no moral; in the Renard stories wickedness more often triumphs than justice.

Most popular of all are the *fabliaux*,[3] the humorous short stories in verse, sometimes written, sometimes recited. These stories, the product of authors of various social classes, are enjoyed by all kinds of audiences. Some have folk tale origins, some are drawn directly from life. Their common ingredient is humor, often bawdy. Certain characters recur: the merchant, usually older than his wife, cuckolded, swindled, beaten; the young man, often a student, who outwits the husband; the lecherous priest who is his rival. The women, treacherous, lustful, and faithless, may be beaten by their husbands but always manage to get the better of them.

Finally, there are the romances, normally in verse, but sometimes in a combination of verse and prose, or even entirely in prose. Best known of the composers of these courtly tales, after Chrétien de Troyes, is Marie de France, who composed many of her romances (which she called "lays") on Arthurian themes. The authors of many thirteenth-century romances are unknown, but their work is characterized by a high degree of sophistication and realistic detail. Love stories like *Galeran* or *The Kite* deal with star-crossed lovers, united in a happy ending; picaresque tales like *Joufroi* carry a knightly hero through various adventures amorous and military, none of which is treated very seriously.

One of the best is the Provençal romance *Flamenca*. At her wedding feast, Flamenca's husband, Archimbaud of Bourbon, sees the king, as he leads her from a tourney, familiarly embrace her, accidentally touching her breast. Archimbaud misinterprets the gesture and is devoured by jealousy. He tears his hair and beard, bites his lips and grits his teeth, eschews society, can finish nothing he starts, understands nothing that is spoken to him, babbles nonsense, and watches his wife all the time. Word spreads about his affliction, and soon all Auvergne is resounding with songs, satires, and sayings on the subject. He grows worse. He ceases to bathe. His beard resembles a badly mowed wheat field; he tears it out in tufts and puts them in his mouth. In short, he is like a mad dog. A jealous man is not wholly sane.

Flamenca's life becomes cruel. Archimbaud has her shut up in a tower with two young servants, Alis and Marguerite, and spies on them by a peephole in the kitchen wall. They are only allowed to leave this prison to go to church on Sundays and feast days, and then Archimbaud forces them to sit in a dark corner, closed off by a thick screen as high as Flamenca's chin. Only when they stand for the reading of the Scripture can they be seen, and instead of letting them go to the altar for communion, Archimbaud has the priest come to them. Flamenca is not permitted to take off her veil or gloves. Only the little clerk who brings her the book for the Kiss of Peace can see her face.

Two years pass. As it happens, next door to Archimbaud's house is a bathing establishment[4] where he takes his wife on occasion to distract her, always searching the premises first and then standing guard outside. When Flamenca is ready to leave, she rings a bell and her husband opens the door, as usual overwhelming her with reproaches: "Will you be ready to leave this year or the next? I was going to give you some of the wine the host sent me, but I've changed my mind. I won't let you go to the baths again for a year, I assure you, if you drag it out like today." The servants insist that it is their fault; they bathed after Madame. "You like water better than geese," declares the jealous one, biting his nails.

Enter the hero of this piece, a knight named Guillaume de Nevers, handsome, with curly blond hair, a high and broad white forehead, black arched eyebrows, laughing dark eyes, a nose as straight as an arrow shaft, well-made ears, a fine and amorous mouth, a slightly cleft chin, straight neck, broad shoulders and chest, powerful muscles, straight knees, arched and graceful feet. This fine fellow has studied in Paris and is so learned that he could run a school anywhere. He can read and sing better than any clerk; he can fence; he is so agile that he can put out a candle with his foot when the candle is stuck in the wall over his head. Furthermore, he is rich, and he has the tastes of a gentleman—tourneys, dances, games, dogs, and birds. He is generous, too, and always pays more than the asking-price, gives away his profits from tourneys, is liberal with his men. He is more expert at making songs than the cleverest jongleur.

This paragon has never been in love, but he has read the best authors and knows that he must soon have this experience. Hearing of Flamenca's beauty and her misfortunes, he decides that she shall be his lady, and goes to Bourbon full of delicious hopes.

He puts up at the bathing establishment, so that from his window he can gaze up at the tower where Flamenca is imprisoned. He goes to church and impresses everyone by reciting a prayer in which he says the sixty-two names of God, in Hebrew, Greek, and Latin. Flamenca arrives, and when she uncovers her head to receive the holy water, he has a glimpse of her hair; at the reading of the Gospel, when she rises to cross herself, he sees her bare hand and is seized by emotion. A moment later, when the acolyte brings her the breviary to kiss, he sees her mouth. Asking for the book when the service is over, he kisses the same page.

That night in a dream Guillaume discovers what he must do. The next day he rents the entire bathing establishment, explaining that he needs solitude. Everyone else moves out; then he orders workers to dig a tunnel between his apartments and the room where Flamenca bathes. Next he flatters the priest into sending his clerk to Paris to study, and undertakes to serve in his place. Now, Sunday after Sunday, a dialogue takes place. When Guillaume brings Flamenca the breviary to kiss, he sighs, "Alas!" The following week she replies, "Why do you sigh?" The next week, Guillaume tells her, "I am dying."

During that week the tunnel is finished. On Sunday she answers, "Of what?" On Rogation Day, he says, "Of love"; the following Sunday she asks, "For whom?" On Pentecost he replies, "For you." She replies a week later with an ambiguous, "What can I do about it?"

He admires her cleverness and promises "fair Lord God" that he will give all his income in France to the Church and the bridge-building brotherhood if He will let him have Flamenca—he will even give up his place in Paradise.

The dialogue continues. "Cure me," Guillaume demands; on St.-Jean's Day she ripostes, "How?" and, in taking the book, brushes his fingers with hers. On Sunday he answers, "I know a way." Flamenca's servants advise her to reply, "Take it"—though she is not sure it is honorable to give in so quickly.

The next day Guillaume tells the host and hostess that they may move back to their bathing establishment. In church Guillaume and Flamenca regard each other tenderly, and he says, "I have taken it." Another month is occupied

by the following exchange: "How then?" "You will go."
"Where?" "To the baths." "When?" "Soon." She hesi-
tates, in spite of the urgings of her maidens. At last she
announces to them, "I will answer yes, for I see that otherwise I could not go on living." Then she faints. Archimbaud runs in with cold water and throws it in her face, and
she persuades him that she is ill and needs to visit the baths.
The following Sunday, she says a single word: "Yes."

As usual, Archimbaud conducts the three women to the
baths and they bar the door after him. At that moment
Guillaume raises the stone at the end of the tunnel and
appears, candle in hand. He invites the ladies to pass into his
apartments through the tunnel. With characteristic thought-
fulness, he has brought two friends, Ot and Clari, for the
maidens Alis and Marguerite. For four whole months the
six lovers continue to meet. They live in perfect happiness.

Flamenca is now self-confident. She approaches her
husband and demands that he restore her liberty on condition that she promises to behave as well as she has up to the
present moment. He agrees, washes his head, forgets his
functions as turnkey, and becomes once more the man of
the world. As a result Flamenca is soon surrounded by ladies
and knights, and finds it impossible to visit the baths without at least seven ladies accompanying her. She sends
Guillaume away . . .[5]

13.

The New Theater

*Paradise is to be made in a raised spot, with
curtains and cloths of silk hung round it. . . . Then
must come the Saviour clothed in a dalmatic, and
Adam and Eve be brought before him. Adam is to
wear a red tunic and Eve a woman's robe of white,
with a white silk cloak; and they are both to stand
before the Figure . . . And the Adam must be well
trained to speak composedly, and to fit gesture to the
matter of speech. Nor must they foist in a syllable or
clip one of the verse, but must enounce firmly and
repeat what is set down for them in due order.*
—Stage directions for LE MYSTÈRE D'ADAM

City people are enjoying a revival in the theater as well
as in books. The theater of Greece and Rome was
lost with the Dark Ages, but an entirely new drama
is growing up in, of all places, the church. With many of its
thirty-odd holidays retaining a festive touch of paganism—
the Yule log, the pranks and garlands of May Day, the
schoolboy games of Shrove Tuesday—the Church has long
tolerated a variety of irreverent customs. On the Feast of the
Holy Innocents choirboys change places with bishop, dean
and other cathedral officials, conduct services, and lead a
torchlight procession. The Feast of the Circumcision sees
even more unlikely sights as the minor clergy lead an ass

183

into church, drink wine and munch sausages before the altar, wear their vestments inside out and hold their books upside down, while they punctuate the service with hee-haws. They sing and dance in the streets, often choosing songs that shock elderly parishioners.

A celebration of holidays in a different spirit has led to the rebirth of the theater. "Troping"—embroidering parts of the service with added words and melodies—especially at Easter and Christmas, is the source of this development. In the ninth century a trope was added to the opening of the Easter service in the form of a dialogue between the three Marys and the angel at the tomb, sung by two halves of the choir, or a soloist and the choir. Soon this trope, which begins *Quem quaeritis in sepulchro?* ("Whom do you seek in the sepulchre?") was transferred to the end of the Easter matin service, and dramatic action was added, with costumes and properties. Next an older ceremony was incorporated; a cross was wrapped in cloth on Good Friday and laid in a small stone sepulchre constructed near the altar, sometimes over the tomb of a wealthy burgher or a noble who provided for it in his will. A lamp was placed and vigil kept until Easter morning, when the cross was removed during matins and laid upon the altar, symbolizing the Resurrection. The *Quem quaeritis* was used at the end of this ceremony, as a climax. New scenes were added, with the apostles Peter and John and Mary Magdalen.

In its present form, in the thirteenth century, the play is presented at the end of the Easter matin service. A priest representing the angel at the tomb, dressed in white vestments and holding a palm in his hand, quietly approaches the sepulchre. Then the three Marys, also played by priests, two dressed in white and one (Magdalen) in red, their heads veiled, come bearing thuribles with incense, walking sadly and hesitantly, as if looking for something. A dialogue begins, chanted in Latin:

> *The Angel (gently):* Whom do you seek in the sepulchre, O followers of Christ?
>
> *The Three Marys:* Jesus of Nazareth.
>
> *The Angel:* He is not here, He has risen as He prophesied. Go, announce that He is risen from the dead.
>
> *The Three Marys (turning to the choir):* Hallelujah, the Lord is risen today!
>
> *The Angel (calling them back):* Come and see the place. (*He rises and lifts the veil which hides the sepulchre, showing that the cross that represents Christ's body is gone.*)

Now the apostles Peter and John appear, Peter dressed in red and carrying keys, John in white, holding a palm. In accordance with the Gospel, John reaches the sepulchre before Peter, but Peter enters first. He holds up the gravecloth in which the cross was wrapped during the vigil, and a dialogue ensues between the apostles and the three Marys, ending with the antiphon, "The Lord is risen from the tomb," and the placing of the gravecloth upon the altar.

Two of the Marys depart, leaving Mary Magdalen behind at the tomb. The risen Christ appears to her. At first she mistakes him for a gardener, and approaches him weeping; but he warns her, "Touch me not!" With a cry of recognition, she prostrates herself at his feet—a moment of true theater.

The performance ends with the triumphant hymn *Te Deum Laudamus* ("We praise Thee, God"), at the conclusion of which all the bells ring out together.

A Christmas play has evolved in a similar way, starting with another trope, *Quem quaeritis in praesepe?* ("Whom do you seek in the manger?") First it was merely sung by two parts of the choir; then it was dramatized; an Epiphany play of the visit of the Magi was added; and finally a meeting with Herod, the first individualized role in medieval drama. Herod's is a star role, his violent personality suggesting histrionic potential. Episodes of the Slaughter of the Innocents and the lament of Rachel complete the cycle.

Another play sometimes presented during the Christmas season is *The Prophets*. Its origin is not a chant, like that of the Easter and Christmas plays, but a sermon said to have been delivered by St. Augustine, part of which is often used as a lesson for the Christmas offices. In this sermon the lector calls upon the Jews to bear witness to the Christ out of the mouths of their own prophets. He summons Isaiah, Jeremiah, Daniel, Moses, David, Habakkuk, Simeon, Zacharias, Elizabeth, and John the Baptist, and bids each to speak in turn. The reading of the sermon develops into a dramatic dialogue between the priest and the prophets, to which is added a miniature drama of Balaam and the ass. Balaam addresses the ass, "Why do you loiter, obstinate beast? My spurs are splitting your ribs and your belly." The ass, played by a choirboy in a donkey's skin, replies, "I see an angel with a sword before me, forbidding me to pass, and I fear that I will be lost." Sometimes this play about the prophets is tacked on the end of the basic Christmas play. One version brings St. Augustine himself onto the stage, plus a Boy-Bishop, a devil, and a comic Archsynagogus, satirizing the Jewish faith.

All these playlets, growing out of the liturgy and chanted as part of the service, are done entirely in Latin, and so are only visually comprehensible to most of the lay audience. But during the course of the twelfth century passages in the vernacular occurred in several plays, such as the *Raising of Lazarus*, by a pupil of Abélard's named Hilarius, and the Beauvais *Play of Daniel*, one of the masterpieces of medieval drama. The popularity of this innovation doubtless led to the production, late in the century, of the first play (at least the first to survive) written entirely in French, *Le Mystère d'Adam*. Widely played at Easter throughout the thirteenth century, *Adam* retains Latin only in the stage directions and a few interpolations. As if to symbolize its liberation from the liturgy, the play is performed in the open air, outside the church. A platform built on the church steps serves as stage, an arrangement which allows the church itself to represent the dwelling of God. The verses are no longer chanted, but recited. The first scene is Paradise, strewn with flowers and greenery and trees with fruit hung from their branches. A "Figure" representing an abstraction of God appears, and Adam and Eve are brought before him, Adam wearing a red tunic and Eve a white dress with a white mantle. They stand before God, Adam with calm visage, Eve with a more modest air.

The lesson is read in Latin: "In the beginning God created Heaven and earth, and created man in His own image and after his likeness." The choir then chants, again in Latin: "And the Lord God formed man of the dust of the ground. and breathed into his nostrils the breath of life, and man became a living soul."

Now the dialogue begins, in French. God instructs Adam and Eve in their duties and leads them into Paradise, where He points out the forbidden fruit, then retires into the church, leaving Adam and Eve to walk about Paradise in delight. But a pack of demons run out on the stage with grotesque gestures, approaching Paradise from time to time and slyly pointing out the forbidden fruit to Eve. The Devil himself appears, confronts Adam, and tempts him to pick the fruit, but Adam remains firm. With downcast countenance the Devil retreats to the doors of Hell, where he holds council with the other demons. Then he makes a sally among the audience, stirring a noisy reaction, and returns to Paradise, this time addressing Eve. With smiling face and flattering air, he tells her that she is more intelligent than Adam. Eve replies that Adam is a little hard. "Though he be harder than Hell," the Devil promises, "he shall be made soft." He praises her beauty. "You are a gentle and tender thing, fresh as a rose, white as crystal . . . You are too tender and he is too hard. But nevertheless you are wiser and more courageous . . ."

Eve makes a show of resistance. The Tempter departs. Adam, who has been watching mistrustfully, reproaches her for listening. Now a serpent rises by the trunk of the forbidden tree. Eve puts her ear to his mouth, then takes the fruit and presents it to Adam. He eats, realizes his sin, and throws himself on his knees. Out of sight behind the curtain, he puts off his red tunic and dons a garment of fig-leaves. He rises and begins his lament. When God reappears, Adam and Eve hide in a corner of Paradise, and when called upon they rise but crouch in shame and weep. They confess their sin, Adam blaming his error on Eve, Eve on the serpent. God pronounces his curse on them and on the serpent, and drives them out of Paradise, barring the gate with an angel dressed in white who bears a shining sword in his hand. God withdraws into the church.

Adam takes up a spade and Eve a hoe, and they begin to cultivate the earth and sow it with wheat. After they have sown, they sit down to rest, gazing at Paradise and weeping. While they are thus occupied, the Devil sneaks in, plants thorns and thistles in their garden, and escapes. When they see the thorns and thistles, they are smitten with grief and throw themselves on the ground, beating their breasts, and once more Adam reproaches Eve. Now the Devil reenters with three or four of his demons, carrying iron chains and fetters, which they place on the necks of Adam and Eve. The luckless pair are hauled off toward Hell (underneath the platform), from which other demons come to meet them, reveling at their perdition. Smoke arises, the devils exclaim in glee, clashing pots and kettles, and caper about the stage.

This is the favorite part of the play for the audience. There are two more brief acts, one the story of Cain and Abel, who are also dragged off to Hell at the end, the demons beating Cain as they go but treating Abel somewhat more gently. Finally, there is a brief version of *The Prophets*, which winds up the entertainment.

A trouvère from Arras named Jean Bodel has gone still further in removing drama from the church. His *Play of St. Nicholas*, written at the beginning of the thirteenth century, is based on one of the legends of that saint in which he is entrusted with the treasure of a rich man (in this case a pagan king, who becomes a Herod-figure of violent speech and gesture); thieves steal the treasure and St. Nicholas restores it. This simple story is developed into a full-length play with colorful and individualized characters. The thieves are given picturesque names—Click, Pinchdice, Razor—and roles to match. Another play believed to be written by Bodel, *Le Courtois d'Arras*, is a version of the story of the Prodigal Son, with Arras as its background. Both plays are set in the streets and taverns of a thirteenth-century town, with innkeepers, thieves, and other real-life figures.

With plays staged outside the church, with dialogue the audience can understand and scenes that are more and more secular, the theater has outgrown its confining cradle.[1] Though for a long time to come it will draw heavily on religion for its themes, it now stands on its own feet as an independent art.

14.

Disasters

Pestilence ravaged the country that year; many were consumed inwardly by the sacred fire; their bodies rotted; their entrails turned black as coal; they died miserably or had the even worse misfortune to live after having lost feet and hands to gangrene, and finally many were cruelly tortured by a contraction of nerves.

—SIGEBERT DE GEMBLOUX

Few Troyens alive in 1250 remember the decade of the 1180s, but everybody has heard tales of it. In a space of eight years three of the five major disasters that commonly befall medieval cities struck Troyes. In 1180 the Seine overflowed its banks in the worst flood recorded in the city's annals, inundating streets and houses and taking a heavy toll of people 'and animals. Four years later a crop failure in Champagne resulted in one of the worst famines the city has ever experienced. Finally, one night in 1188 fire broke out in the fair quarter near the Abbey of Notre-Dame-aux-Nonnains, crossed the canal to the old *cité*, gutted the cathedral and the new church of St.-Etienne, damaged the count's palace, razed the public baths, destroyed hundreds of houses, and consumed thousands of pounds' worth of fair merchandise.

Precautions against these recurring disasters are totally

inadequate. Crop surpluses are never enough to make possible a rational system of storage. Even great lords cannot put aside enough grain to carry them through a famine. The Lord of Brienne, scion of a famous Crusading family, was reduced by the famine of 1184 to robbing the Abbey of St.-Loup, something, he confessed later, "which I ought not to have done, but it was to provision my castle."

The first effects of a food shortage are rumors, hoarding, and black-marketing. The prices of both grain and bread are regulated in ordinary times, and even the size and weight of the round loaf. But bakers have many tricks for reducing the actual content of the standard loaf, and when grain is in short supply they are not slow to use them. Worse than the bakers are the speculators, who evade laws limiting the amount of grain a single individual can purchase, and who illegally buy up from farmers before the grain reaches the city market. The council and the provost may take extraordinary measures, and if the shortage is severe and prolonged, speculators dangle from the gallows. During a famine the clergy parade the relics of the cathedral. The knot of beggars at the church door grows into a crowd, and churchgoers must force their way through the whining, hand-stretching throng of men, women and children.

Famine is often accompanied by its sister, pestilence. Even a merely severe winter often leaves a city population prey to mysterious maladies, such as the scurvy that decimated St.-Louis' Crusading army in Egypt. Epidemic afflictions of skin, mouth, lungs, and other organs, such as that chronicled by Sigebert de Gembloux in Champagne and Flanders in 1089, recur unpredictably. The fourteenth century will experience a visitation of the Black Plague beside which all previous contagions will seem mild.

As for floods, inland Troyes is lucky in comparison with

cities situated on larger rivers or in exposed coastal regions. The cities of the medieval Netherlands undergo repeated devastation despite their dikes. Once a storm finds a weak or low dike, the reciprocal flow of the tides through the hole swiftly widens the gap. The death toll for one thirteenth-century Dutch flood is over fifty thousand.

Open-flame illumination and heating make fire a year-round hazard in every section of town. The cheek-by-jowl timber-frame dwellings and shops, sometimes sharing party walls, form a perfect avenue for the flames. Householders are theoretically forbidden to have straw roofs or wooden chimneys, but even these elementary precautions are hard to enforce. An effective measure, stone party walls, has been thought of, but only the rich can afford to build in stone. Buckets of sand and tubs of water quench many fires in early stages, but once furnishings, floors, and partitions take flame little can be done except to pray, and form a bucket brigade—measures about equally effective. If the season is wet and the wind from the right direction, damage may be limited to a few houses or a single street. If the season is dry and the wind fresh and contrary, a large part of a city may be doomed.

The chronicle that records the fire of 1188 gives few details except for the fact that the Devil made an appearance in Troyes shortly beforehand, and was exorcised by a priest with a vial of holy water. But a vivid account of a fire of the same era is that of Gervaise, a monk of Canterbury, in 1174:

> At about the ninth hour, during an extraordinarily violent south wind, a fire broke out . . . by which three houses were half-destroyed. While the citizens were assembling and bringing the fire under control, cinders and sparks carried aloft by the wind were deposited upon the church, and being driven between the joints of the lead roof, remained there among the old timber

rafters, to which they soon set fire; from these the fire was communicated to the larger beams and braces, no one yet perceiving . . . .

But beams and braces burning, the flames rose to the slopes of the roof; and the sheets of lead yielded to the increasing heat and began to melt. Thus the raging wind, finding a freer entrance, increased the fury of the fire; and the flames beginning to show themselves, a cry arose in the churchyard: "The church is on fire!"

Then the people and the monks assemble in haste, they draw water, they brandish their hatchets, they run up the stairs, full of eagerness to save the church, already, alas, beyond help. When they reach the roof and perceive the black smoke and scorching flames that pervade it throughout, they abandon the attempt in despair, and thinking only of their own safety, make all haste to descend.

And now that the fire had loosened the beams from the pegs that bound them together, the half-burnt timbers fell into the choir below upon the seats of the monks; the seats, consisting of a great mass of woodwork, caught fire, and thus the mischief grew worse and worse . . . .

And now the people ran to the ornaments of the church, and began to tear down the *pallia* and curtains, some that they might save, some to steal them. The reliquary chests were thrown down from the high beam and thus broken, and their contents scattered; but the monks collected them and carefully preserved them against the fire . . . .

Not only was the choir consumed in the fire, but also the infirmary, with the chapel of St. Mary, and several other offices in the court; moreover many ornaments and goods of the church were reduced to ashes.

Besides these peacetime calamities, there is always the possibility of war. Here at least people in the city enjoy an advantage over the peasants in the villages. When the feudal army rides, it sets fire to everything it cannot carry off, but the walls of a city like Troyes are nearly always proof against such depredations. The besieging army of Hugo of

La Marche and Peter of Brittany was easily held at bay outside Troyes in 1230. Even an enemy armed with a formidable array of siege engines and missile weapons has a difficult time breaking into a walled city. A feudal army can rarely be kept in the field longer than a month or two. The military obligation of vassals does not extend further, and mercenary troops are too expensive for any but a very wealthy prince bent on a highly important objective, such as a Crusade. Ordinarily, the attacker must within the limits of a short campaign muster either an overwhelming assault force to scale the walls at many points simultaneously, or a powerful enough battery of siege engines to knock down walls or gates. He has a third alternative, if the ground is favorable, and if the defense is insufficiently alert: mining.

The overwhelming assault force may prevail when the stronghold under attack is a castle with a weak garrison. A tightly-packed city of ten thousand citizens, like Troyes, is unlikely to succumb even to a very large storming party, because there are enough men night and day to keep an alert guard at every point of the two-thousand-yard rampart. When the assault force approaches, under cover of a "castle," or movable wooden platform, to fill in the ditch around the walls and plant scaling ladders, the garrison can quickly concentrate at the threatened point or points. Lofty walls, and especially round towers, give the defenders all the advantage in the contest of arrows, bolts, and missiles. Combustibles can be flung down on the attackers' castle, and even if some of the storming party gain a foothold on the wall, they can be isolated by the fire from the neighboring towers, for the space in front of the wall is always kept clear of any cover. The towers project, so that they can bring flanking fire to bear on attackers scaling the wall.

Siege of a City. Sketch by Viollet-le-Duc, who restored the fortified
medieval city of Carcassonne, shows how the assailant succeeded in
collapsing the outer wall of the city by digging a "mine" under it,
then setting fire to the timbering. The defenders countered by
hastily erecting a timber fortification inside the breach.

The old-fashioned Roman siege engines have been much improved. The Romans employed only tension and torsion as motive power. Medieval military engineers have added the counterweight, which provides both more power and greater accuracy. A trebuchet, or counterweight engine, consists of a long firing pole balanced on a pivot, or cross-pole, in turn mounted on a pair of uprights. The firing pole is not set on its mid-point, but on a point about a quarter from its butt end, which is faced toward the enemy. The long end is pulled down, the missile placed in a cavity or sling, and secured by a wooden catch worked by a winch, while the butt end is loaded with wedge-shaped weights of iron or stone. When the catch is released, the counter-weight drops, sending the missile flying. On more sophisti-cated models, the counterweight can be moved closer or farther from the pivot, increasing or decreasing the range. A couple of zeroing-in shots permit a good engineer to fire with considerable accuracy. The missile is ordinarily a heavy stone, though variants include combustible materials and occasionally the heads of enemies. Some military experts prefer a simpler model of counterweight engine, worked by ropes pulled down by men. This is inferior in range and accuracy, but it has the advantage of being highly man-euverable, so that several may be quickly brought to bear on a single weak point in the enemy's defenses.

Artillery, however, is no monopoly of the attackers. In the crypts of the towers of Troyes' ramparts, a great number of dismantled engines stand ready for assembly, together with a supply of stone ammunition.

How effective catapult artillery is against a stone wall depends on the wall. Some old walls, made of a thin shell of rough-cut stone covering an earth core, can be battered to pieces. But a good modern wall, laid in even courses locked into a rubble core, can defy all the engines an enemy can bring to bear, as has been repeatedly demonstrated by the redoubtable though weakly garrisoned Crusader forts in Syria.

The attackers' third alternative, mining, is the most promising, provided soft ground can be found. Against a castle it is particularly effective, because the mine can be driven under either a section of the wall or under the main keep. No explosive is involved—the mine is "discharged" simply by setting fire to the timbering which supports the mine roof. As the timbers burn, the ground above collapses. At one siege in Syria the Saracen engineers first undermined and collapsed a tower in the curtain wall. But the garrison, composed of Knights of St. John, successfully fought off the subsequent assault and reestablished the barricade in the rubble of the tower. The Saracens then dug a mine into the interior of the castle, directly under the keep, and invited the Franks to send their own engineers to inspect it. When the Frankish engineers reported back that the discharge of the mine would cause the certain collapse of the keep, the Knights agreed to surrender on terms— marching out and abandoning the castle to the Saracens.

The proper defense against the mine is the countermine. Ten years ago a memorable duel of mine and countermine took place between defending and attacking engineers at Carcassonne. The seneschal of the city, William des Ormes, reported that the Albigensian rebels, under Raymond Trencavel, viscount of Béziers, found their siege artillery of little avail and so switched to mining.

> The rebels began a mine against the barbican [fortified tower] of the gate of Narbonne [wrote the seneschal]. And forthwith we, having heard the noise of their work underground, made a countermine, and constructed in the inside of the barbican a great

and strong wall of stones . . . so that we retained full half the barbican when they set fire to the hole so that when the wood burned a portion of the front of the barbican fell.

They then began to mine against another turret . . . We countermined, and got possession of the hole which they had excavated. They began therefore to run a mine between us and a certain wall and destroyed two embrasures . . . But we set up there a good and strong palisade between us and them.

They also started a mine at the angle of the town wall, near the bishop's palace, and by dint of digging from a great way off they arrived at a certain wall . . . but when we detected it we made a good and strong palisade between them and us, higher up, and countermined. Thereupon they fired their mine and flung down some ten fathoms of our embrasured front. But we made hastily another good palisade with a brattice and loopholes, so none among them dared to come near us in that quarter.

They began also a mine against the barbican of the Rodez gate, and kept below ground, wishing to arrive at our walls, making marvelous great tunnel. But when we perceived it we forthwith made a palisade on one side and the other of it. We countermined also, and having fallen in with them, carried the chamber of their mine.

Altogether the assailants drove seven different mines, starting from the cellars of houses in the suburb outside. A final attempt to storm the barbican failed, and the approach of a royal relieving army forced Trencavel to raise the siege.

This was an exceptionally determined effort. In the skirmishing warfare more normal in the thirteenth century, a walled city can usually assure its safety merely by closing its gates on the approach of an enemy force.

15.

Town Government

"I am a good lawyer," said Renard. *"Often I've made right out of wrong and wrong out of right, as it suited me."*

—ROMAN DE RENARD

Medieval cities enjoy a great deal of individual liberty, varying degrees of self-government, and little democracy. Their charters, many of which were written in the twelfth century, are principally grants of freedom from feudal obligations—the head tax, the labor service, the tax at will, the marriage tax—in return for payment of a cash impost. Limits are set for their military service, they are allowed to operate their own law courts for lesser crimes ("low justice") and, usually, they are permitted a mayor and council.

The charter is essentially a compact between the burghers and their seigneur, or a contract for which the commune is the collective bargaining agent.

The mayor and council may be elected by the heads of the corporations (masters of the guilds), or they may simply replace themselves at intervals by "co-optation," that is, by naming their own successors. Whatever the method, the result is to place town government in the hands of wealthy burghers closely allied in interest to their prince. Typically a small number of families monopolize political power.

In Venice twenty-seven families supply half the members of the 480-man Grand Council. Some families are represented on the same city council for generations and even centuries. The Lanstiers sat on the town council of Arras for three hundred years. The more sophisticated the town's economic life, the more it participates in international commerce, the more this oligarchic tendency is exaggerated. In Pisa thirty families monopolize the government throughout the thirteenth century.

The commune of Troyes does not include everyone who lives in the city. It is restricted to the "Third Estate"— merchants and craftsmen. Knights who have houses in town may not belong. The clergy too—bishop, abbot, canons, priests and monks—are excluded. But if a knight or a clerk goes into business, not only may he join, he must. On the other hand, members of the commune do not necessarily live in the city; some live in the suburbs but do business in the city.

Members of a commune invariably take an oath, swearing on the relics that they will faithfully guard the life and possessions of their dear lord, his lady, and his children, and sustain them against all men and women whomsoever, and at the same time be loyal to every member of the commune, not aid foreigners against the burghers, obey the mayor, pay their part of the debts of the city, and be good and loyal burghers.

Under the mayor and the town councillors serve a bureaucracy of officials, treasurers, clerks, and magistrates. The town watch guards the ramparts by day and patrols the streets by night. In case of attack, the watch is supplemented by the whole militia. Often a charter specifies that "all who have sworn the communal oath must join the defense, none may remain at home, except one sick, infirm or so poor that he must himself take care of his sick wife or children."

Nearly all charters promise the seigneur *ost et chevauchée* (military service) but on varying terms. That of Troyes exempts moneychangers and fair merchants while the fair is taking place. Laon, whose charter was one of the earliest in northwest Europe, owes a fixed quota: one hundred and twenty foot sergeants and three wagons. Arras has a more advanced arrangement: the town is obligated to supply either a thousand foot sergeants or three thousand livres, a cash sum sufficient to hire a thousand soldiers for the summer. Many towns have demanded and won geographical and political limits to their military service. The citizens of Brai-sur-Somme are required to march only in case of general war or an expedition for the faith, and for either purpose no farther than Reims and Châlons, Tournai and Paris, at their own expense. Men of Poitiers do not have to cross the Loire, those of Chaumont and Pontoise can stop at the edge of the Seine or the Oise.

Recently a new turn has been given to the question of military service. With the growth of proletarian discontent many towns are taking care to restrict the privilege of arms to the wealthy. In Troyes only those citizens possessing *vingt livres vaillant* ("twenty pounds' worth of property") are authorized to own a crossbow and fifty bolts.

Of the two aspects of the charter, individual liberty and self-government, the former is much the more important. The constitutional history of Troyes is a vivid illustration of this fact of medieval life. Though traces of town government appeared in the late twelfth and early thirteenth century, Troyes apparently did not receive a charter until 1230, when Thibaut the Songwriter, financially embarrassed by his war with Peter of Brittany and Hugo of La Marche, signed a formal guarantee of the citizens' ancient privileges and in addition established a Town Council. The councilmen, thirteen in number, were appointed directly by Thibaut; from their company they elected a mayor. The council's function was, quite baldly, to raise money. Members of the commune of Troyes, freed from all servile imposts, were required to pay a fixed annual cash levy, based on the amount of their property. The *taille* (tax) was assessed at a rate of six deniers per livre on movable property, two deniers per livre on real estate. It was the job of the mayor and council to obtain a sworn statement from each burgher of the precise value of his property. But the richest burghers, among whom the councilmen were doubtless numbered, did not have to make such a statement; they were permitted the option of paying a flat rate of twenty livres.

The tax system specified by the charter of Troyes has been popular for some time, but by mid-century two other kinds of taxation have appeared: the cash poll tax and the sales tax. All three reflect the changing fiscal situation, in which sovereign counts, dukes, and kings are succeeding in touching the rapidly growing liquid wealth of the city burghers. The petty lords of the countryside have no such sources of income, and so are losing ground financially to the heads of incipient national states.

Another major source of revenue is the cause of violent wrangling among the competing authorities. This is justice. Whoever administers justice keeps the fines and forfeits, so kings, counts, barons, bishops, and burghers quarrel jealously over jurisdiction. One of the significant provisions of the Magna Carta protects the English barons against loss of their lucrative courts to the king. Like most charters, that of Troyes of 1230 reserved for the count "high justice"—jurisdiction over murder, rape, and robbery. He was also awarded two-thirds of the fines for false measure—an important matter in a fair town—and all cases concerning his churches, knights, fiefs, and Jews. For a yearly cash payment he relinquished other kinds of justice to the town.

In Champagne, cases reserved for the count are heard by his provost. This office is usually filled by a burgher, who works on a commission basis, pocketing a share of the fines he levies. A provost is usually not above accepting gifts, though the practice is officially frowned on. For many of the offenses he tries the penalty is death and confiscation of property. A murderer with wealthy relatives stands a better chance of escaping the gallows than a poor man—a situation not confined to the Middle Ages.

Hanging is a painful death, because the drop technique has not yet been invented, and death comes by strangulation. Torture is rarely employed. If the provost feels it is necessary to extort a confession, he may have a prisoner's teeth extracted, or have him toasted over a fire, or given a stretch on the rack. But few provosts are so fastidious as to insist on a confession. They prefer to listen to the evidence and give the word to the hangman. Traitors, witches, and heretics are burned at the stake, executions in the latter two categories being accompanied by numerous prayers. On the other hand, thieves may be let off with a taste of the branding iron, or a lopped-off hand, and youthful first offenders may escape with a flogging. It even happens that a poor man who steals a shirt is freed after a brief imprisonment on the grounds that he is ill and the offense is small. The crypt under the old castle is used for confinement of those awaiting trial. Actual prison sentences are rare.

The town tries cases involving petty theft, fraud, and

minor assault. It also hears litigation concerning commercial transactions and property. The mayor and four or five councilmen act as judges, listening to the evidence and delivering their verdict unanimously. A few typical recorded cases[1] give the flavor of thirteenth-century urban court problems:

A burgher has discovered some silver wine cups belonging to him in the possession of another townsman, who proves that he purchased them from a tin merchant, who in turn declares that he bought them from a fourth man. Hauled into court, the fourth man swears that he is "pure and innocent," the unvarying formula of the accused, and calls to witness the uprightness and honesty of his life. He is not, however, able to give a convincing account of how he came into possession of the cups, which are ordered returned to the rightful owner. The accused man is sent to the crypt until the judges can hear further witnesses. A woman whose son has been hanged for fatally assaulting another young man in a tavern by bashing his head with a heavy flagon is accused by the victim's relatives of instigating the crime. They want a money payment, but are disappointed. The mayor after due deliberation declares the woman innocent. A knight who owns a house on which the tenant has not paid any rent for a year demands permission to seize the tenement's doors and shutters, which is granted, with a fraction of the sale going to the court. A woman who keeps a lodging house is summonsed for creating a "vile nuisance." She has had a wooden pipe built from the privy chamber of her house to the gutter, rendering it evil-smelling and sometimes blocking it up. The neighbors bring her into court, where she is fined six deniers and ordered to remove the pipe within forty days.

Civil and criminal law are not yet clearly distinguished.

Traces of the old Germanic custom, by which every offense was personal, and murderers paid money ransoms to the relatives of their victims, survive in the mid-thirteenth century. It is difficult to prosecute a felon without the testimony of his victim or his victim's relatives, and sometimes a killer can still buy his freedom by compensating the family (paying *wergild*).

Together with this view of crime as a civil offense, the early Middle Ages also preserved the barbarian customs of duel and ordeal. By 1250 judicial duel is officially forbidden nearly everywhere but is still widely practiced. Even peasants often settle their disputes with cudgels. Legal or not, the loser or his family must pay a heavy fine, and if the quarrel is settled before the combat takes place, fines must still be paid, so that the seigneur does not lose his profit.

But trial by ordeal has fallen into disrepute. Formerly a man was allowed to prove his innocence by thrusting his hand into hot water, or picking up a hot iron, or risking drowning. But in the view of the thirteenth century, sensibly expressed by Frederick II, the ordeal "is not in accord with nature and does not lead to truth . . . How could a man believe that the natural heat of glowing iron will become cool or cold without an adequate cause . . . or that because of a seared conscience the element of cold water will refuse to accept the accused? . . . These judgments of God by ordeal which men call 'truth-revealing' might better be called 'truth-concealing.' "

Roman law is slowly superseding *wergild*, as well as duel and ordeal; court trial, examination of witnesses under oath, and even the use of trained lawyers are becoming more common. Rediscovery of such collections as the *Digest* of Justinian has led to a renaissance of law, coinciding with the more sophisticated needs of reviving commercial life. The markets and fairs, and especially the Fairs of Champagne, have given a powerful impetus to the development of merchants' law.

There is a third law court in most towns—that of the bishop. Here again revenue is of prime importance, and the bishop will fight with every weapon in his spiritual arsenal to defend his court against encroachment from town or provost. Even a clerk in minor orders who has no intention of becoming a priest can insist on being tried in the ecclesiastical court, where he is certain to be more gently treated than by town magistrate or provost. In the bishop's court the law is a composite of Scripture, oral tradition, precedents in Roman and Germanic law, decrees of Church councils, and legislation by the Pope. The celebrated Gratian brought this hodgepodge into an orderly system in the twelfth century, and at the same time founded a whole methodology by posing one text against another and reconciling them.

Roman law is now taught in law schools at Montpellier, Orléans, Angers, Bologna, Reggio, and other places, but Paris teaches only canon law. Lawyers are not particularly popular. Their pretensions are resented, and their pedantic interpretations irritate everyone. They insist on exact forms and formulas. But they are improving the administration of justice and pointing the way to guarantees for the accused that a future age will regard as indispensable.

A jurisdictional dispute among the courts of a town sometimes becomes a bigger legal cause than the case that was originally to be tried. In 1236 the mayor and councillors of Laon imprisoned three men who the canons of the cathedral thought should be tried in the ecclesiastical court. The town officials refused to hand over the prisoners, where-

upon the canons issued bans of excommunication against
the councillors. But the parish priest to whom the bans were
given sided with the town and refused to publish them. The
canons excommunicated the priest. Priest and townsmen
took the case all the way to Rome and won a favorable
judgment, enforced by a papal excommunication against the
canons. The same priest savored the revenge of entering the
church at Vespers, lighted candle in hand, pronouncing the
sentence, and turning the candle upside down.

Many regions are beginning to enjoy a medieval advance
in jurisprudence—the court of appeals. The Parlement of
Paris and the Parliament of London are two of the most
famous. Another is taking shape in Troyes—the Council
and Tribunal of the Count of Champagne, meeting from
time to time in the *Grands Jours de Troyes*. In its origins
no more than the count's court sitting in judicial session, it
will develop into a regularly appointed body of chief
vassals, leading burghers and prelates, and will serve as trial
court for the nobility and appeals court for the lower
classes.

The Charter of 1230 may have sufficed for Thibaut's
financial needs in 1230, but a little more than a decade later
it no longer did. Probably the minor Crusade of 1239, in
which Thibaut distinguished himself, plunged him into
fresh debts. In any case the mayor and council proved
incapable of raising enough money for their sovereign, and
so without ceremony he turned them out of office. In their
place he installed a group headed by an enterprising
Cahorsin financier named Bernard de Montcuc, who had
arrived in Troyes some years earlier as a moneychanger.
Together with his associates, who included two of his
brothers, Bernard undertook to advance Thibaut four

thousand three hundred pounds (*livres Tournois*) a year for five years—a thousand at the Hot Fair, two thousand at the Cold Fair, and the remainder at the Fair of Bar-sur-Aube. With these loans Thibaut could pay off his debts and presumably have enough to live on. Bernard and his consortium were repaid by two means: first, a special sales tax over the five-year period levied at four deniers per livre (one-sixtieth) on all merchandise sold in Troyes, and second, the farming out of low justice. As a sop to the businessmen of Troyes, those paying the sales tax were exempted from military service. To clear the way for these revenues politically, Thibaut appointed Bernard and his friends to serve in turn as mayors throughout the emergency.

Thus in Thibaut's view the government of Troyes is little more than a money-raising agency. Though the Troyes burghers doubtless grumbled at first, their acceptance of the Montcuc scheme and their generally passive attitude toward the charter indicate a lethargy toward political affairs that differentiates them sharply from most other townsmen. In many cities charters have been won after violence and bloodshed, and once won are jealously guarded. The difference in the Troyen attitude is unquestionably a reflection of the vast advantages accruing to the burghers of Troyes from their fairs. Though their political liberties have proved illusory, their individual liberties are genuine. They possess freedom without self-government, and as long as the fairs prosper they will be satisfied.

Troyes is not the only town to suffer from a prince's follies, and at the head of the list of princely follies stands crusading. Burgher discontent has played a major role in the decline of the crusading business since Peter the Hermit. In 1095 idealism caused many people to do foolish things, but by the thirteenth century ordinary people have lost their appetite for warfare, while princes and barons have grown more cautious about selling estates to equip armies. Nowadays only princes who can exact large contributions from their towns can think about Crusading. In most of France and Flanders the principal form of such contributions is the feudal "aid," originally a gift to a lord on the occasion of a daughter's marriage or a son's knighting —a ham from one peasant, a sack of grain from another. In the more affluent, urbanized society of the thirteenth century, the aid is a cash payment. When a sovereign requests it, his towns must assess themselves. No town is happy about an aid, and some find it thoroughly objectionable. Douai, in Flanders, paid 32,600 livres over a period of twenty years for a variety of needs and extravagances of its counts and countesses. Noyon went bankrupt, the goods of its burghers being seized to pay creditors.

Two years ago, in 1248, Louis IX, valiant and devout king of France, went on crusade. The king's idealism about the Holy Land was shared by few of his subjects or peers. Some two thousand eight hundred knights and eight thousand foot sergeants were recruited, nearly all on a mercenary basis. Jean de Joinville, seneschal of Champagne, accompanied the king, who was a personal friend, with reluctance. Later he described his departure from home: "I never once let my eyes turn back towards Joinville, for fear my heart might be filled with longing at the thought of my beautiful castle and the two children I had left behind." The happiest result of the expedition, in fact, is Joinville's own memoir of it, which adds a leaf to Troyes' literary laurels. After a rather brilliant beginning, in a successful amphibious assault on Damietta, the expedition bogged down in the swampy upriver country around the fortress city of Mansourah. Famine and scurvy turned the camp into a hospital and charnel house, and the survivors were easily taken prisoner by the Saracens. The queen ransomed the king by trading Damietta, after which Louis ransomed Joinville and the other knights by paying four hundred thousand livres. Originally the sultan demanded five hundred thousand, but when the king unhesitatingly agreed, the equally chivalrous sultan knocked off a hundred thousand livres, commenting, "By Allah, this Frank does not haggle!"

The money was raised on the spot by a bit of pressure on the wealthy Knights Templar, but is now in the process of being paid by the king's subjects, mainly the burghers of his cities, already touched for sizeable aids, and facing still more bills for Louis' new fortifications in Syria. It is hardly surprising that quite a few burghers identify themselves with the wrong side of the debate between Crusaders and non-Crusaders that is a favorite subject of the trouvères. They feel that after all, "it is also a good and holy thing to live quietly at home, in friendship with neighbors, taking care of children and goods, going to bed early and sleeping well." If the sultan of Egypt should take it into his head to invade France, they will be ready to pay an aid, and take up their pikes and crossbows besides. But they do not see the wisdom of journeying far over the sea to die, and die expensively at that.

16.

The Champagne Fair

There are ten fairs in the land of France,
One at Bar, another at Provins,
Another at Troyes and a fourth at Lendit,
And three in Flanders, and the eighth at Senlis,
The ninth at Cesoirs, the tenth at Lagny.

—GARIN DE LOHERAIN

The Hot Fair of Troyes, celebrated in song and story, is the most important of the six Fairs of Champagne, which are divided unequally among four towns stretching across the county from its easternmost to westernmost borders. Geography and season make the first two fairs of the cycle,[1] those of Lagny and Bar-sur-Aube, the smallest. Lagny is close to Paris, Bar on the edge of Burgundy, a hundred miles east. The Lagny Fair is held in January–February, that of Bar next in March–April. Third in the calendar year comes the May Fair of Provins, running through May and June, followed by the Hot Fair, or Fair of St.-Jean, held in Troyes at the height of summer in July and August. The distance from Provins to Troyes is only forty miles, and many fair clients pack up at Provins to unpack again in Troyes. The next fair, in September–October, is the Fair of St.-Ayoul in Provins, and again there is heavy inter-fair traffic. Finally comes the Fair of St.-Rémi, the Cold Fair of Troyes, in November and December. These four, in the two neighboring cities, lasting through the good traveling weather, form the major loci of this un-rivaled marketplace for wholesale merchants and money-men from Flanders, Italy, England, Germany, Spain, and even more distant places.

The Hot Fair is the climax of weeks of preparation. Apprentices have been up early and late, sewing, cleaning, sorting, finishing, storing, and repairing. The big halls and little stalls of the fair area have been put in order for their guests, as have the hostels and houses used for lodgings. In the taverns the dice are freshly cleaned, a precaution that may prevent a few knife fights. The cadre of regular prostitutes has been reinforced by serving wenches, trades-women, and farmers' daughters. Cooks, bakers, and butchers have added extra help and lengthened their families' working hours.

An army of officials ensures that all goes smoothly. At their head are two Keepers of the Fair, chosen from the ranks of both nobles and burghers. They are appointed by the count at the excellent stipend of 200 pounds (livres) a year, expense allowances of 30 pounds, and exemption from all tolls and taxes for life. Their chief assistants, the keepers of the Seal, receive 100 pounds apiece. A lieutenant of the Fair commands the sergeants, a hundred strong, who guard the roads and patrol the fair. There are tax collectors, clerks, porters, roustabouts, and couriers. Notaries[2] attest all written transactions. Inspectors check the quality of merchandise. Finally, heralds scour the countryside to advertise the fair to the rustics.

The hubbub of the fair is as sweet a sound to the count as to the citizens of Troyes. Notaries, weighers, and other fee collectors divide their earnings with him. Thieves and bandits come under his high justice, their booty confiscated in his name. Sales taxes, the "issue" fee levied on departing merchandise, and other charges go to the count. So do rents on many stalls, booths, halls, stables, and houses. The bishop profits, too, drawing a sizeable income from rents, as do burghers and knights of Troyes. The Knights Templar draw revenues from their monopoly of wool weighing.

In return for all the fees and charges, the visiting merchants get freedom and protection. Fair clients are guaranteed security for themselves and their merchandise from the day of arrival to the day of departure, sunrise to sunset. At the height of the fair the streets are even lighted at night, making them almost safe.

Merchants are not only protected from bandits and robber barons, but from each other, and in fact today this is the more important protection of the two. Crimes committed at the fair are answerable to special courts, under the supervision of the Keepers of the Fair, but both town and provost try cases too, and law enforcement becomes a lively three-way competition. The special courts were actually created because the foreign merchants demanded protection against the other two agencies. Merchants can choose which court they will be tried in, and the most important cases fall to the courts of the fair. Energetic measures are taken to ensure collection of debts. A debtor or a swindler will be pursued far beyond the walls of Troyes and stands little chance of escaping arrest if he shows his face at another fair. This is not all. He is liable to arrest in any city of Flanders or northern France, and if he is Italian he will be least safe of all in his home town, for the keepers of the Fair will threaten reprisal against his fellow townsmen if they do not assist in bringing him to justice. The extent to which these guarantees are actually enforced was graphically demonstrated eight years ago when a caravan of merchants was set upon by robbers on the highway between Lodi and Pavia. It was ascertained that the bandits were from Piacenza. The aggrieved merchants reported the offense to the keepers of the Champagne Fairs, who promptly and effectively threatened to exclude the merchants of Piacenza unless restitution was made.

These protections, together with a general diminution of lawlessness and improved physical conditions for travel, have brought merchants from all over Europe in steadily increasing numbers. Throughout the yearly cycle the stream of traffic to and from Champagne never ceases.

But merchants can trade at the fair without making the journey in person. A regular contract form known as a "letter of carriage" exists for the purpose: "Odon Bagnasque, carrier, promises to Aubert Bagnaret to transport at his own cost, including tolls, with risks of robbery falling to Aubert, six bales from Marseille to Troyes, from the day of this act to Christmas, in exchange for a horse given by Aubert." Or they can enter into a form of partnership developed by the Italians, known as the *commenda*, by which a younger man undertakes the risks of a journey in return for a quarter of the profits, while an older merchant puts up the capital. When the young businessman has some capital of his own, he can alter the agreement and put up a third of the capital, taking half the profit. This and other forms of contract are so common in Italy that a Genoese patrician dying in 1240 left no property but his house and a portfolio of *commenda* investments.

The fair, though primarily a wholesale and money market for big business, is also a gala for common folk. Peasants and their wives, knights and their ladies, arrive on foot, on horses, on donkeys, to find a bargain, sell a hen or a cow, or see the sights. Dancers, jugglers, acrobats, bears, and monkeys perform on the street corners; jongleurs sing on the church steps. Taverns are noisily thronged. The whores, amateur and professional, cajole and bargain.

For a farmer or backwoods knight, the fair is an opportunity to gape at such exotic foreigners as Englishmen, Scots, Scandinavians, Icelanders, and Portuguese, not to mention Provençaux, Frenchmen, Brabanters, Germans, Swiss, Burgundians, Spaniards, and Sicilians. Most numerous are the Flemings and the "Lombards," a term which includes not only men from Lombardy, but Florentines, Genoese, Venetians and other north Italians. The rustic visitor hears many languages spoken, but these men of many nations communicate with little difficulty. Some of the more learned know Latin, and there are always plenty of clerks to translate. But the *lingua franca* of the fairs is French; though there is little sense of French nationality, and though French is not universally spoken throughout the narrow realm of the king of France, nearly every merchant and factor at the fair can acquit himself in this tongue. French is already acquiring exotic words which the Italians have picked up from their Arab business contacts. Eventually *douane, gabelle, gondran, jupe, quintal, recif*, and many more will find their way into French. English will acquire *bazaar, jar, magazine, taffeta, tariff, artichoke, tarragon, orange, muslin, gauze, sugar, alum, saffron*.

The first week of the fair is occupied with the merchants' entry—registration, unpacking, setting up displays. Then the fair opens with a ten-day Cloth Market. The Italian merchants pass from one to another of the halls of the famous cloth cities, examining the bolts, which have already been subjected to a rigid inspection at home, for every cloth town guards its reputation like Caesar's wife. It is an offense to sell defective cloth abroad; below-grade or irregular material must be marketed locally. Each kind of wool is folded in a different way, both to make it identifiable and to display its special virtues. An expert can recognize at a glance the cloths of Douai, Arras, Bruges, Tournai or Ypres—towns which, together with a number of others of the Low Countries and northern France, form the "Hanse of the Seventeen Towns," an association of wool producers who have agreed to sell their cloth only at the Champagne Fairs.

Each town has its own standard bolt—those of Provins and Troyes are twenty-eight ells long; those of Ghent thirty, except for the scarlets, which are thirty-six; those of Ypres twenty-nine ells, and so forth. A special official is on hand to explain the different lengths. The ell itself varies in other parts of Europe, but here it is the standard ell of Champagne, two feet six inches. An iron ruler of this length is in the hands of the Keepers of the Fair. Against it all the wooden rulers in use have been measured.

The tables in the cloth halls are a kaleidoscope of colored bolts, ranging from ecru, uncolored and little finished, through gray, brown, vermillion, rose and scarlet. The reds, highly prized and expensive, are a specialty of the famous *Arte di Calimala* of Florence, whose agents at the fair buy undyed cloth and sell dyed. Here and there is cloth heavy with gold and silver thread. Though wool predominates, there are also silks, mostly from Lucca; cotton from Italy, France, and Flanders; flax in the form of linen for sheets, sacks, purses, and clothing, and of hemp for nets, ropes, bowstrings, and measuring lines.

Bargaining finished, deals concluded and notarized, and arrangements made for the transfer of goods, the sergeants close the Cloth Market with the traditional cry of "Hare!

Hare!" and attention turns to the next order of business. This is "*avoir de poids*," goods that must be weighed—sugar, salt, alum, lacquer, dyes, grain, wines. These come from a diversity of places—salt from Salins in Franche-Comté, sugar from Syria, wax from Morocco and Tunisia. But just as the king of textiles is wool, the prince of avoir de poids is spices. They are the fabulous commodities that alone sustain a trade by pack train, galley, camel caravan, and Arab dhow. There are literally hundreds of spices; one medieval list names two hundred and eighty-eight.[3] The Italian merchants themselves do not know where all the spices come from. They load their precious cargoes at Constantinople, or Acre, or Antioch, or Tripoli, and if they question their Arab suppliers, they receive a shrug or a strange answer. Cinnamon, they may be told, comes from the nest of a bird of Arabia who favors this aromatic fruit as building material. Cassia trees grow in glens or lakes watched over by ferocious winged animals. Another opinion holds that the spices are harvested by the Egyptians, who stretch nets across the Nile.

Few of the merchants at the Hot Fair believe these fairy tales. They know the spices come from the distant East, from coasts and islands no European visits, lost in a fog of fourth-hand knowledge. It is not difficult for them to credit the costs involved in the arduous and perilous freightage over thousands of leagues. Tolls must be paid by the dozens, and caravans guarded. Losses must be made up for in the prices. No wonder a pound of mace at the fair is worth as much as three sheep.

The very mystery of the spices adds something to their desirability. Their basic value is twofold: as flavoring for meat whose toughness needs long cooking, and as preservatives. For these two purposes, one spice surpasses all others:

pepper. This small black wrinkled berry has become a metaphor—"dear as pepper." It is not the most expensive spice; saffron and cinnamon are much costlier. But at four sous a pound it is expensive enough, and by far the most popular of the spices. Pepper merchants sell it retail by the peppercorn; a housewife may buy just one if she wishes.

Its popularity and costliness cause pepper to be guarded like diamonds. Longshoremen who handle it are closely watched and frequently searched. Crossbows and blades bristle on the galleys that bring it through the Mediterranean, and in the pack trains that carry it through the Alpine passes and across the hills and plains of Burgundy and Champagne.

All these precautions do not protect the pepper from depredations of a different kind—those of grocers, wholesalers and middlemen, any of whom may mix a bit of something with it—perhaps a few peppercorns confected from clay, oil, and mustard, difficult to distinguish from the genuine article. At the fair, experts scrutinize every batch of pepper with eyes, fingers, and nose. The arguments that ensue add to the din around St.-Jean.

When a spice deal is consummated, the merchandise is taken to a weighing station. The weighing, too, is followed by several pairs of alert eyes. Only responsible merchants are permitted inside the spice halls and the weighing station.

Other food products besides spices do a brisk retail business, as celebrated in a contemporary verse:

> A Laigny, à Bar, à Provins
> Si i a marcheand de vins
> De blé, de sel et de harenc . . .
>
> [At Lagny, Bar, and Provins
> There are sellers of wine,
> Grain, salt, and herring.]

Among the comestibles are meat and cheese (that of Brie is already celebrated) and, above all, wine. The wines of Champagne—Reims, Epernay and Bar-sur-Aube—are popular, but the principal wine sold at the Champagne Fairs is that of Auxerre, a few miles south of Troyes. (Wine is too bulky a commodity to be shipped far, except by water.)

Dyestuffs are also included in avoir de poids. Some are produced in Flanders and sold to the Italians, some sold by the Italians to the Flemings and Champenois. The greatest demand is for indigo, from India, which the Italians buy in the Syrian ports. Alum, an essential to the dyeing as to the tanning process, is now produced in Spain as well as Egypt and the East. The Italians produce certain other dyes, violets and reds, from lichen and insects—tricks they have learned from their Moslem suppliers, either by observation or espionage.

During this part of the fair, a host of commodities is sold, ranging from raw materials like skins and metals to finely worked handicrafted products. Armorers buy iron from Germany and steel from Spain. Lead, tin, and copper are on hand, from Bohemia, Poland, Hungary, and England. Furs and skins sold by local dealers compete with imports from across the Rhine and even from Scandinavia. Then there are luxury goods from the East, imported by the Italians: camphor, ambergris, musk, rubies, lapis lazuli, diamonds, carpets, pearls, and ivory tusks. The Champagne Fairs are a source of supply for the ivory carvers of Reims, Metz, and Cologne, whose intricate masterpieces, ivory replicas of castles and cathedrals, are on display. So is the art of the Italian and local goldsmiths and silversmiths, and astonishing work in ebony, such as carved chess sets from the Far East. Amid the shoes and leather displayed, the famous Spanish cordovan is in the limelight.

The happy uproar of opening day does not diminish during the weeks that follow. Bargaining is conducted with zest and vehemence. Faults are found with the merchandise: there are complaints that cloth has been stretched, flax left out all night in the damp to increase in weight; that wine has been falsely labeled. The loudest bargaining, the bitterest disputes and the most frequent invocations of the saints are heard in front of the small stalls. Big companies like the Bardi and Guicciardini of Florence, the Bonsignori and Tolomei of Siena, and the Buonconti of Pisa have reputations to maintain for quality and probity.

Throughout the month following the Cloth Market, however, the busiest section of the Fair is the money-changers' area near St.-Jean. The commerce of which the Champagne Fairs are the focus has stimulated a lively flow of foreign exchange, and the fairs themselves are the natural center of this money trade. Travelers who are not fair clients may visit Troyes simply to have their money changed or to buy letters of credit. Essentially private businessmen, the twenty-eight moneychangers are at the same time functionaries of the fair. Half of them are Italians, many from Siena. The other half are Jews and Cahorsins.

The standard coin of the fairs is the *denier de Provins* (Provins penny). A strong currency, of high and stable relative value, it has even inspired an Italian copy, the "Provinois of the Senate," minted in Rome for fair-bound merchants. But dozens of other pennies of widely varying worth also put in an appearance. Moneychanging is governed by strict regulations. One ironclad rule directs the changer to remove from circulation all debased or false coins. Exchange rates on all kinds of money are posted, the quotations made in terms of one sou (twelve pennies) of Provins.

Moneychangers, such as these shown in Chartres Cathedral window, were the principal bankers of the thirteenth century. Some of those who held tables at Troyes became wealthy patricians.

But the moneychangers' function at the fair is not limited to providing a standard medium of exchange for the merchants' use. They are also the focus of a very extensive system of credit.[4] This operates in several ways. A certain Florentine house is a regular purchaser of cloth at the fairs.

But the company's cargoes of spices and luxury goods, which they sell in Champagne, do not always arrive on time. Therefore they keep a balance to their account with the moneychangers so that their agents are never without funds. Further, they can deposit Florentine money in Florence or Genoa and have the money paid to their agent at Troyes in silver of Provins.

Or an Italian merchant may borrow a sum in Genoa in local currency, pledging as security the goods he is shipping to Champagne, and specify that repayment is to be made in money of Provins at the Fair. If the goods are entrusted to a third party, the contract may specify that they travel at the creditor's risk.

An even more sophisticated method of credit is employed by the big Italian houses. Instead of sending a pack caravan to arrive during the opening week, the firm dispatches a courier with a bill of lading for its agent in Champagne. The agent buys cloth on credit and sends it off to Italy. When his firm's merchandise arrives, in time for the avoir de poids market, the agent turns seller and negotiates credit transactions in reverse, acquiring enough paper for his spices to cover his cloth debts.

Apart from credit transactions and currency exchange, the fair moneychangers do a great deal of business in straight loans. The "Lombards" are notable pawnbrokers. Behind his moneychanging stall a Lombard may have a back room full of rings, paternosters, and silver plate. Not only businessmen, but all classes use the fairs as banking places. Princes, barons, bishops all borrow at the Hot Fair and promise to repay at the Fair of St.-Ayoul. Not all this lucrative loan business is in the hands of the moneychangers, but they are generally involved, as are the notaries (who are also frequently Italian).

Sometimes a merchant borrows at one fair and promises to repay in installments at the next three or more, as he sells his goods. This sort of arrangement is taken care of in the closing days of the fair, during the debt settlement (*paga-mentum*), a time of general liquidation of the promises to pay that have accumulated on all sides. Among other things, the system of dating loans from one fair to another helps solve the problem of variant calendars.[5] Venetian, Pisan, and Florentine merchants do not agree on when the year begins, or even what year it is.

An ever more complex financial system is taking shape. A merchant's promise to pay may itself be sold at a discount, and a third party may appear at the subsequent fair to claim the debt. A merchant of Florence may buy a stock of cloth from a merchant of Ghent at the May Fair of Provins, and promise to pay twenty pounds at the Hot Fair of Troyes. The two take their "Letter of the Fair," spelling out the agreement, to the Keeper of the Fair, and have it witnessed and sealed with the fair seal. The Fleming then has in his possession a negotiable piece of paper, which he may use to pay for his own purchases of pepper and cinnamon. The Letter of the Fair makes it possible to execute a considerable proportion of the fair's business without recourse to the moneychangers, and without the need for handling large sums of cash.

Thus in the cheerful clamor of the fair, the jingle of silver is quietly being replaced by the rattle of the abacus and the scratching of the quill, turning bales and bolts into livres and deniers, and recording them in notarial documents.

Here, more than in anything else in this busy, know-ledgeable, money-oriented city of shopkeepers, lies a portent of the future.

After 1250

The growing financial sophistication evident at the Hot Fair of Troyes in the year 1250 led in succeeding decades to a paradox not uncommon in history. The Champagne Fairs became so successful that they made themselves obsolescent.

Historians used to blame politics for the fourteenth-century decline of the fairs. The dynasty of Thibaut the Great came to an end with the marriage of Jeanne de Navarre, only surviving grandchild of Thibaut the Song-writer, to King Philip the Fair, whose taxes and wars were once believed to have ruined the fairs. But there was sufficient evidence of trouble before Philip. His predecessor in Champagne was an Englishman, Edmund of Lancaster, who married Jeanne's widowed mother, Blanche of Artois. Edmund and Blanche raised taxes to a point where in Troyes' sister city, Provins, the mayor sought to ease the burden of his fellow burghers by lengthening the weavers' hours of labor. Workmen rioted and killed the mayor and several of his councillors. Repression and reprisal followed.

Social relations were growing complicated. The hallowed formula of three estates—clergy, nobility, and common folk—was never very realistic, even at the height of feudalism. By the late thirteenth century the "third estate" included bankers, engineers, salesmen, doctors, and poets along with peasants and proletarians. The topmost group of

this class, the "patricians," played a more and more active
social and political role. While in cities like Provins they
importuned their feudal lords to help them punish unruly
workers, in other places they stoutly contested their lords'
rights to military service and aids. The refusal of Bourges to
contribute to St.-Louis' quixotic enterprise of 1270, upheld
by the Parlement of Paris, gave the crusading business a
final push into the grave.

But class war was not more responsible than taxes for the
decline of the Champagne Fairs. An unparalleled school for
banking, bookkeeping, and merchandising, the fairs helped
kill themselves by nourishing more efficient methods of
doing business. The grandson of the Italian businessman who
struggled over the Alpine passes, at the head of his pack
train, stayed home in his countinghouse and struggled over
accounts. Traveling partners were replaced by permanent
factors stationed in the principal cities of the north. (The
Paris factor of the famous Bardi firm of Florence in the
early fourteenth century had a bright son named Giovanni
Boccaccio.) Ultimately the old overland route of the spice
and cloth trade was itself superseded. As early as 1277 a
venturesome Genoese galley rounded Gibraltar and crossed
the stormy Bay of Biscay to the English Channel, though it
was some time before shipping became safe enough to
compete in cost with land transport. For shipments by both
land and sea, the business tycoon of the fourteenth century
took advantage of another new business technique—cargo
insurance.

A variety of calamities, some natural and some man-
made, befell Troyes, Champagne, and western Europe
generally in the fourteenth century. Philip the Fair's war
with Flanders interrupted the fairs. Agriculture suffered a
number of bad harvests, one in 1304 bringing famine in

Troyes, and others affecting various regions in the 1320s. Edward III of England prepared for his expedition in quest of the crown of France by borrowing a quarter of a million pounds from Italian, Flemish, German, and English moneymen and then declaring bankruptcy, bringing ruin to the mighty firms of Bardi and Peruzzi. Finally the appalling catastrophe of the Black Death (1348–50) shook the entire agricultural and commercial structure of the West.

But even without war, famine and pestilence, there is reason to believe that the boom had temporarily run its course. Exactly what caused the slowdown of the fourteenth and early fifteenth centuries remains a mystery. Even if increasing taxes did not kill the Champagne Fairs, they may have contributed to the big depression. Some scholars point to the growth of monopolies. An example is the tanners of Troyes, who became rich and powerful by cartel buying and selling. Even more striking is the story of the butchers of Paris, who in 1260 acquired a perpetual lease on the twenty-five municipal butcher stalls of the city. In the course of a hundred years their number shrank to six families, none personally engaged in the trade, but all very wealthy and playing a major political role in the Hundred Years' War.

In the second round of the war, starring Henry V and Joan of Arc, Troyes enjoyed a brief prominence, first in 1420 as the scene of Henry's marriage to Catherine of France, consecrated in St.-Jean, and next in 1429 by Joan's capture of the city *en route* to crowning the dauphin at Reims. But Troyes was on the downgrade. Though it remained a bishopric and continued to serve as a local center for commerce and manufacture, it had long ceased to be either a political capital or a nucleus of international trade. Paris, capital of a powerful central monarchy, took over as the major economic hub, growing to a metropolis of more than a hundred thousand by the end of the war (1453). London, capital of a rival kingdom and port for England's growing wool-cloth industry, was not much smaller. Across the Channel, Antwerp, the best port on the coast, rode the crest of the new seaborne commerce, leaving behind the old cloth towns of Flanders—Ypres, Saint-Omer, Arras, Douai. In Germany, Hamburg and Lubeck, on either flank of the Danish peninsula, led the cities of the Hanseatic League on a brilliant career of commercial and political supremacy in the Baltic, monopolizing trade and fisheries, fighting wars with kings and collecting tolls.

In southern France some of the old cities (Avignon, Montpellier) declined, while others (Marseille, Lyon) held their own. In Italy, Florence rose to ever new heights under the leadership of a parvenu banking house, the Medici, as did Milan under the Visconti. Genoa crushed its ancient rival, Pisa, then met with difficulties in its turn and lost most of its far-flung colonial empire, though it remained a major financial center on the strength of its banking *savoir-faire*. With the downfall of its maritime rivals, Venice became the unchallenged queen of the Mediterranean, a position so glamorous that it was some time before Venetians became aware that the Mediterranean itself was losing importance through the opening of a sea route to the East and the discovery of a New World in the west. That the discovery was made by an experienced Genoese sailor, hired by the queen of the Atlantic maritime kingdom of Castile, was not surprising.

America had of course been discovered before, but Leif Ericson, Bjarni Herjulfson, and their companions brought along only the limited technology of the Old World's tenth century. The difference between the Viking explorers and Columbus is the difference between the early and late

Middle Ages. The Vikings had no wheeled plows, no felling axes, no iron harrows, no horse collars or horseshoes, no overshot waterwheels, no wealth of handicrafts to conciliate the aborigines, and no firearms (introduced in western Europe in the fourteenth century) to coerce them. Neither did they have the booming market for gold, silver, and furs that provided a lively stimulus for the Spaniards, English and French.

The Commercial Revolution, as modern scholars have named it, supplied the economic and technological basis for exploitation of the New World. At the same time it laid the foundations in mining and metallurgy, banking and merchandising, for the momentous developments in north-west Europe in the sixteenth, seventeenth, and eighteenth centuries. The descendants of the craftsmen, merchants, and moneylenders of thirteenth-century France, England, Germany, and Flanders steadily augmented their power, toppling thrones, overturning churches, burying hallowed customs and taking over the privileges of the privileged classes. Without the Commercial Revolution of the Middle Ages, neither the French Revolution nor the Industrial Revolution is conceivable.

Like a number of other sleepy old towns, Troyes received a stimulus from the Industrial Revolution. It even regained a modicum of its ancient status, developing its own manu-facturing specialty, knitwear, and winning the honorable title of leader of the nightcap industry. Its worst fire, in 1524, wiped out the rich and populous commercial quarter, destroying the cloth halls, the Templar commandery, the Belfry (formerly the Viscount's Tower), and seriously damaging the churches of St.-Pantaléon, St.-Jean, and St.-Nicolas. Four and a half centuries of wear and tear, including the invasion of 1940 and the liberation of 1944, have further depleted the town's medieval heritage. A few buildings weathered every rack, among them the Hôtel-Dieu-le-Comte, largely rebuilt, the Abbey of St.-Loup, which now houses a library and museums, and the cathedral with its stained glass. The "old quarter" of Troyes today, which includes the old fair quarter, actually dates from the rebuilding after the fire. Much of the original street layout remains: Cats' Alley is still only seven feet wide, with the housetops leaning against each other.

An intangible relic also survives. Among such ancient professions as that of gem cutter, precious-metal worker, and apothecary, "Troy weight," with its medieval ratio of twenty pennyweight to the ounce and twelve ounces to the pound, is still in use—a last souvenir of the great days of the Champagne Fairs.

Genealogy of the Counts of Champagne

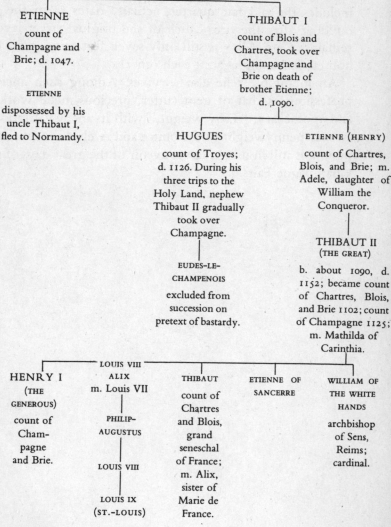

EUDES

count of Chartres, Tours, and Blois, cousin of Etienne, last of the line of Vermandois, disputed county with King Robert of France and won; 1019 seized Troyes, took name of count of Champagne. Killed in battle, 1037.

ETIENNE

count of Champagne and Brie; d. 1047.

ETIENNE

dispossessed by his uncle Thibaut I, fled to Normandy.

THIBAUT I

count of Blois and Chartres, took over Champagne and Brie on death of brother Etienne; d. 1090.

HUGUES

count of Troyes; d. 1126. During his three trips to the Holy Land, nephew Thibaut II gradually took over Champagne.

EUDES-LE-CHAMPENOIS

excluded from succession on pretext of bastardy.

ETIENNE (HENRY)

count of Chartres, Blois, and Brie; m. Adele, daughter of William the Conqueror.

THIBAUT II
(THE GREAT)

b. about 1090, d. 1152; became count of Chartres, Blois, and Brie 1102; count of Champagne 1125; m. Mathilda of Carinthia.

HENRY I
(THE GENEROUS)

count of Champagne and Brie.

LOUIS VIII
ALIX
m. Louis VII

PHILIP-AUGUSTUS

LOUIS VIII

LOUIS IX
(ST.-LOUIS)

THIBAUT

count of Chartres and Blois, grand seneschal of France; m. Alix, sister of Marie de France.

ETIENNE OF SANCERRE

WILLIAM OF THE WHITE HANDS

archbishop of Sens, Reims; cardinal.

HENRY I
— (THE GENEROUS) —

HENRY II (THE YOUNG)

b. 1166; count of
Champagne 1181–1192;
king of Jerusalem
1192–1197; d. 1197 at
Acre. His mother Marie
was regent until his
majority in 1187.

b. 1127; count of
Champagne 1152–1181;
m. Marie, daughter of
Louis VII and Eleanor of
Aquitaine. Eleanor
afterward m. Henry II of
England and bore Richard
the Lionhearted and John,
making Marie half sister to
three kings:
Philip-Augustus, John, and
Richard.

THIBAUT III

b. 1179; count of
Champagne 1·197–1201;
m. Blanche of Navarre;
d. 1201 on eve of Fourth
Crusade. His mother
Marie was regent from
1192 until his majority in
1198.

THIBAUT IV
(THE SONGWRITER)

b. 1201; count of
Champagne 1201–1253;
king of Navarre
1234–1253; m. Gertrude
de Habsburg (or de
Dabo); annulled, no issue;
Agnes de Beaujeu, one
daughter; Marguerite de
Bourbon, four sons, three
daughters.

THIBAUT V

count of Champagne,
king of Navarre
1253–1271; m. Isabelle,
daughter of St.-Louis.

HENRY III (THE FAT)

count of Champagne,
king of Navarre
1271–1274; m. Blanche of
Artois, niece of St.-Louis,
who after his death m.
Edmund of Lancaster.

JEANNE DE NAVARRE

m. Philip IV (the Fair),
grandson of St.-Louis,
king of France, 1285–1314.

LOUIS X (THE BRAWLER)

king of France and
Navarre 1314–1316.

Notes

PROLOGUE

1. *the count of Vermandois:* During the ninth century Troyes was held by a miscellaneous succession of non-hereditary counts, including Adelerin, the abbot of St.-Loup. The first of the Vermandois counts to reign in Troyes was Héribert, who died in 943. His son Robert, who repelled Bishop Anségise's effort to recover power in the city, died without issue and was succeeded by his brother Héribert, with whose son Etienne (d. 1015) the dynasty came to an end.

2. *a cardinal . . . an abbot:* Jacques de Vitry and Guibert of Nogent.

3. *population:* All figures are conjectural. Estimates of city populations for the Middle Ages are obtained from a base figure, such as the number of hearths in a tax list, men in a communal army or fleet, signatories to a treaty, members of a key profession (such as notaries), etc., multiplied by a coefficient representing the assumed relation of the base to the total population.

CHAPTER 1. TROYES: 1250

1. *city wall:* The walls of Troyes have long since been replaced by boulevards. The description of the wall given here is based on that of neighboring Provins, built in the same period and still standing, including the handsome Porte-St.-Jean.

2. *Viscount's Tower:* A mere anachronism in the thirteenth century. But in the next century it regained importance, becoming the "belfry," stronghold of the burghers and hall of municipal government.

3. *paved with stone:* Probably. A document of 1231 attests that the section of the thoroughfare immediately west of Troyes was paved. City pavements were rare outside Italy, although in Paris Philip Augustus is said to have paved some streets in the early thirteenth century.

CHAPTER 2. A BURGHER'S HOME

1. *oiled parchment:* Glass was seldom used even in the houses of the wealthy. In England, where great nobles possessed scattered estates, they sometimes carried glazed casements from one residence to another. Wooden shutters were also common.

2. *table manners:* These injunctions are taken from three sources: *Roman de la Rose* and Robert of Blois's *Chatoiement des Dames*, both thirteenth century, and *Disciplina Clericalis*, written in the eleventh century by Petrus Alfonsus, a converted Spanish Jew, translated into French at the end of the twelfth century and popular in the thirteenth.

CHAPTER 3. A MEDIEVAL HOUSEWIFE

1. *at three-hour intervals:* The eight services of canonical office celebrated by the Church were (approximately):

Matins at midnight	Sext at midday
Lauds at 3 A.M.	None at 3 P.M.
Prime at 6 A.M.	Vespers at 6 P.M.
Tierce at 9 A.M.	Compline at 9 P.M.

In its simplest form, the clepsydra was similar to the sand-glass, with hour-levels marked as water dripped through an aperture. Elaborate mechanical clepsydras were also made, which with their trains of cogged wheels were ancestors of modern clocks. A drawing of Villard de Honnecourt shows an escapement, one of the basic mechanisms of clockwork.

The remarkable scientist and scholar Gerbert, who became Pope Sylvester II, is said to have invented the mechanical clock in 996, but the clock he had constructed at Magdeburg was doubtless a water clock, as were other clocks described during the following three centuries. In 1360 the first unquestionably mechanical clock in the modern sense was built by De Vick for Charles V of France.

2. *A fat capon costs six deniers:* Most of the commodity prices cited here and elsewhere in the text are drawn from the massive compendium of the Vicomte d'Avenel, who gathered price and wage figures in western Europe from 1200 to 1800. Original sources are cited in his work.

3. *gardens:* These plants are taken from John of Garlande's thirteenth-century dictionary.

4. *members of normally male professions:* Cf. Villon, "Les Regretz de la belle Héaulmière."

5. *abbess of Notre-Dame:* When Pope Urban IV wanted to build a church on the site of his father's shoe shop, he found himself embroiled with the abbess on whose seigneury the construction impinged. She led an armed party that attacked and demolished the work in 1266.

6. *wipe . . . one's nose:* Langlois, who edited Robert of Blois's *Chatoiement des Dames* for modern readers, suggests that the injunction is intended as humor, and is not a true indication of manners.

CHAPTER 4. CHILDBIRTH AND CHILDREN

1. *Birth records:* When Jeanne of Champagne was betrothed in 1284 an extensive investigation was necessary to determine her birth date.

CHAPTER 5. WEDDINGS AND FUNERALS

1. *demolish . . . portico:* Evidently the portico was repaired later, because the projecting statues are still a feature of Notre-Dame-de-Dijon.

2. *Jongleurs:* From instructions written for jongleurs of Provence.

CHAPTER 6. SMALL BUSINESS

1. *the hundred and twenty guilds of Paris:* In 1268, 120 crafts registered and wrote out their statutes at the invitation of Etienne Boileau, provost of Paris.

Preserved in the *taille* (tax list) of Paris for the year 1292 are the numbers of practitioners of the regulated crafts, by then totaling 130. The principal ones:

366 shoemakers
214 furriers
199 maidservants
197 tailors
151 barbers
131 jewelers
130 restaurateurs
121 old-clothes dealers
106 pastrycooks
104 masons
95 carpenters
86 weavers
71 chandlers
70 mercers
70 coopers
62 bakers
58 water carriers
58 scabbard makers
56 wine sellers
54 hatmakers
51 saddlers
51 chicken butchers
45 purse makers
43 laundresses
43 oil merchants
42 porters

42 meat butchers
41 fish merchants
37 beer sellers
36 buckle makers
36 plasterers
35 spice merchants
34 blacksmiths
33 painters
29 doctors
28 roofers
27 locksmiths
26 bathers
26 ropemakers
24 innkeepers
24 tanners
24 copyists
24 sculptors
24 rugmakers
24 harness makers
23 bleachers
22 hay merchants
22 cutlers
21 glovemakers
21 wood sellers
21 woodcarvers

2. *confiscation:* In 1268 Thibaut V, preparing to go on the last Crusade, again confiscated the goods of Troyen Jews and burned thirteen.

CHAPTER 7. BIG BUSINESS

1. *silver-copper-zinc pennies:* Though the basic coin of the Middle Ages was called denier in France, penny in England, pfennig in Germany, etc., it was universally written in Latin, *denarius*, as was the pound (*libra*) and

shilling (*solidus*), which accounts for the odd abbreviations of modern English coinage, the last relic of the medieval money system.

2. *grosso* (*groat*): St.-Louis issued a *gros tournois* even larger than the *grosso* in 1266, and Edward I of England a still larger groat in 1270. Simultaneously gold coinage returned for the first time since the Dark Ages, first in Italy, then in France and England. The French gold coin, *écu*, was valued at 10 *gros tournois*, or 120 *deniers de Provins*, or one-half *livre*.

CHAPTER 8. THE DOCTOR

1. *fewer than a half dozen doctors:* This is a fairly safe conjecture. In Paris in 1274 there were eight qualified physicians, a number which rose rapidly to 29 in 1292. On the other hand, 38 men and women of Paris in 1274 were identified as practicing medicine without benefit of a diploma. In the fourteenth century, the Faculty of Medicine of the University of Paris launched a vigorous war against the unlicensed practitioner.

2. *medical textbooks:* Pietro d'Abano, Taddeo Alderotti, Lanfranc, Henri de Mondeville, and others added much new work in the later thirteenth century.

CHAPTER 9. THE CHURCH

1. *no benches or pews:* Lecoy de la Marche, in *La chaire française*, insists that there were benches in the churches, on the grounds that otherwise people could not have fallen asleep (they were the butts of many clerical jokes and diatribes). Others feel that the congregation could

have slept as soundly on cushions and portable seats.

2. *sermon on the Christian virtues:* This sermon was preached to pilgrims at Notre-Dame of Amiens.

3. *oratorical tricks:* These were employed by the famous Paris preacher Jacques de Vitry, cardinal-archbishop of Acre.

4. *process of canonization:* Details of procedure were fixed in the thirteenth century, and beyond a fourteenth-century refinement have scarcely changed since.

CHAPTER 10. THE CATHEDRAL

1. *names of the masters:* Our earliest source of information about the builders of St.-Pierre is the cathedral accounts from 1293 to 1300. One Master Jacopo Lathomo (the Stone Cutter) is mentioned in a legacy of 1295–6 to the cathedral, and French scholars speculate that he may have been an architect who worked on the cathedral about 1270. The first certain reference to an architect in the records is to Master Henri, whose expenses for a trip with a servant are recorded in 1293–4; the next year he goes to the quarry on Ascension Day with Masters Richer and Gautier; in 1295–6 Renaudin, valet of the masons, presents himself to Henri at Auxerre, so that they may visit the quarry at Dangis; the following year they are at Dangis again. In 1297–8 Geoffroi of Mussy-sur-Seine takes over the job.

In 1920 a French scholar, de Mély, published in the *Revue archéologique* the then astonishing number of over five hundred architect-engineers in France alone. Many more medieval builders have been identified since. In 1954 John Harvey published a dictionary of English medieval architects.

2. *The builders' plans:* Very few survive. Parchment was precious and was commonly scraped and reused. An extant plan of Strasbourg Cathedral dates from the thirteenth century.

3. *iron clamps:* Metallic reinforcement of masonry was common—windows, steeples, and pinnacles made use of wrought iron for clamps, stays, tie-rods, and dowels.

4. *the bell is long-waisted:* When change-ringing became popular at the end of the Middle Ages, shorter-waisted bells were cast because it was easier to raise and ring them.

5. *choir vault:* The steeply pitched timber roofs of Gothic churches do not touch the vaulting beneath. The sketch-book of Villard de Honnecourt shows timbering built up from the tops of the piers, at the point of the springing of the arches, and secured by wooden ties. The timber roof was apparently then erected and the vaulting finished under cover. Rafters were about fourteen inches apart, often covered with leading.

6. *Gothic architecture:* Hans Straub, in his *History of Civil Engineering*, names four structural developments of the Gothic builders: (1) the distinction between bearing pillars and nonbearing walls; (2) the pointed arch, which is "statically efficient," that is, can carry heavy loadings; (3) vault-supporting ribs in place of the Roman solid vaults; (4) buttresses and flying buttresses.

7. *Deathbed bequests:* Among the legacies to the Troyes cathedral in 1298–9 is that of Pierre, the town hangman.

8. *the master glazier has no secrets:* Art has its own historical laws, and there is undeniably a charm in twelfth- and thirteenth-century glass which the work of later centuries does not have, probably because in later days

the use of the medium to its best advantage, as a mosaic of colored light, was sacrificed to realistic representation.

9. *St.-Bernard:* The great ascetic's viewpoint was not entirely abandoned by the later Middle Ages, and certainly found an echo in the Protestant movements of the fifteenth and sixteenth centuries. Sale of indulgences to pay for church-building, especially St. Peter's in Rome, was a powerful stimulus to discontent, and the very magnificence of church architecture remained an irritant to some.

CHAPTER II. SCHOOL AND SCHOLARS

1. *Nicolas of Clairvaux:* Translated by John Benton in *Annales de Bourgogne*.

2. *seven liberal arts:* A fifth-century writer named Martianus Capella, in a romance called *The Wedding of Philology and Mercury*, which remained popular throughout the Middle Ages, personifies the seven arts as women, distinguished by their varying clothing, implements, and coiffures.

3. *Alexandre of Villedieu's* Doctrinale: Through the fourteenth and fifteenth centuries the *Doctrinale* remained the universal grammar of Europe.

4. *a map of the world:* Several twelfth- and thirteenth-century maps are extant, including the world disk in Hereford Cathedral (late thirteenth century), which depicts imaginary continents and seas with fabulous beasts; the Psalter Map (c. 1230); and the Ebstorf Map (from the same period as the Hereford Map.)

5. *five in northwest Europe:* No German universities came into existence until the fourteenth century. By the end

of the Middle Ages there were some eighty European universities, two-thirds of which were in France and Italy.

6. *no university buildings:* The movement toward permanent buildings did not get seriously under way until the fifteenth century. At Paris, the only remaining monuments of the thirteenth-century university are the old church of St.-Julien-le-Pauvre, where university meetings were often held, and the cathedral from which the university sprang. Bologna has no university buildings from earlier than the fourteenth century. At Bologna, where classes were sometimes very large, popular professors lectured in public buildings or in the open air. At Cambridge, the oldest college, Peterhouse (thirteenth century) has only parts of its earliest buildings; Merton, at Oxford, also preserves some original fragments.

7. *theology:* Theology did not become prescribed training for the priesthood until the Counter Reformation.

CHAPTER 12. BOOKS AND AUTHORS

1. *booksellers:* The Paris *taille* of 1292 lists 8 bookstores, 17 bookbinders, 13 illuminators, and 24 clerk-copyists. At least in Paris, most booksellers were also tavernkeepers: *Nicholas l'Anglois, librairie et tavernier.* By 1323 there were 28 bookstores.

2. *libraries:* By 1290 the Sorbonne had 1,017 volumes; by 1338 it had 1,722. Other libraries were expanding at a similar rate, suggesting the economic context for the fifteenth-century development of movable type.

3. *fabliaux:* Because of their well-advertised ribaldry, the

fabliaux were once attributed exclusively to the non-noble class, a notion modern scholars have discarded.

4. *bathing establishment:* Bourbon-l'Archimbault, where the story takes place, remains a spa today.

5. This romance survives in a single mutilated thirteenth-century manuscript at Carcassonne, which terminates abruptly shortly after this point. It is hard to see how the author could have improved on the ending as it stands.

CHAPTER 13. THE NEW THEATER

1. *the theater has outgrown its confining cradle:* Secular and comic elements multiplied in both mysteries (Biblical—like the Adam play) and miracles (saints' lives—like the play of St.Nicholas). Herod developed into a melodramatic villain, the Magdalen's early life was explored, obscure Biblical personages were expanded into comic characters. Finally plays exploited purely secular themes. Adam de la Halle's *Jeu de Robin et de Marion*, based on the story of Robin Hood and presented at the Court of Naples in 1283, interspersed dialogue with songs and dances. It has been called the first comic opera.

In the fourteenth century guilds and corporations took over the religious drama, usually assigning Biblical scenes to appropriate trades—the story of Jonah to the fishmongers, the Marriage at Cana to the wine merchants, the building of the ark to the plasterers, the Last Supper to the bakers. In the second half of the fourteenth century, the great cycles of mystery plays were founded at Chester, Beverly, London, York, and Coventry, unfolding the principal stories of the Bible in sequence. Though amateurs, the actors were paid: account books for the York cycle list such items as "20 d. [pence] to God, 21 d. to the demon, 3d. to Fauston for cock crowing, 17 d. to two worms of conscience." The morality play, whose characters were virtues and vices and other abstractions, as in *Everyman*, became popular in the fifteenth century.

CHAPTER 15. TOWN GOVERNMENT

1. *typical recorded cases:* Two are patterned after a court report published by Maurice Prou and Jules d'Auriac in *Actes et comptes de la commune de Provins de l'an 1271 à l'an 1330;* one is cited by Paul Vinogradoff in Crump and Jacob's *Legacy of the Middle Ages* (see Bibliography, Chapter 2); the fourth, that involving the lady with the gutter pipe, is from a *Speculum* article by Ernest L. Sabine (see Bibliography, Chapter 2).

CHAPTER 16. THE CHAMPAGNE FAIR

1. *the cycle:* Our knowledge of the divisions of the six Fairs of Champagne comes partly from the *Extenta* of 1276–1278 (see Prologue), partly from an earlier document surviving in six variant texts. The generally agreed-on dates are:

Lagny: January 2 to February 22.

Bar-sur-Aube: Opened between February 24 and March 30, closed between April 15 and May 20.

Mai de Provins: Opened between April 28 and May 30, closed between June 13 and July 16.

St.-Jean de Troyes (Hot Fair): July 9–15 to August 29–September 4.

St.-Ayoul de Provins: September 14 to November 1 (All Saints'
Day).
St.-Rémi de Troyes (Cold Fair): November 2 to December 23.

In addition to the great international fairs, there were
a number of small trade fairs in Champagne, at Bar-
sur-Seine, Châlons-sur-Marne, Château-Thierry, Nogent, Reims and other places. Troyes itself had three
small fairs, the Fair of Clos, that of Deux Eaux, and
that of the Assumption.

2. *notaries:* "It is certain," says O. Verlinden in the *Cambridge Economic History*, "that there existed at the
Champagne Fairs a real records department." Hardly a
fragment survives. A single leaf, from a register of the
Hot Fair at Troyes of 1296, drawn up by an Italian
notary, contains fifteen deeds mentioning merchants
from Piacenza, Genoa, Milan, Asti, Como, Savona,
Florence, Montpellier, Narbonne, Avignon, Carpen-
tras, and St.-Flour.

3. *two hundred and eighty-eight spices:* Pegolotti of Florence
(1310–1340), whose list may include a few variants or
duplications.

4. *an extensive system of credit:* The Riccardi of Lucca
declared that they could borrow up to 200,000 pounds
at a single fair.

5. *the problem of variant calendars:* The calendar was in a
state of confusion, principally because of a widespread
disagreement over when the new year began. January 1
was the first day of the Roman civil year, and the
revival of the study of Roman law led to the use of this
reckoning in some places, but it was the rarest of all the
modes of dating the beginning of the year. In some
places, the month in which the Passion and Resurrection

were believed to have occurred, was considered the first month, but not everywhere, which led to some curious situations for a traveler. March 1 was officially celebrated as the beginning of the year in Venice. At Pisa, on the other hand, the year was reckoned from the presumed date of the Annunciation, that is from March 25 preceding A.D. 1. In Florence the years of the Incarnation were dated from March 25 a year later. In other places the year began on Christmas or Easter.

In a treatise on medieval timekeeping Reginald L. Poole (see Bibliography, Chapter 2) imagines a traveler setting out from Venice on March 1, 1245, the first day of the Venetian year; finding himself in 1244 when he reached Florence; and after a short stay going on to Pisa, where he would enter the year 1246. Continuing westward, he would return to 1245 when he entered Provence, and upon arriving in France before Easter (April 16) he would be once more in 1244. However, this confusion would not much discommode him, for he would think not in terms of the year but of the month and day, or the nearest saint's day.

Bibliography

General

BLOCH, MARC, *Feudal Society*, trans. L. A. Manyon. London, 1961.

BOISSONNADE, P., *Life and Work in Medieval Europe*, trans. Eileen Power. New York, 1964.

Cambridge Economic History of Europe, Vol. II: *Trade and Industry in the Middle Ages*, ed. M. Postan and E. E. Rich. Cambridge, 1952. Vol. III: *Economic Organization and Policies in the Middle Ages*, ed. M. Postan, E. E. Rich, and Edward Miller. Cambridge, 1963.

Cambridge Medieval History, 8 vols. New York, 1936.

DOWNS, NORTON, ed., *Basic Documents in Medieval History*. Princeton, 1959.

ESPINAS, GEORGES, *La vie économique et sociale au moyen âge*. Fontenay-le-Comte, 1946.

EVANS, JOAN, *Life in Mediaeval France*. Oxford, 1925.

FARAL, EDMOND, *La vie quotidienne au temps de Saint Louis*. Paris, 1938.

GAUTIER, LEON, *Chivalry*, trans. D. C. Dunning. New York, 1965.

HEER, FRIEDRICH, *The Medieval World*, trans. Janet Sondheimer. London, 1961.

LATOUCHE, ROBERT, *The Birth of Western Economy*, trans. E. M. Wilkinson. London, 1961.

LE GOFF, JACQUES, *La civilisation de l'occident médiéval*. Paris, 1964.

LOPEZ, ROBERT S., *The Birth of Europe*. New York, 1967.

MUNDY, JOHN H., and RIESENBERG, PETER, ed., *The Medieval Town*. Princeton, 1958.

PAETOW, L. J., *Guide to the Study of Medieval History*. New York, 1931.

PAINTER, SIDNEY, *French Chivalry*. Baltimore, 1940.

————, *A History of the Middle Ages*. New York, 1956.

PIRENNE, HENRI, *Economic and Social History of Medieval Europe*, trans. Kegan Paul. London, 1936.

————, *A History of Europe from the Invasions to the Sixteenth Century*. New York, 1939.

————, *Medieval Cities*, trans. Frank D. Halsey. Princeton, 1925.

————, *Mohammed and Charlemagne*, trans. Bernard Miall. New York, 1939.

RÉAU, LOUIS, *La civilisation française au moyen âge*. Paris, 1958.

REYNOLDS, ROBERT L., *Europe Emerges, Transition Toward an Industrial World-Wide Society*. Madison, Wis., 1961.

SÉE, HENRI, *Histoire économique de la France*. Paris, 1939.

SOUTHERN, R. W., *The Making of the Middle Ages*. New Haven, 1953.

STEPHENSON, CARL, *Medieval History*. New York, 1935. Also, fourth edition, ed. and rev. Bryce Lyon, New York, 1962.

THATCHER, OLIVER J., and MCNEAL, EDGAR, *A Source Book for Medieval History*. New York, 1905.

Special, by Chapter

PROLOGUE

ALENGRY, CHARLES, *Les foires de Champagne*. Paris, 1915.

BENTON, JOHN F., ed., *Town Origins*. Boston, 1968.

BOSERUP, ESTER, *The Conditions of Agricultural Growth*. London, 1965.

BOUTIOT, T., *Histoire de la ville de Troyes et de la Champagne méridionale*. Troyes, 1870.

CHAPIN, ELIZABETH, *Les villes de foire de Champagne*. Paris, 1937.

CROZET, RENÉ, *Histoire de Champagne*. Paris, 1933.

D'AROBOIS DE JUBAINVILLE, M. H., *Histoire des et des comtes de Champagne*. Paris, 1865.

ESPINAS, GEORGES, *Deux fondations de villes dans l'Artois et la Flandre française X^e-XVe siècles*. Paris, 1946.

GUILBERT, ARISTIDE, *Histoire des villes de France*. Paris, 1845.

LONGNON, AUGUSTE, *Documents rélatifs au comté de Champagne et de Brie, 1172–1367*. 3 vols. Paris, 1904.

LOPEZ, ROBERT S., "Some Tenth Century Towns," in *Medievalia et Humanistica*, 1955.

LUCHAIRE, ACHILLE, *Les communes françaises à l'époque des Capétiens directs*. Paris, 1911.

——, *Social France at the Time of Philip-Augustus*. New York, 1929.

PIRENNE, *Economic and Social History*.★

RUSSELL, J. C., *Late Ancient and Medieval Population*. Philadelphia, 1958.

STEPHENSON, CARL, *Borough and Town, a Study of Urban Origins in England*. Cambridge (Mass.), 1933.

WHITE, LYNN, *Medieval Technology and Social Change*. Oxford, 1963.

——, "Technology and Invention in the Middle Ages," in *Speculum*, 1940.

CHAPTER I. TROYES: 1250

ADELSON, HOWARD L., *Medieval Commerce*. Princeton, 1962.

ALENGRY, *Les foires de Champagne*.★

ANDERSON, R., *Examples of the Municipal, Commercial and Street Architecture of France and Italy from the 12th to the 15th Century*. Edinburgh, n.d.

BENTON, JOHN, "Comital Police Power and the Champagne Fairs," a paper presented before the American Historical Association, December 28, 1965.

BOURQUELOT, FELIX, "Etudes sur les foires de Champagne au XIIe, XIIIe et XIVe siècles" in *Mémoires présentés par divers savants à l'Académie des Inscriptions et Belles-Lettres*, Deuxième série. Paris, 1865.

BOUTIOT, T., *Dictionnaire topographique du département de l'Aube*. Paris. 1874.

——, *Histoire de la ville de Troyes*.★

CHAPIN, *Les villes de foire de Champagne*.★

EVANS, MARY, *Costume Throughout the Ages*. Philadelphia, 1930.

FRANKLIN, ALFRED, *La vie privée au temps des premiers Capétiens*. Paris, 1911.

A History of Technology, Vol. II, ed. Charles Singer, E. J. Holmyard, A. R. Hall, and Trevor Williams. Oxford, 1956.

HOLMES, URBAN TIGNER, JR., *Daily living in the Twelfth Century, Based on the Observations of Alexander Neckam in London and Paris*. Madison, Wis., 1952.

HOLMES, URBAN TIGNER, JR., and KLENKE, SISTER M. AMELIA, O. P., *Chrétien, Troyes and the Grail*. Chapel Hill, N.C., 1959.

KOHLER, CARL, *A History of Costume*. London, 1928.

LACROIX, PAUL, *Costumes historiques de la France*. Paris, 1860.

MUNDY and RIESENBERG, *Medieval Town*.★

ROSEROT, ALPHONSE, *Troyes, son histoire, ses monuments des origines à 1790*. Troyes, 1948.

SALUSBURY, G. T., *Street Life in Medieval England*. Oxford, 1939.

CHAPTER 2. A BURGHER'S HOME

BEMIS, ALBERT, and BURCHARD, JOHN, *The Evolving House*.Cambridge, 1933.

CRUMP, C. G., and JACOB, E. F., ed., *The Legacy of the Middle Ages*. Oxford, 1926.

Disciplina Clericalis. Heidelberg, 1911.

FRANKLIN, *Vie privée*.★

HOLMES, *Daily Living*.★

LANGLOIS, Charles-Victor, *La vie en France au moyen âge de la fin du XIIe au milieu du XIVe siècle, d'après des moralistes du temps*. Paris, 1925.

POWER, EILEEN, trans. and ed., *The Goodman of Paris*. London, 1928.

SABINE, ERNEST L., "Latrines and Cesspools of Medieval London," in *Speculum*, 1934.

SALUSBURY, *Street Life*.★

WOOD, MARGARET, *The English Mediaeval House*. London, 1965.

WRIGHT, LAWRENCE, *Clean and Decent*. London, 1960.

★See earlier citation

CHAPTER 3. A MEDIEVAL HOUSEWIFE

D'AVENEL, VICOMTE G., *Histoire économique de la propriété, des salaires, des denrées et de tous les prix en général depuis l'an 1200 jusqu'en l'an 1800.* 7 vols. Paris, 1898.

BEARD, MARY, *Women as a Force in History.* New York, 1946.

CRUMP and JACOB, *Legacy of the Middle Ages.★*

FRANKLIN, *Vie privée.★*

History of Technology.★

HOLMES, *Daily Living.★*

LANGLOIS, *Moralistes.★*

LECOY DE LA MARCHE, A., *La chaire française au moyen âge.* Paris, 1886.

———, *La société au treizième siècle.* Paris, 1888.

MILHAM, WILLIS, *Time and Timekeepers.* New York, 1923.

POOLE, REGINALD L., *Medieval Reckonings of Time.* New York, 1935.

POWER, *Goodman of Paris.★*

ROGERS, JAMES E. THOROLD, *Six Centuries of Work and Wages.* New York, 1884.

ROSEROT, *Troyes.★*

SALUSBURY, *Street Life.★*

STENTON, DORIS, *The Englishwoman in History.* London, 1957.

WRIGHT, RICHARDSON, *The Story of Gardening.* New York, 1934.

CHAPTER 4. CHILDBIRTH AND CHILDREN

ARIES, PHILIPPE, *Centuries of Childhood,* trans. Robert Baldick. London, 1962.

DELARUE, PAUL, ed., *The Borzoi Book of French Folk Tales.* New York, 1956.

FRANKLIN, *Vie privée.★*

GAUTIER, *Chivalry.★*

HOLMES, *Daily Living.★*

LANGLOIS, *Moralistes.★*

THORNDIKE, LYNN, *A History of Magic and Experimental Science During the First Thirteen Centuries of Our Era.* 8 vols. New York, 1964.

CHAPTER 5. WEDDINGS AND FUNERALS

CRUMP and JACOB, *Legacy of the Middle Ages*.★

FRANKLIN, *Vie privée*.★

GAUTIER, *Chivalry*.★

GEIRINGER, KARL, *Musical Instruments: Their History in Western Culture from the Stone Age to the Present*. New York, 1945.

HOLMES, *Daily Living*.★

LANGLOIS, CHARLES-VICTOR, *La société au XIII siècle d'après dix romans d'aventure*. Paris, 1914.

LECOŸ DE LA MARCHE, *La chaire française*.★

PARRISH, CARL, *A Treasury of Early Music*. New York, 1958.

POWER, *Goodman of Paris*.★

SACHS, CURT, *The History of Musical Instruments*. New York, 1940.

THORNDIKE, *Magic*.★

CHAPTER 6. SMALL BUSINESS

ADELSON, *Medieval Commerce*.★

D'AVENEL, *Histoire économique*.★

BOSERUP, *Conditions of Agricultural Growth*.★

BOUTIOT, *Histoire de Troyes*.★

Cambridge Economic History, Vol. III.★

CHAPIN, *Villes de foire de Champagne*.★

DION, ROGER, *Histoire de la vigne et du vin en France des origines au XIVe siècle*. Paris, 1959.

DUBY, GEORGES, *L'économie rurale et la vie des campagnes dans l'Occident médiéval*. Paris, 1962.

EMERY, RICHARD, *The Jews of Perpignan in the Thirteenth Century, an Economic Study Based on Notarial Records*. New York, 1959.

ESPINAS, GEORGES, *La vie urbaine de Douai au moyen âge*. Paris, 1913.

FRANKLIN, *Vie privée*.★

GUILBERT, *Histoire des villes*.★

History of Technology.★

★See earlier citation

Holmes, *Daily Living.*★

Lanel, Luc, *L'Orfèvrerie.* Paris, 1949.

Luchaire, *Social France.*★

Marcus, Jacob R., *The Jew in the Medieval World, a Source Book, 315–1791.* Cincinnati, 1938.

Mazaros, J. P., *Histoire des corporations françaises d'arts et métiers.* Paris, 1878.

Millett, F. B., *Craft Guilds of the Thirteenth Century in Paris.* Kingston (Ont.), 1915.

Mundy and Riesenberg, *Medieval Town.*★

Rabinowitz, Louis, *The Social Life of the Jews of Northern France in the XII–XIVth Centuries.* London, 1938.

Robert, Ulysse, *Les signes d'infamie au moyen âge, Juifs, Sarrasins, hérétiques, lépreux, cagots et filles publiques.* Paris, 1891.

Rogers, *Work and Wages.*★

Roth, Cecil, "The Jews in the Middle Ages," *Cambridge Medieval History,* Vol. VII. New York, 1932.

Saige, Gustave, *Les Juifs du Languedoc antérieurement au XIVe siècle.* Paris, 1881.

Salusbury, *Street Life.*★

Shneidman, J. Lee, *The State and Trade in the Thirteenth Century.* Madrid, 1958.

Stephenson, Carl, *Medieval Institutions.* Ithaca, 1954.

Technology in Western Civilization, ed. Melvin Kranzberg and Caroll W. Pursell, Jr. New York, 1967.

Thrupp, Sylvia, *The Merchant Class of Medieval London, 1300–1500.* Chicago, 1948.

———, *A Short History of the Worshipful Company of Bakers of London.* London, 1933.

White, Lynn, "Technology and Invention."★

CHAPTER 7. BIG BUSINESS

Adelson, *Medieval Commerce.*★

Alengry, *Foires de Champagne.*★

BOUTIOT, *Histoire de Troyes*.*

Cambridge Economic History, Vol. II: *Trade and Industry and the Middle Ages*, ed. M. Postan and E. E. Rich. Cambridge, 1952.

Cambridge Economic History, Vol. III.*

Cambridge Medieval History (Cecil Roth).*

CAVE, ROY C., and COULSON, HERBERT H., ed., *A Source Book for Medieval Economic History*. New York, 1938.

CHAPIN, *Villes de foire de Champagne*.*

CIPOLLA, CARLO M., "Currency Depreciation in Medieval Europe," in *Change in Medieval Society*, ed. Sylvia Thrupp. New York, 1964.

———. *Money, Prices and Civilization in the Mediterranean World, Fifth to Seventeenth Century*. Princeton, 1956.

CROZET, *Histoire de Champagne*.*

EMERY, *Jews of Perpignan*.*

ESPINAS, GEORGES, ed., *Sire Jean de France, Sire Jacques le Blond, les origines du capitalisme*. Lille, 1936.

ESPINAS, *Vie économique et sociale*.*

FRANKLIN, *Vie privée*.*

GODEFROY DE PARIS, *Chronique, suivie de la taille de Paris en 1313*. Paris, 1827.

HERLIHY, DAVID, *Pisa in the Early Renaissance: a Study of Urban Growth*. New Haven, 1958.

History of Technology.*

HOLMES, *Daily Living*.*

LECOY DE LA MARCHE, *Société au treizième siècle*.*

LESTOCQUOY, J., *Les villes de Flandre et d'Italie sous le gouvernement des patriciens (XIᵉ–XVᵉ siècles)*. Paris, 1952.

LUCHAIRE, *Social France*.*

MUNDY and RIESENBERG, *Medieval Town*.*

PIRENNE, *Economic and Social History*.*

POWER, EILEEN, *The Wool Trade in English Medieval History*. London, 1941.

SAYOUS, EDOUARD, *La France de St. Louis d'après la poésie nationale*. Paris, 1866.

*See earlier citation

THOMSON, DANIEL, *The Weavers' Craft, a History of the Weavers' Incorporation of Dunfermline.* Paisley, Scotland, 1903.

WENGER, O. P., *Les Monnaies.* Lausanne, n.d.

CHAPTER 8. THE DOCTOR

D'AVENEL, *Histoire économique.*★

BARTHOLOMEW ANGLICUS, *Medieval Lore.*★

BOUTIOT, *Histoire de Troyes.*★

CASTIGLIONI, ARTURO, *A History of Medicine,* trans. E. B. Krumbhaar. New York, 1946.

FRANKLIN, *Vie privée.*★

HOLMES, *Daily Living.*★

INGLIS, BRIAN, *A History of Medicine.* New York, 1965.

JOHN OF SALISBURY, *Metalogicon,* trans. and ed. Daniel D. McGarry, Berkeley, 1955.

SAIGE, *Les juifs de Languedoc.*★

THORNDIKE, *Magic.*★

WALKER, KENNETH, *Story of Medicine.* New York, 1954.

CHAPTER 9. THE CHURCH

D'ARBOIS DE JUBAINVILLE, *Histoire des ducs et des comtes.*★

CLARKE, W. K., *Liturgy and Worship.* London, 1950.

DANIEL-ROPS, HENRI, *Cathedral and Crusade.* London, 1956.

DAWSON, CHRISTOPHER, *Mediaeval Religion and Other Essays.* London, 1934.

DIX, GREGORY, *The Shape of the Liturgy.* Westminster, 1943.

GEIRINGER, KARL, *Musical Instruments.*★

HOLMES, *Daily Living.*★

LEA, HENRY CHARLES, *History of the Inquisition in the Middle Ages.* New York, 1888.

LECOY DE LA MARCHE, *La chaire française.*★

Réalités, June 1965, "The Saints Go Marching On."

REESE, GUSTAVE, *Music in the Middle Ages*. New York, 1940.

ROSEROT, *Troyes*.★

RUNCIMAN, STEVEN, *The Medieval Manichee*. New York, 1961.

TOYNBEE, MARGARET, S. *Louis of Toulouse and the Process of Canonization in the Fourteenth Century*. Manchester, 1929.

WALKER, WILLISTON, *A History of the Christian Church*. New York, 1959.

CHAPTER 10. THE CATHEDRAL

ADAMS, HENRY, *Mont-St. Michel and Chartres*. Boston, 1913.

BRIGGS, MARTIN S., *The Architect in History*. Oxford, 1927.

——, *A Short History of the Building Crafts*. Oxford, 1925.

CHOISY, AUGUSTE, *Histoire de l'architecture*, 2 vols. Paris, 1899.

DANIEL-ROPS, *Cathedral and Crusade*.★

DU COLOMBIER, PIERRE, *Les chantiers des cathédrales*. Paris, 1953.

HAMLIN, TALBOT, *Architecture through the Ages*. New York, 1940.

HARVEY, JOHN, *English Mediaeval Architects: a Biographical Dictionary Down to 1550*. London, 1954.

——, *The Gothic World, 1100–1600*. London, 1950.

HEADLAM, CECIL, *The Story of Chartres*. London, 1902.

History of Technology.★

KNOOP, DOUGLAS, and JONES, G. P., "The English Medieval Quarry," in *Economic History Review*, November 1938.

——, *The Medieval Mason*. Manchester, 1933.

LAVEDAN, PIERRE, *French Architecture*. London, 1956.

NICHOLS, J. R., *Bells through the Ages, the Founders' Craft and the Ringers' Art*. London, 1928.

PARKER, JOHN HENRY, *ABC of Gothic Architecture*. Oxford, 1910.

PEVSNER, NIKOLAUS, *An Outline of European Architecture*. London, 1943.

PRENTICE, SARTELL, *The Voices of the Cathedral*. New York, 1938.

ROSEROT, *Troyes*.★

SHELBY, L. R., "The Role of the Master Mason in Medieval English Building," in *Speculum*, 1964.

★See earlier citation

STRAUB, HANS. *A History of Civil Engineering*, trans. E. Rockwell. London, 1953.

VON SIMSON, OTTO, *The Gothic Cathedral*. New York, 1962.

CHAPTER 11. SCHOOL AND SCHOLARS

D'ANDELI, HENRI, *The Battle of the Seven Arts*, ed. L. J. Paetow. Berkeley, 1914.

ARIES, *Centuries of Childhood*.

BENTON, JOHN, "Nicolas de Clairvaux à la recherche du vin d'Auxerre, d'après une lettre inédite du XIIᵉ siècle," in *Annales de Bourgogne*, XXXIV (1962).

CROMBIE, A. C., *Medieval and Early Modern Science*. New York, 1959.

CRUMP and JACOB, *Legacy of the Middle Ages.*★

CURTIUS, ERNST ROBERT, *European Literature and the Latin Middle Ages*. New York, 1953.

FRANKLIN, *Vie privée.*★

GUIBERT DE NOGENT, *Autobiography*, trans. C. C. Swinton Bland. London, 1925.

HASKINS, CHARLES HOMER, *The Renaissance of the Twelfth Century*. Cambridge (Mass.), 1927.

———, *The Rise of the Universities*. New York, 1923.

———, *Studies in the History of Mediaeval Science*. Cambridge (Mass.), 1927.

HOLMES, *Daily Living.*★

JERVIS, W. W., *The World in Maps, a Study in Map Evolution*. New York, 1937.

JOHN OF GARLAND, *Morale Scolarium*, ed. L. J. Paetow. Berkeley, 1927.

JOHN OF SALISBURY, *Metalogicon.*★

KIBRE, PEARL, *The Nations in the Medieval Universities*. Cambridge (Mass.), 1948.

———, *Scholarly Privileges in the Middle Ages*. Cambridge (Mass.), 1962.

LANGLOIS, CHARLES-VICTOR, *La connaissance de la nature et du monde au moyen âge*. Paris, 1911.

LEACH, A. F., *The Schools of Medieval England*. London, 1915.

LECOY DE LA MARCHE, *La chaire française*.

L'Image du Monde de Maître Gossoulin, trans. into modern French, O. H. Prior. Paris, 1913.

PAETOW, LOUIS J., *The Arts Course at Medieval Universities with Special Reference to Grammar and Rhetoric*. Champaign, Ill., 1910.

RASHDALL, HASTINGS, *The Universities of Europe in the Middle Ages*. Oxford, 1936.

SANFORD, VERA, *A Short History of Mathematics*. Boston, 1930.

THATCHER and McNEAL, *Source Book*.*

THORNDIKE, LYNN, "Elementary and Secondary Education in the Middle Ages," in *Speculum*, 1940.

——, *Magic*.*

——, ed., *University Records and Life in the Middle Ages*. New York, 1944.

CHAPTER 12. BOOKS AND AUTHORS

BENTON, JOHN F., "The Court of Champagne as a Literary Center," in *Speculum*, XXXVI (1961).

CHRÉTIEN DE TROYES, *Yvain*, trans. André Mary. New York, 1963.

CROSLAND, JESSIE, *Medieval French Literature*. New York, 1956.

FARAL, EDMOND, *Les jongleurs en France au moyen âge*. Paris, 1910.

FRANKLIN, *Vie privée*.*

GUILLAUME DE LORRIS and JEAN DE MEUNG, *Le roman de la Rose*, trans. André Mary. Paris, 1949.

HASKINS, *Renaissance of the Twelfth Century*.*

HELLMAN, ROBERT, and O'GORMAN, RICHARD, ed. and trans., *Fabliaux, Ribald Tales from the Old French*. New York, 1965.

HOLMES, *Daily Living*.

HOLMES, URBAN TIGNER, JR., *A History of Old French Literature*. New York, 1962.

LANGLOIS, *Moralistes*.*

——, *La société française*.*

*See earlier citation

McCulloch, Florence, "The Funeral of Renard the Fox in a Walters Book of Hours," in *Journal of the Walters Art Gallery*, Baltimore, 1962–3.

Ogg, Oscar, *The 26 Letters*. New York, 1948.

Rashdall, *Universities*.★

Rutebeuf, *Oeuvres complètes*, 2 vols., ed. Edmond Faral and Julia Bastin. Paris, 1959–60.

Thorndike, Lynn, "More Copyists' Final Jingles," in *Speculum*, 1956.

CHAPTER 13. THE NEW THEATER

Chambers, E. K., *The Medieval Stage*. Oxford, 1903.

Le courtois d'Arras, in *Jeux et sapience du moyen-âge*, ed. Albert Pauphilet. Paris, 1941.

Frank, Grace, *The Medieval French Drama*. Oxford, 1954.

Le Jeu de St. Nicholas, in *Jeux et sapience*.★

Lecoy de la Marche, *La chaire française*.★

Le mystère d'Adam, in *Jeux et sapience*.★

Young, Karl, *The Drama of the Medieval Church*. Oxford, 1933.

CHAPTER 14. DISASTERS

Boutiot, *Histoire de Troyes*.★

Castiglioni, *History of Medicine*.★

Crozet, *Histoire de Champagne*.★

Gies, Joseph, *Bridges and Men*. New York, 1963.

Guilbert, *Histoire des villes de France*.★

Lot, Ferdinand, *L'art militaire et les armées au moyen âge*. Paris, 1946.

Luchaire, *Communes françaises*.★

Oman, Charles, *A History of the Art of War in the Middle Ages*. New York, 1924.

Willis, R., *The Architectural History of Canterbury Cathedral*. London, 1845.

CHAPTER 15. TOWN GOVERNMENT

BENTON, JOHN, "Comital Police Power and the Champagne Fairs."*

BIBOLET, FRANÇOISE, "Le role de la guerre de cent ans dans le développement des libertés municipales à Troyes," in *Mémoires de la Société académique d'agricultures, des sciences, arts et belles-lettres du département de l'Aube*, Vol. XCIX, 1939–1942. Troyes, 1945.

BOUTIOT, *Histoire de Troyes.**

BRISSAND, JEAN, *A History of French Public Law*, trans. James N. Garner. Boston, 1915.

CROZET, *Histoire de Champagne.**

CRUMP and JACOB, *Legacy of the Middle Ages.**

D'ARBOIS DE JUBAINVILLE, *Histoire des ducs et des comtes.*

DOWNS, *Basic Documents.**

ESPINAS, GEORGES, *Les finances de la commune de Douai des origines au XVe siècle*. Paris, 1902.

GUILBERT, *Histoire des villes de France.**

HAZELTINE, HAROLD D., "Roman and Canon Law in the Middle Ages," *Cambridge Medieval History*, Vol. V. New York, 1929.

HEEREN, A. H. L., *Essai sur l'influence des croisades*. Trans. from German to French by Charles Villers. Paris, 1808.

JOINVILLE, JEAN DE, and VILLEHARDOUIN, GEOFFROI, *Chronicles of the Crusades*, trans. M. R. B. Shaw. Baltimore, 1963. (Containing Villehardouin's *Conquest of Constantinople* and Joinville's *Life of St. Louis*.)

LEFÈVRE, ANDRÉ, "*Les finances de la Champagne au XIIIe et XIV siècles*," in *Bibliothèque de l'École des Chartes*, 4th series, IV and V. Paris, 1868–9.

LESTOCQUOY, J., *Les villes de Flandre et d'Italie.*

LUCHAIRE, *Communes françaises.**

MUNDY, JOHN H., *Liberty and Political Power in Toulouse, 1050–1230*. New York, 1954.

MUNDY and RIESENBERG, *Medieval Town.**

PIRENNE, *Social and Economic History.**

*See earlier citation

PROU, MAURICE, and D'AURIAC, JACQUES, *Actes et comptes de la commune de Provins de l'an 1271 à l'an 1330.* Provins, 1933.

ROSEROT, *Troyes.*★

RUNCIMAN, STEVEN, *A History of the Crusades.* Cambridge, 1951.

SABINE, "Latrines and Cesspools."★

SAYOUS, *La France de St. Louis.*★

SMAIL, R. C., *Crusading Warfare, 1097–1193.* Cambridge, 1956.

SOCIÉTÉ JEAN BODIN, *Recueils, La Ville.* Brussels, 1954.

STEPHENSON, *Borough and Town.*★

STEPHENSON, *Medieval Institutions.*★

STONE, E. N., trans., *Three Old French Chronicles of the Crusades.* Seattle, 1939.

THATCHER and MCNEAL, *Source Book for Medieval History.*

CHAPTER 16. THE CHAMPAGNE FAIR

ADELSON, *Medieval Commerce.*★

ALENGRY, *Les foires de Champagne.*★

D'AVENEL, *Histoire économique.*★

BAUTIER, R. H., "Les foires de Champagne," in *Recueils Jean Bodin,* Vol. V, *La foire.* Brussels, 1953.

BENTON, "Comital Police Power."★

BLOCH, *Feudal Society.*★

BOURQUELOT, FÉLIX, *Etudes sur les foires de Champagne.*★

BOUTIOT, *Histoire de Troyes.*★

Cambridge Economic History, II, III.★

CHAPIN, *Les villes de foire de Champagne.*★

CIPOLLA, *Money, Prices and Civilization.*★

CROZET, *Histoire de Champagne.*★

FACE, R. D., "Techniques of Business in the Trade Between the Fairs of Champagne and the South of Europe in the Twelfth and Thirteenth Centuries," in *Economic History Review,* 1958.

GUILBERT, *Histoire des villes de France.*★

HEATON, HERBERT, *Economic History of Europe.* New York, 1936.

HUVELIN, P., *Essai historique sur le droit des marchés et des foires.* Paris, 1897.

LOPEZ, ROBERT S., and RAYMOND, Irving W., *Medieval Trade in the Mediterranean World.* New York, 1955.

PIRENNE, *Economic and Social History.*★

POIGNANT, SIMONE, *La foire de Lille.* Lille, 1932.

SÉE, *Histoire économique.*★

STEPHENSON, *Medieval Institutions.*★

THATCHER and McNEAL, *Source Book.*★

★See earlier citation

Index

99–100
solidus (sou, shilling), 99–100,
220, 237
Sorbonne, 241
sou (see solidus)
Spain, 5, 24, 25, 113, 219
spices, 15, 31, 44, 48, 217–218,
222, 223, 225, 244
sports (*see* recreations)
"Strada Francesca," 23
Strasbourg, 21
cathedral, 129, 139
street-cleaning, 30–31
streets, 12, 77
of Troyes, 28, 30–33, 47–48,
83, 87, 93, 97
sugar, 48, 217
Sugar, abbot of St.-Denis, 14, 136,
141
surgeons, 114–115
surnames, 77–79
Sylvester I, pope (Gerbert), 234
synagogue, 95, 125–126

taille (see taxes)
tailors, 77, 89
tanners, 30, 83–85, 226
tapestry, 37
taverns, 86, 212, 215
taxes, 17, 199, 202, 208, 224–225,
235
Templars, order of, 31, 48, 104,
210, 213, 228
textbooks, 109, 113–114, 171, 175,
237
theater, 183–189, 242–243
Theodoric of Lucca, 115
theology, 155, 165, 241

Thibaut I, the Trickster, count of
Champagne, 13, 230
Thibaut II, the Great, count of
Champagne, 14, 17, 18,
230
Thibaut IV, the Songwriter
(*le Chansonnier*), count of
Champagne, 18, 19, 20, 21,
52, 106, 125, 130, 132, 134,
167–169, 201–202, 207–208,
224, 231
revenues of, 20–21, 213
Thibaut V, count of Champagne,
231, 236
"Third Estate," 200, 224
three-field system, 11
timbering, 145, 239
timekeeping, 46, 234
tolls, 25
torture, 133, 203
Toulouse, 21
town council, 53, 199, 200, 202,
204, 207
town watch (*see* police)
toys, 63
translations, 113–114, 161
transportation, 25, 88, 141, 217–
218
treaties, commercial, 25
trebuchet, 196
Trencavel, Raymond, viscount of
Béziers, 197–198
trial by combat, 205
trial by ordeal, 205
"Tricasses," 1
trivium (see liberal arts)
trope, 184, 185
trouvères, 107, 168, 210
I